GOOD NEIGHBORS:
AFFORDABLE FAMILY HOUSING

D E S I G N
F O R
L I V I N G

GOOD NEIGHBORS:
AFFORDABLE FAMILY HOUSING

TOM JONES, WILLIAM PETTUS, AIA, MICHAEL PYATOK, FAIA
FOREWORD BY CHESTER HARTMAN;
EDITED BY SALLY B. WOODBRIDGE

McGraw-Hill
New York   Washington D.C.   San Francisco
Montreal   Toronto

First published in Australia in 1997
Second Edition 1998
The Images Publishing Group Pty Ltd
ACN 059 734 431
6 Bastow Place, Mulgrave, Victoria 3170
Telephone (61 3) 9561 5544 Facsimile (61 3) 9561 4860

National Library of Australia Cataloguing-in-Publication Data

    Good Neighbors
        Good Neighbors: Affordable Family Housing

        Bibliography.
        Includes Resource Guide/Index.

        ISBN 0 07 032913 3

This edition published in North America by McGraw-Hill,
a division of The McGraw-Hill Companies, Inc.

Edited by Patricia Sellar
Co-ordination: Willie Pettus

Designed by Blur Pty Ltd, Mulgrave, Australia
Film separations by Scanagraphix, Australia
Printing by Everbest Printing, Hong Kong

Contents

(6) **Acknowledgments**

(7) **Introduction**

(8) **Foreword** by Chester Hartman

Part One: Who Lives in Affordable Family Housing?

(13) Chapter one: Families in Need
(21) Chapter two: Meet Your Neighbors (Profiles)

Part Two: Factors Influencing Affordable Family Housing Design

(29) Chapter three: Community Needs and Context
(39) Chapter four: Policy, Finance, and Regulations
(47) Chapter five: The Design Process

Part Three: Case Studies of Affordable Family Housing

(61) Chapter six: Guide to the Case Studies
(67) Chapter seven: The Northwest and Northern California
(125) Chapter eight: The Southwest and Southern California
(151) Chapter nine: The Central States
(165) Chapter ten: The Northeast
(205) Chapter eleven: The South
(217) Chapter twelve: Additional Case Studies of Merit

(249) **Resource Guide:** Special Characteristics Guide

Comparative Description Index

Using the Guides and Indexes:

Names and telephone numbers of architects, developers, contractors and consultants

Acknowledgments

This book was made possible by a substantial grant from the National Endowment for the Arts to Asian Neighborhood Design. The authors would like specially to thank Mina Berriman for funding the book as the former Director of the Design Arts Division of the National Endowment for the Arts. It was her belief that affordable housing can and ought to be good architecture that inspired and supported us in our efforts. We would like also to thank Charles Zucker, Senior Director for Community Design and Development at the American Institute of Architects for funding the companion slide library. It was his many years of devotion to architecture as a social art which encouraged us to celebrate the works of others in our profession. We would like to thank Wells Fargo Bank, the Bank of America, and the Vanguard Public Foundation for grants that underwrote the purchase price of a limited number of copies of the book. These books are being distributed to non-profit agencies and their members in conjunction with educational programs concerning affordable housing design.

This book is the result of the hard work, generosity, and creativity of many people. The search for excellent case studies was made infinitely easier by our Advisory Committee: Richard H. Bradfield FAIA, Lawrence K. Cheng AIA, Anthony Costello AIA, David Cronrath, Clark S. Davis AIA, Roberta M. Feldman, Pliny Fisk III, Jody Gibbs, Joan Goody FAIA, Robert Herman FAIA, Steve Johnson AIA, Jackie Leavitt PhD, Conrad Levinson, Philip A. Morris, John V. Mutlow FAIA, William Rawn AIA, Christopher A. Rose AIA, ASID, Garth Rockcastle AIA, Ron Shiffman, Tony Schuman, Cynthia Weese FAIA, Henry William Wenzel AIA, and Charles B. Zucker.

For their generosity in supplying information and artwork, we would like to thank the following: the architectural firms, developers, and sponsors who contributed their work as case studies; the firms who sent in examples of their work which could not be included; the photographers, who generously donated their photographs for use for the book and the slide library. For their willingness to be profiled in Part One "Meet Your Neighbors", we thank all the families who gave us the time and permission for interviews and photographs. We thank Janet Delaney for her assistance with the interviews.

For her invaluable and hard work researching and tracking down information, we are very grateful to research associate Mashal Afredi. For their assistance with proofing and co-ordination we thank Meri Furnari and Caryn Tamar.

We thank Chester Hartman, for writing a strong Foreword that clearly states the social and political context in which affordable housing must be built. We would like to thank Sally B. Woodbridge, for her patience and skill editing and refining many drafts of the text, and for her advice on publication issues. Finally, we are indebted to Images Publishing, for their excellent design work, their flexibility and help with many aspects of the publication process, and for helping us to tell the world about this important area of American architecture.

Introduction

This extensively researched book is a testament to the ability of communities to build excellent affordable housing for families using creative vision, perseverance, and scarce resources. Presented from a variety of points of view, it showcases buildings designed by William Rawn Associates, Donald MacDonald Architects, Cooper Robertson Partners, Pyatok Associates, Solomon Inc., Marquis Associates, UDA Architects and Planners, and many others. The housing is developed by a multitude of community-based non-profit and for-profit development corporations, including BRIDGE Housing, McCormack Baron and Associates, established agencies such as the YWCA, Habitat for Humanity, local Housing Authorities, and grass-roots organisations that run on shoe-string budgets. This book engages the reader in an understandable and visually rich survey of outstanding affordable family housing developments. Examples range from small towns to inner-city locations throughout the United States. Citizen advocacy groups, government decision-makers, students, architects, and planners, especially in communities and towns lacking positive examples of well-designed affordable housing, will find this book an invaluable educational resource.

We briefly address the history of affordable housing in the USA, and explain how such housing is developed with a mix of government and private financing today. Profiles of residents precede a clear description of how to work with skilled architects and landscape architects to design housing that works best for the resident families as well as for their neighbors. A major theme of the book is the achievement of compatibility with existing neighborhood conditions while providing contemporary housing at higher densities. Additional themes include the provision of useable public and private open space, the creation of appropriate vehicular and pedestrian access and circulation, and the incorporation of special amenities for residents of all ages. At every level, from the neighborhood and site plan to the dwelling layout, well-designed affordable housing creates pride of place for residents, and reinforces pride among neighbors.

Grants from the National Endowment for the Arts and the American Institute of Architects (AIA), have made the book and a companion slide collection possible. These awards come in part as a result of the efforts of Tom Jones (Development Director of Asian Neighborhood Design), Michael Pyatok, FAIA, and other architects, to develop the curriculum of the NEA and AIA program called Design for Housing. This program has convened architects, developers, property managers, and public officials in different regions of the country to improve design in affordable housing, from individual design decisions to the public policy level. Many participants recognized a strong need for an illustrated resource useable by professionals and affordable housing advocates around the country to educate the public and policy makers about the design and development of affordable housing. This book meets that need.

Michael Pyatok FAIA
Tom Jones
Willie Pettus AIA

Oakland/San Francisco, California

Foreword

Chester Hartman

As this Foreword is being written, the picture for affordable housing is grim, with little hope for amelioration in the near future. HUD's housing subsidy budget is being drastically cut; remaining subsidy programs are being shifted largely to the voucher/certificate approach, which throws money in to cover the gap between market costs and household incomes, rather than lowering housing costs or creating new affordable housing. There are serious proposals to abolish HUD altogether; and there is an all-out attack on so-called "safety net" programs across the board. All this is happening at a time of widespread and increasing general poverty and housing affordability problems. Over 36 million Americans lived below the poverty line in 1992 compared with the 1965 figure of 33 million. And the median rent:income ratio for all renters in 1994 was 30 per cent, compared with 23 per cent in 1970.

We are moving steadily away from, rather than attempting to fulfill, the National Housing Goal of a decent home and suitable living environment for every American family, first enunciated nearly 50 years ago in Congress Preamble to the 1949 *Housing Act*, and reiterated by Congress several times since. A great many causal factors are involved in this dramatic shift in priorities. Not primary, but likely important, is the popular perception that social programs generally, housing in particular, don't work. Media portrayals of the nation's primary low-rent housing program, public housing projects, focus on the obvious failures: Chicago's Cabrini Green and Robert Taylor Homes, St Louis' Pruitt Igoe, Boston's Columbia Point. However unfair it is to base sweeping judgments on a minority of failures, the vast majority of public housing projects provide decent living environments, have huge waiting lists, and are by far the best option available, when compared with what the private market has to offer. There is a clear need to put forth convincing examples of where low-rent housing works. And that in large part is a question of design. We (the general public) tend to form our opinions about housing developments on the basis of looks. Those huge miles-long towers lining South State Street in Chicago turn us off, and rightly so—they are seen as intimately related to the enormous social problems we read about in those developments.

Analogously, we form positive reactions about the housing, the people who live there, the life inside, when we see a well-designed, well-landscaped, thoughtfully-planned housing development. Such projects—and there are hundreds of them around the country, built and owned by public agencies, non-profit and profit-oriented developers—must be brought to everyone's attention if there is to be a serious approach to providing decent, affordable housing for all Americans. And that is the purpose of this book. At present, in the immediate past, and earlier in the 19th and 20th centuries, a great many endeavors to provide decent housing for the poor have held to high design standards and the resultant rewards—in resident satisfaction, lower maintenance costs, durability—have been impressive. And so this book deals with the central issue of design excellence in affordable housing. While "design excellence" is perhaps a somewhat subjective term, "affordable" is less so. To be sure, there are important definitional questions to be answered: "Affordable" to whom? Are we talking about the physical housing unit/building/development itself (how it is financed, its final construction or occupancy costs) or the relationship of the physical object to those who occupy it? In other words, does a given housing unit become "affordable" or "unaffordable" as occupants of differing financial capabilities use it, or as the financial capabilities of a given household change?

Ideally, all housing should be affordable to those who live in it—the consequences of the housing not being affordable are unpleasant, even severe. Our society, in certain instances, establishes affordability standards, sometimes legally applicable (in the case of some government programs), sometimes the prevailing practices of mortgage lenders, landlords and other private housing actors. Often these are referred to as "rules-of-thumb", nicely expressing the imprecise, ad-hoc quality of the concept and measure (after all, in relative terms, people's actual thumb sizes vary enormously). When the federal government established the public housing program in the 1930s, it set 20 per cent as the portion of income each tenant would be charged. As tenants' income-based rents increasingly were unable to cover sharply rising operating costs, local housing authorities were forced to increase rents, leading to severe affordability problems for their tenants, whose rents in some cases rose to 50 per cent and more of their income. A series of amendments to the public housing program in 1969–71 increased federal subsidies and at the same time placed a 25 per cent cap on the amount of a tenant's income that could be charged for rent. Then, when Ronald Reagan became President, one of the first acts of his Office of Management & Budget in 1981 was to raise that "affordability standard" to 30 per cent of income—no rationale, other than to reduce the need for government subsidies by extracting more money from poor tenants. And among the mid-1995 Republican Congressional proposals to reduce the federal deficit and budget (which may be law by the time this book is in print) is raising the mandated tenant contribution above 30 per cent.

Recently, University of Massachusetts housing economist Michael Stone has provided us with an important conceptual and policy critique of affordability standards. Stone argues against the notion of a fixed housing expense:income ratio standard altogether. What a family can afford to pay for its housing ought to be, and realistically is, a function both of household size and household income. That is, the larger the number of people in the household, the more that household must spend for food, clothing, transportation, medical care and other non-shelter necessities. Ideally, at any given income level, the proportion of income devoted to housing should decrease as household size increases, if these other basic needs are to be met. Similarly, the lower the household's income, the lower the proportion of its income it can afford to devote to housing, if it is to satisfy as well basic needs for food, clothing and so on. In reality, for most households, housing is a fixed expense, usually required a month in advance, the financial and social costs of not meeting which are severe. By contrast, food consumption, the other major expense item in most lower-income families' budgets, is far more flexible in nature. One can immediately and drastically decrease food expenditures by not eating out, changing the quality, quantity and frequency of meals, etc. One cannot correspondingly reduce housing costs substantially and immediately by telling the landlord or mortgage-holder that the living room and some of the bedrooms won't be used for the next few months. Families understandably seek to keep these fixed housing costs to a minimum, as rent or mortgage payments represent the overriding first claim on disposable income.

By any definition of "affordability", the country has a housing affordability problem of staggering proportions. The 1991 American Housing Survey data showed that 6.3 million renter households are paying 50 per cent or more of their income for housing, of which 3.6 million are paying 70 per cent or more. Using detailed minimum budget data from the Bureau of Labor Statistics, updated with Consumer Price Index data, Stone arrives at this mind-boggling conclusion: some 14 million US households cannot afford to spend a single cent for housing if they are to have sufficient income left for the non-shelter basics the government says are the minimum needed. The terrible problem of outright

homelessness is the ultimate affordability problem. Estimates, censuses and studies of the problem yield quite different numbers, and, of course, the homeless are not easily counted. A recent Columbia University study, reported in the *American Journal of Public Health*, found that at some time in the five-year period 1985–90, 5.7 million people had been literally homeless—that is, sleeping in shelters, bus/train stations, abandoned buildings, etc., and 8.5 million reported some type of homelessness (involving bunking with relatives or friends). Lifetime homeless figures were 13.5 million people at some point literally homeless, 26 million experiencing some type of homelessness.

Against this totally depressing contextual background, what can be said about this country's efforts to produce "affordable housing"? There's a long history here, going back well into the 19th century and the various reform efforts by churches, settlement houses and private philanthropists; through to the full range of government efforts at the federal, state and local level that began in earnest in the 1930s and continue right up to the present; to the more recent efforts on the part of non-profit sponsors (unions, religious entities, etc.) and locally-based community development corporations, triggered in large part by the partial retreat of federal support that began in the early 1980s with the ascendancy of the Reagan–Bush Administrations.

There have been marked successes, as well as marked failures, in this arena. The chapters that follow discuss these in detail, and draw out the most important lessons as to what creates each of these outcomes. The total effort, however, is minuscule compared with the need. Public and government-assisted housing programs, in all their forms, by both non-profit and for-profit developers, have produced only some 5 million units in 60 years, and the current production rate is down to a dribble. And a great many of these units are in fact being transferred out of the affordable stock or removed altogether, through undermaintenance, demolition, and conversion to condominiums or market-rate rent levels. While impressive affordable housing developments—in design and social terms—are being created all over the country, the reality is that the sum total of all this work is meeting only a tiny fraction of what is needed if the National Housing Goal is to become a reality any time in the next 10–20 years.

A crucial misconception that has dogged US housing policy with respect to lower-income households is the belief that subsidized housing by nature should be transitory—transitory accommodations. That concept underlay introduction of the public housing program in the New Deal 1930s—that public housing was for what Stanford University law professor Lawrence Friedman termed "the submerged middle class"—those (white) middle-class households laid low by the ravages of The Depression, but who, after a few short years of support, would be back on their feet and on to middle-class life. That underlying conception was the rationale for building far fewer housing units than the number of needy families: over time, these units would be recirculated to others in need. By and large, Friedman's characterization of and predictions for the initial occupants of public housing were accurate; came World War II and the post-war recovery, these families moved out of the housing projects to the suburbs (aided, of course, by other government programs, most notably FHA mortgage insurance and federally-aided highway construction). In their place came a less economically mobile (and less white) population, in large part displaced by urban renewal and these same highway programs, and with consequent priority for admission to public housing. For a range of reasons—having largely to do with the country's economic and racial structure—a large proportion of these replacement families, and their children, have continued to need and become more or less permanent residents of government-subsidized housing.

This newer reality—that very large segments of our population require, and desire, permanently affordable housing—has yet to permeate the society's consciousness. Nor have we created or even thought seriously about the kinds and scale of programs needed to ensure decent, permanently affordable housing for all. Public housing projects, in all too many instances, gave inadequate consideration to good design. This was understandable, as it often was hard to find sites and, once one was in hand, the goal was to cram as many units as possible onto the land. And since the housing would be temporary, that also suggested less need for high-quality design. But with the more realistic approach to creating permanently affordable housing for a very large portion of American households, we need to raise good design to a paramount place. And that is not just a question of aesthetics. Well-designed permanently affordable housing must be well located, well managed, have adequate facilities, and be responsive to residents' needs—in short, such developments must provide the setting for stable, safe, satisfactory family life and neighboring, and access to employment, schools, transportation, health services, commerce and all of the other elements that make up "a suitable living environment".

So let us look to the models and lessons about design excellence in affordable housing that this book offers. The examples presented herein clearly show that neighborhood quality and national equity goals can be advanced through the provision of affordable housing. And, underlining the point made at the beginning of this Foreword, it is no exaggeration to assert that unless we place good design at the forefront of all efforts—by public agencies, non-profit and profit-oriented developers—to produce affordable housing, we will not succeed in securing the public and political support needed to mount programs of the scale required to meet the nation's extreme and growing housing crisis.

But we must also see the need to engage in the political struggles that can put solving the nation's housing affordability problem on the front burner. That means, as a precondition, vastly increasing the amount of government subsidies, in order to cover the chasm between housing costs and household incomes. If it helps to win political support, these funds might legitimately be characterized as a wage subsidy that eases the crunch on employers and also frees up household income to consume goods and services, further boosting a local economy. The irony of the nation's current housing subsidy system is that, even before current draconian cuts, the amount of indirect subsidies given to those least in need—via the homeowner deduction feature of the income tax system, which allows deduction from one's taxable income base of all property

taxes and virtually all mortgage interest payments—was many times the amount of direct subsidies to lower-income households. Simply matching this $67 billion homeowner subsidy with an equivalent amount of direct subsidies would be a major first step.

A second necessary reform is to tie government subsidies to structures of financing, ownership and management that permit creation of units that are permanently affordable to lower-income households. The case-studies in this book show how housing costs can be drastically lowered once housing is removed from the for-profit sector with its need to maximize returns at all stages in the housing process: land acquisition, financing, insurance, design, construction, buying/selling, management. Housing owned by resident co-operatives or community-based non-profit corporations have as their goal providing, on a long-term basis, the best housing for the lowest cost, not treating housing as a commodity to yield the largest pecuniary return. Radical reform in the financing, ownership and management of housing is a necessary condition for creating truly affordable units.

The benefits of such an approach are manifold. Stable, mixed-income communities can be created and maintained, communities in which those employed locally can afford to live. Where family housing costs are reasonable and affordable, there is adequate budget to accommodate other needs, with lessened budget-related tensions in family life. Resident involvement in the design process will produce more satisfactory housing and communities. Employment and job ladders for local residents can be created, in construction, management, social services and related commerce. A balanced, integrated local economy keeps cash within the community, rather than having it flow out to outside investors and landlords. Well-designed housing can and should provide the basis for a true community-building process. That is what we mean by "design excellence in affordable family housing".

1. See "America's New War on Poverty", ed. Robert Lavelle & the Staff of Blackside, Inc. (San Francisco: KQED Books, 1995).

2. "The State of the Nation's Housing: 1995" (Cambridge, MA: Joint Center for Housing Studies of Harvard University).

3. Michael E. Stone, "Shelter Poverty: New Ideas on Housing Affordability" (Philadelphia: Temple University Press, 1993).

4. Bruce Link *et al.*, "Lifetime and Five-Year Prevalence of Homelessness in the United States", *American Journal of Public Health*, December 1994, pp. 1907–1912.

5. For a comprehensive program embodying this set of radical reforms, see "The Right to Housing: A Blueprint for Housing the Nation" (Washington, DC: Institute for Policy Studies Working Group on Housing, 1989).

Tomas Prosek

PART ONE: WHO LIVES IN AFFORDABLE FAMILY HOUSING?

CHAPTER ONE:
FAMILIES IN NEED

Affordable family housing is developed for families with some form of government assistance to insure that housing costs do not consume too much of that family's income. Who are these families and why do they need affordable housing? They are often our neighbors, the people we see on the bus, our children's playmates, and the workers in our communities.

Families in need

They are people who have been paying a high percentage of their income on rent, often living in overcrowded or substandard conditions. Their problem is easy to identify; their jobs do not pay them sufficient income for them to participate in inflated local housing markets, either as renters or homeowners, without paying more than 30 per cent of their incomes for housing. As much as any of us, they need and deserve to live in healthy, affordable places where they can raise their children and have enough every month to pay their other bills. Despite a severe shortage in many areas, all over the country families are living in well-designed, government-subsidized housing. In this chapter you will meet some of these people, and read about why they and many others need well-designed affordable housing.

What is "affordable housing"?

According to the federal government, housing is considered affordable if it consumes no more than 30 per cent of a household's income. For very low-income families 30 per cent may be too much to allow enough for the rest of the family expenses (see the Foreword for more detail). Many families in America pay far more than 30 per cent on housing every month, and this situation has been getting worse. "From 1978 to 1993, the percentage of very-low-income households (see sidebar for definition) paying more than 50 per cent of their income for housing, rose by 34 per cent to more than one-third.[1]"

The high cost of housing compared to wages in many areas of the country—particularly in metropolitan areas—is one of the main reasons for this burden.[2] The supply of affordable housing stock, already inadequate, has dwindled as more affluent households have competed for housing and, as a result, have driven up prices. In addition, the expiration of HUD subsidies on some buildings, the demolition of many buildings, and other factors, have caused the removal of an average of 130,000 units affordable to low-income households from the market annually between 1985 and 1991.[3]

As the number of low-rent units has fallen, the number of low-income renters has risen. In 1970, there was a surplus of low-rent units—7.4 million low-rent units and 6.5 million low-income renters. In 1993, the shortage of affordable housing for low-income households reached 4.7 million units.[4] In 1993, over 900,000 households were on the waiting lists for public housing, and nearly 1.4 million households were waiting for privately-owned subsidized housing. Countless other households, which are overpaying, do not appear on lists; many housing authorities have closed their waiting lists because the need is so much greater than the supply.[5] Homelessness, overcrowding, and unsanitary conditions have been some of the results of the loss of affordable housing. In view of this situation, community-based developers and enlightened housing authorities have been attempting to redress this growing shortfall.

Who lives in affordable housing?

Most residents of affordable family housing work. Of the six and one half million families with children below the poverty line in 1994 in the US, 64 per cent are employed.[12]

Willie Pettus

Who needs affordable housing?

A family is considered "low-income" if the household income is below 80 per cent of an area's median income (AMI), below 50 per cent is called "very-low-income", and below 25 per cent is called "extremely-low-income". In 1990, over 40 per cent or almost 20 million families with children in the US were considered low-income. Many of these families had incomes below the poverty line—$11,522 for a family of three in 1993.[6] In 1993, 14 per cent of all US households were in this category.[7] For example, in Alameda County, California, (1995) the area median income was $55,400 for a family of four. A typical family of four qualifying for affordable housing makes about $30,000 a year—or two breadwinners each earning about $8/hr. In 1995, rents in Oakland, California for a 3-bedroom apartment averaged $1,100/mo.— about $13,200/year, or 45 per cent of that family's income.[8]

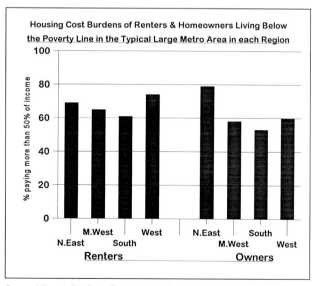

Source: *A Place to Call Home: The Low Income Housing Crisis in 44 Major Metropolitan Areas*, Center on Budget and Policy Priorities. p.54

Contrary to the myth that low-income renters receive disproportional subsidies, homeowners with annual incomes over $65,000 received over $40 billion of Federal housing subsidies in 1989 in the form of tax deductions related to homeownership. Only a small percentage of these families paid more than 30 per cent of their incomes for housing.[9] Homeowners received this bonus from the government, simply because they have the privilege of owning their own home(s); yet in the early 1980s the Reagan Administration cut the HUD budget (which primarily aided lower-income renters) from about $30 billion to about $9 billion.[10] Further cuts in housing programs proposed by Congress in 1995 will make the rent burden for poor families much worse, while the mortgage interest deduction for homeowners remains untouched.

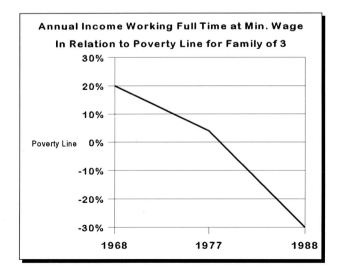

Annual Income Working Full Time at Min. Wage In Relation to Poverty Line for Family of 3

Someone working full time at minimum wage in 1968 was 20 per cent above the poverty line. Someone working full time at minimum wage in 1988 was 26 per cent below the poverty line.[11]

These people often work in the communities where they live, providing goods and services for the town and region. These are relatively low paid, essential service jobs such as teachers, nurses, entry-level firemen and police officers, restaurant workers, farmworkers and mechanics.

Low-income renters

For many families with low incomes, rental housing is the only form of housing within their reach. About 37 per cent of households in the US are renters, and of these about 60 per cent, or about 19.5 million households, earn incomes at or below 80 per cent of the median income for their region.[13] One reason that many families are paying too much rent is the lack of adequate public assistance to compensate for the market's inability to serve them. Despite the federal government's pledge in 1949 to provide a decent home and a suitable living environment for every American family, only about one-third of renter households below the poverty line receive public assistance in some form for housing.[14] The total federal housing subsidy in 1989 was about $14 billion for renters with incomes below $20,000 a year. These households received an average housing subsidy of $300 per month. Meanwhile, middle- and upper-income homeowners received an average of $326 per month in mortage interest deductions.[15]

Low-income homeowners

About 19 million, or 32 per cent, of all homeowner households are low-income—they earn below 80 per cent of the median income in their region. Although only about 1.2 million, or about 6 per cent, receive any housing assistance from the government, another 17 per cent or over 3 million low-income households are paying more than 50 per cent of their income for housing.[16] In most cities, most homeowners below the poverty line are paying over 30 per cent of their incomes for housing. This problem is particularly bad in major cities around the country, ranging from Boston to Miami to San Diego, which have undergone growth spurts and become magnets for more affluent households.[17]

In most areas, new affordable housing for low-income families is rental because it is the type of housing most affordable to households in need. However, given the opportunity, many families with low incomes would prefer owning their own homes, and there are some subsidy programs that private and non-profit developers around the country are using to make this possible. Although rental housing is typically less expensive to develop on a per unit basis than homeownership for low-income families, many communities also prefer low-income homeownership to rental housing because they perceive it as more stable, and politically less controversial.

Still, it is important to note that the financial responsibilities of homeownership can be hard for low-income families to assume—only people above a certain income level can qualify. Significantly higher subsidies—often twice as much as for rental housing—are required to make homeownership affordable for those who qualify on a long-term basis. Often the local government will make up part of the gap with a second mortgage that need not be repaid when the buyer sells if the housing is kept affordable to low-income families. This action prevents speculation and maintains the stock of affordable homes. A lease-to-purchase program can make homeownership possible for first-time buyers who have trouble making a down payment. With some developers, such as Habitat for Humanity, homeowners can participate in the construction to build up "sweat equity", thereby reducing the price of the home. This can also create a sense of community among new homeowners and their neighbors who help build their own and each other's homes.

Limited equity co-operatives

Co-ops and mutual housing offer a middle ground between renting and owning that gives the resident a stake in the property, without the possibility of making a profit on the housing as a commodity. A limited-equity co-op is owned by a non-profit corporation; the residents are shareholders, each purchasing a share (like a down payment or deposit) in the co-op. The residents' monthly payments cover the operating costs and a proportional share of the mortgage. The residents earn interest on their original investment, often at a savings or money market account rate. If a resident moves out, the new resident shareholder purchases the share for the original amount plus the accrued interest. Usually, the non-profit has first right of refusal, thus ensuring that the housing remains affordable. As co-owners, residents manage the corporation's property, and engage services to ensure effective management. Co-op housing may resemble good quality rental or homeownership housing—in fact some rental developments become limited equity co-ops in later years.

"Co-housing" is a term used to describe an intentional community, a social arrangement that typically a group of homeowners may choose in order to share resources and other aspects of their life. The housing usually includes shared facilities for eating, working, and socializing; shared childcare is a big asset for working families. Sharing facilities, equipment and even meals can save families money and time.

Diversity in affordable family housing

Family structure

Single-parent families are one of the fastest growing groups in need of affordable housing. From 1980 to 1990, the number of single parents under 34 years old with children increased by almost 25 per cent. Today, nearly one-third of all families headed by women are in poverty.[18] With limited sources of income and young children, these families require more than shelter. Childcare, job training and counseling services are often critical for a single parent to find and hold a job, while after school programs and children's recreational activities allow parents to work a full day.

Another family type inadequately served by the private housing market is large families. In many cities two-bedroom units are common, three-bedroom apartments are less so, and four- and five-bedroom units are virtually non-existent.[19] Families are forced into overcrowded conditions until children are old enough to find their own place. Larger families may include grandparents living at home or other extended family groups. In recognition of this problem

Parkside Gables, mutual housing in Stamford, Connecticut.
See p. 180 See p. 180   *Fred George*

Nancy Canady and her two children Sheena and Che, resident manager of new affordable family rental housing in Oakland, California.
                                    Michael Pyatok

What is overcrowded and substandard?

Overcrowded and substandard housing is a major problem in the United States. In 1991, it was conservatively estimated that 2.5 million low-income households lived in housing that was inadequate due to lack of plumbing, heating, appliances, or physical maintenance. Nationwide, in 1989, one of ten renter households below the poverty line lived in overcrowded conditions (more than one person per room), compared with 4 per cent of renters who were not below the poverty line; 18 per cent of households lived in physically deficient housing. Substandard housing is relatively worse in rural areas and in the South, especially in cities such as New Orleans and San Antonio. Overcrowding is a significant problem for immigrant families in metropolitan areas—in Los Angeles where there is a large population of Latino-Americans three out of every ten households live in overcrowded homes.[20]

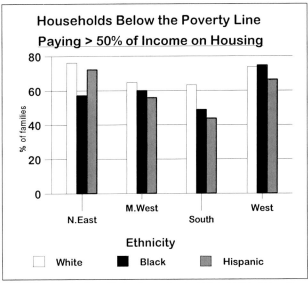

Households Below the Poverty Line Paying > 50% of Income on Housing

Source: *A Place to Call Home: The Low Income Housing Crisis in 44 Major Metropolitan Areas*, The Center on Budget & Policy. See p. 56

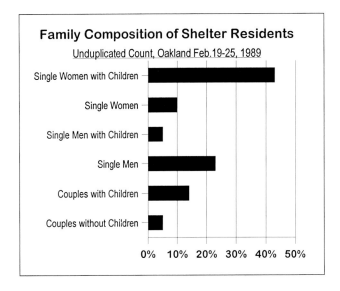

Family Composition of Shelter Residents
Unduplicated Count, Oakland Feb.19-25, 1989

Family Composition of Shelter Residents		
Type	Number	Per cent
Men	660	31 per cent
Women	645	30 per cent
Children	844	39 per cent

Source: *Homelessness in Oakland: 1989 Composite Profile and Unduplicated Count*, Emergency Services Network of Alameda County.

many competitive government-assisted funding programs for affordable family housing give preference to proposals with larger units. Some of these developments are featured in the Case Studies section of the book.

Ethnicity

The housing crisis affects all households below the poverty line regardless of race. In absolute numbers Caucasians make up the majority of poor households with almost 4.2 million renter households (19 per cent) and 3.4 million homeowners (6.5 per cent) below the poverty line in 1993.[21] Throughout the country, Caucasians with incomes below the poverty line paid more for housing than most other groups.[22] However, in relation to their total populations a high percentage of African-American and Hispanic households are in poverty. Of all African-American households, 41 per cent of renters and almost 20 per cent of homeowners have incomes below the poverty line. Almost 36 per cent of Hispanic renters and over 13 per cent of homeowners are below the poverty line.[23] The increase in immigration since 1965 has significantly increased the number of minority families, especially Asian and Hispanic, seeking housing. Many of these families start below the poverty line renting in large "gateway" cities and creating a stronger demand for affordable housing in those communities. Native Americans often live in culturally inappropriate, poorly built and maintained homes on reservations managed by the Bureau of Indian Affairs, a far away agency.

Special needs

Although many people with special needs are single, families below the poverty line may also have members with disabilities or illnesses who need adequate affordable housing. Many of these families require special facilities or services such as wheelchair access or on-site social services. There is a lack of affordable housing and programs for families with special needs. This situation forces some families to be split up and many others to have members who languish indoors in inadequate facilities. Since 1991, most rental apartments and some for-sale housing built with public funds are required by law to make a percentage of the units accessible to people with disabilities. Continually changing design guidelines and regulations require designers to maintain regular contact with local agencies to determine current standards.

Homeless families

The single fastest growing population of homeless people in the US is children. In the San Francisco Bay Area alone, the State of California estimated that over 70,000 parents and children were homeless for at least one night in 1990, a 16 per cent increase over 1989. On any given night, over 20,000 people in the Bay Area compete for about 5,000 shelter beds, a refuge of last resort sometimes perceived to be more dangerous than the streets. Many people on the streets have some form of disability or substance abuse problem. These issues are not easily resolved due to a shortage of social services. Many homeless people work—up to 20 per cent work full or part time—but without the basic support systems that stable families take for granted, holding a job while homeless is extremely difficult.[24] Transitional housing with services is one model that begins to address the complex needs of families working their way back into mainstream life.

Profiles of residents

In the following pages you will meet six families from around the US who demonstrate the diversity of households living in affordable housing developed by community-based developers, partly with government funds. Although each has its own story, these families stand for many others with limited incomes and housing choices. We are grateful for their willingness to be interviewed and photographed for this book.

1. "In Short Supply: The Growing Affordable Housing Gap." The Center on Budget and Policy Priorities, 1995. pp.10–12. "Rental Housing Assistance at a Crossroads: A Report to Congress on Worst Case Housing Need." Table A-4, H.U.D., March 1996.

2. "A Place to Call Home: The Low Income Housing Crisis in 44 Major Metropolitan Areas." The Center on Budget and Policy Priorities, 1992. p.1.

3. "The State of the Nation's Housing, 1994." The Joint Center for Housing Studies of Harvard University, 1994. p.16.

4. "In Short Supply" Op. Cit. p.8.

5. "A Place to Call Home" Op. Cit. p.38.

6. "In Short Supply" Op. Cit. p.8.

7. "The State of the Nation's Housing, 1994." Op. Cit. Exhibit 18, p.14.

8. City of Oakland Office of Housing and Neighborhood Development, 1995.

9. "The Housing Poster" (American Housing Survey Data). The Low Income Housing Service, 1993.

10. "Homelessness in the Bay Area." The Center for Common Cause, San Francisco, 1993. p.6.

11. Ibid. p.11.

12. US Census Data; The Statistical Abstract.

13. "The State of the Nation's Housing, 1994." Op. Cit. Exhibit 22, p.16.

14. "A Place to Call Home" Op. Cit. p.36.

15. "The Housing Poster" Op. Cit.

16. "The State of the Nation's Housing, 1994." Op. Cit. p.16. and Table A-9, p.31.

17. "A Place to Call Home" Op. Cit. p.23.

18. "Homelessness in the Bay Area." Op. Cit. p.11.

19. City of Oakland Office of Housing and Neighborhood Development, 1995.

20. "A Place to Call Home" Op. Cit. pp.25–34.

21. "The State of the Nation's Housing, 1994." Op. Cit. Exhibit 18, p.14.

22. "A Place to Call Home" Op. Cit. Table 6, p.58.

23. "The State of the Nation's Housing, 1994." Op. Cit. Exhibit 18, p.14.

24. "Homelessness in the Bay Area." Op. Cit. p.11.

Tomas Prosek

CHAPTER TWO:
MEET YOUR NEIGHBORS

Profiles of residents of affordable housing.

Name: Hanh and Bich Le Nguyen
Location: Oakland, California
Children: Minh (21)
Occupations:
  Hanh: Maintenance supervisor, student
  Bich Le: Health aide, student
HH Income Range: $16,000–30,000/yr
Rent Range: $430–563/mo
Unit Size: 2 BR/1 BA

Magnus Stark

Janet Delaney

Introduction: Hanh Nguyen and Bich Le live with their son Minh at Frank Mar Housing, a mixed-use development in downtown Oakland. Children yell excitedly as they run across the courtyard. The spicy smells of cooking lingered in their apartment when we met with the Nguyens on a Friday before they went to evening classes.

Hanh: "We came here from Vietnam in 1990. We were sponsored by a family in Albany. I was a pilot during the war, and trained in the US in 1969. Unfortunately we lost the war and my whole family got stuck. We suffered a lot. I was in a concentration camp for 6 years. We tried to escape several times and some of my friends were killed. I was released in 1982."

Bich Le: "When my husband was arrested at the end of the war, the airline I was working for fired me. I had to sell everything I owned, and sold candy, rice and cigarettes on the black market to support my son and my husband when he was in the camp. We were very happy to come here, although when we first arrived we had a lot of trouble. We didn't speak English. I was very afraid and I cried every day. Our sponsor lived in Albany in a very nice, quiet house in the hills. We liked them very much but we felt lonely. We were so happy when we went to Oakland Chinatown, but it was hard because of the distance. Then my husband took this job as maintenance supervisor at Frank Mar Housing and we moved here. The building is beautiful—it is modern, convenient and affordable. It's near transportation, other Asian people, and, most of all, Laney Community College."

Hanh and Bich Le take classes at Laney. Hanh: "I am taking a construction technology course so that I can become a contractor. I wish I was younger and could have started sooner—the war interrupted my studies—but it's better late than never."

Bich Le: "I work at the Vietnamese Health Promotion Project in San Francisco. I work in the Tenderloin with Vietnamese people who have limited English and are afraid to go to the hospital. Preventive health measures are a new concept for Vietnamese women, and we urge them to get checkups every year. I am studying English as a Second Language at Laney. I want to go to University to finish in public health so I can help people more with health issues."

Son Minh: "I went to Albany High School. I graduated in 1992, and went to Laney College for two years to improve my language skills. Now I am at UC Berkeley pursuing a double major in chemistry and biochemistry. I want to go to medical school or perhaps do a Ph.D. in biochemistry. I would like to teach and to help people, especially young people, with health problems."

Hanh: "We have been living here more than three years. We like it a lot, the neighborhood is quiet even though it is downtown. The residents are ethnically diverse, and everyone gets along well. The courtyard is a safe place for children to play, and we have potlucks in the community room at Christmas, Chinese New Year, and Thanksgiving. As maintenance supervisor I know almost everyone here. People like the apartments, although some people have said they wish the patios were smaller so they had more living space.

We are very glad to be here. In Vietnam we have a saying, "We can't have a good life unless we have a safe affordable place to live.""

Name: Gregor Jamroski and Susan Clifford
Location: Seattle, Washington
Children: Sophia (10), Madeleine (8), Aaron (3)
Occupations:
  Gregor: Artist, bookstore owner, teacher
  Susan: Artist, teacher, nursing assistant
HH Income Range: $16,000–28,000/yr
Rent: $600/mo
Unit Size: 3 BR/2 BA

Yannis Paris

Janet Delaney

Introduction: Gregor Jamroski and Susan Clifford live with their three children at Cascade Court in Seattle. The building fits comfortably with its neighbor, the historic Stimson Mansion, in an area of older apartment buildings and tree-lined streets. The sunny courtyard was full of children playing together with parents watching and socializing. Gregor and Susan met with us after dinner.

Gregor: "Before we moved here in November 1994, we were living in a two-bedroom house in South Seattle, spending two-thirds of our income on rent. The first week we were there someone was shot and killed in our alley."

Susan: "I was working as a resident assistant for elderly people for $7 per hour. We were just scraping by, and were on the waiting list for Cascade for two years. When our lease expired we called the management to see if there was an opening and there was! Here we are able to recover from previous years of borrowing, and we feel a lot safer. The neighborhood is a nice mix of families, single people and seniors.

Five years ago rents were doubling every year here and this area was off limits to us financially. The children go to school near here, so being able to live here affordably reduces the stress on all of us and makes family life easier.

It's great to have light and ventilation from both sides and having two bathrooms is nice so we don't have to wait in line. The play structure in the courtyard is a focal point around which families can come together and discuss things."

Gregor: "The kids love playing in the courtyard, and the young ones like to play in the planting beds. Naturally this gets management concerned."

Susan: "I'm interested in helping to create a more interactive play area for the children, like a sandbox. This would help keep them out of the landscaping. Also, if the kids can participate in replanting the beds they will be less likely to tear them up."

Gregor owns a bookstore that features 20th century literature. "When I opened the bookstore, we couldn't afford childcare for Aaron so he came with me to work every day for several years. Now he goes with Susan to work where they have a childcare program."

Susan: "I work in a program making art with seniors. Making art is very therapeutic for people and makes the places they live feel less institutional."

Madeleine proudly gave Gregor a Father's Day present. "I really worked very hard on this," she said. "You have to open it very carefully." As the family gathered around, Gregor opened a beautifully wrapped painting with a copper frame. "That's gorgeous, thank you so much," exclaimed Gregor. He added, "Art is a big part of our lives. We do a lot of art at home—it is very important to the children. In my own artwork I express important themes in society, such as the tension between natural systems and industrial production. I also work at a nearby school teaching art in the enrichment program, and work with Susan in the elderly art program."

Gregor and Susan agree that, "being able to move to Cascade Court was a miracle for us, and living here has made our life as a family easier and more stable."

Name: Sheryl King
Location: Pittsburgh, Pennsylvania
Children: Michael (11), Marcus (8)
Occupation: Hospital worker
HH Income Range: $16,000–20,000/yr
Rent Range: $400–500/mo
Unit Size: 2 BR/1.5 BA

Tim Buckman

Janet Delaney

Introduction: Sheryl King and her two boys live in Crawford Square, just a few blocks from downtown Pittsburgh, on the edge of the Hill district. The area has a rich cultural history full of jazz musicians, basketball players, and political ferment. It also has the largest concentrations of public housing in Western Pennsylvania. During the riots after the assassination of Dr Martin Luther King Jr. several blocks were burned down; Crawford Square, a mixed-income development for renters and homeowners, is built on these blocks. Sheryl spoke with us on a Friday evening after work.

Sheryl: "I grew up in the projects—it used to be safe. People looked out for each other like family, but now it's getting bad, mostly because of the drugs. There are a lot of people trying to clean things up, but I didn't want to raise my kids there. I saw the projects more as a stepping stone to get on your feet. I was able to save enough money to put down a first, last, and deposit and to move into Crawford Square.

I love it here—I have a very nice two-bedroom townhouse with a view of the City from the back porch. It was really nice that they have a program to help low-income families—I was lucky to fit in the bracket of people who qualify. At first the people in the public housing marched against Crawford Square before they knew it was partly for low-income families, but when they realized it was, they were supportive.

I work at Allegheny General Hospital in the Operating Room. I set up surgical kits for the doctors and sterilize the instruments before the operations. We see about 100 cases a day. This is my fourth job—each time I step up, and it's better for me. I

leave the house at about 5.30 every morning to go to work, and I feel secure because the street is well lit. They patrol a lot, and everyone looks out for their neighbors.

My sons go to school near here. The schools are pretty good—as long as they listen and respect the teacher they will learn. They are both on the honor roll; I'm very proud of them.

I want both my boys to go to college some day. If I have to work five jobs, that's my goal. Their dad is an excellent dad—he gets them every weekend, takes them fishing, goes to parents meetings. He went to college, and works two jobs, one at the hospital in distribution and one part time maintenance job. His boys are his life.

My neighbors are pretty diverse—there are blacks and whites here, and we all get along. My neighbor, Lisa, was white, and the kids used to go over there all the time for dinner. We both cried when she moved away. One of my other neighbors is a doctor. We don't see her much because she's so busy. Another one, her son plays pro-football. There are some elderly, and some college students.

I want my children to grow up around other cultures and learn about different types of people. That way, when they go to college they will be able to mix easily with everybody. We all have to live together and work together so we should all get along."

Name: Paula Stone
Location: Boston, Massachusetts
Children: Kenny (9)
Occupation: Homemaker/caregiver
HH Income Range: $15,000–30,000/yr
Rent Range: $215–400/mo
Unit Size: 2 BR/1 BA

Steve Rosenthal

Janet Delaney

Introduction: Paula Stone lives with her son Kenny at Tent City, a mixed-income rental development in the heart of Boston's historic district. Situated at the edge of Copley Square, a busy and dense commercial center, the 100-unit apartment building echoes the four-story brownstone townhouses on nearby tree-lined streets and the high rise towers across the plaza. A regional train and Metro station is across the street, while at the ground level a cafe is filled with passers-by. We met with Paula and Kenny after breakfast.

Paula: "I used to live in Marlboro, a small town outside of Boston. My mother still lives there, and she comes to visit us now and then. My other son is 20 and is in the Navy. He comes to visit when he can. It was nice and quiet in Marlboro, but I moved here to be closer to the hospitals. Kenny has brittle bone disease and needs to go for check-ups on a regular basis. Living here is great for us because we can get around more independently. With the train station across the street we are able go downtown a lot—it's a 5-minute train ride. Right here at Tent City there's something new to do every day."

Kenny: "I like it here because there's a lot of places to go, there's a mall next door, and there's an after-school program where I can do my homework and play. The program starts at 2.30 and ends at 6. Sometimes we go on field trips to the Children's Museum or the circus."

The program is for children from families with a range of incomes. Paula: "The mixed-income population is not an issue; the kids all play together, and they don't care whether or not you have more money."

Kenny: "I take the school bus to school in Brighton every morning. I like reading and math a lot, and my favorite teacher is Maryanne. My dad comes here often—almost every day. Sometimes we go out together, and sometimes we play indoors, or work on the computer."

Paula: "My job is taking care of Kenny. I also serve as the Treasurer of the Residents Alliance, which is made up of tenants and is a liaison between the tenants and management. When there is an issue such as a rent increase, or a maintenance problem, people come to us first, so we can help make things more personalized. I enjoy visiting my neighbors, Trish Miller, who is also on the Alliance, and Ann and Domingo, an older couple. They do a lot of arts and crafts. Their apartment is full of wonderful things.

Architecturally, the building is nice. The grounds are beautiful and all the facilities are accessible for people in wheelchairs, although disabled people each have different needs. Some have to sit with their legs straight, while others have things like oxygen on the back of the chair. This usually means that they need more room to turn around in the apartment, so ideally when you are designing, you should try to leave lots of room. Also, the main doors would be more accessible if they were designed with a remote switch. This would help anyone coming home with two bags of groceries.

Life at Tent City is an experience. I love it here. I feel very lucky to be in a place that is so convenient and with so many different kinds of people."

Name: Anita and James Menifee
Location: Chattanooga, Tennessee
Children: Olympia (9), Jarvis (7)
Occupations:
  Anita: Claims processor at Blue
  Cross/Shield
  James: Sign maker
HH Income Range: $17,200–37,840/yr
Payments Range: $350–500/mo
Unit Size: 3 BR/2 BA

Brian Clements

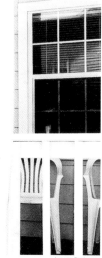

Janet Delaney

Introduction: Anita and James Menifee and their two children live in a quiet, tree-lined neighborhood not far from the center of town. Children ride their bikes and play in the street while mothers sit and chat in the shade of front porches. The neighborhood, called Orchard Village, was built by Chattanooga Neighborhood Enterprises for families with low incomes who had been priced out of the market. We met the Menifees as they returned from Sunday church with Anita's father.

Anita: "This home is all you could dream of. It's the first time we have owned a house. We tried several times before but we didn't have enough income to qualify. We always thought we would have to pay a lot of money that we don't have, but we are only paying $9 more a month than we were paying in rent."

James: "Where we were living before on the Westside, it wasn't a very safe neighborhood. One night we heard a bunch of gunfire and I said to Anita, 'I can't stand it any more,' so we moved. And by the grace of God we're here."

Daughter Olympia: "We have three bedrooms, one for Jarvis and one for me. We have two full baths, one upstairs and one downstairs. There's no waiting in line any more."

Anita: "Olympia's favorite subject at school is spelling—this year she was third in the county spelling bee."

James: "We like to have barbecues in the back yard and the wrap-around porch keeps the house cooler. It can get burning hot here in the summer. The neighbors here are pretty friendly —some are single mothers and some are elderly. We look out

for each other here. Whenever I cut the grass I usually cut my neighbor's grass, because she has allergies, and it always looks funny when only one side of the lawn is cut.

We were both born and raised here in Chattanooga, a block away from each other. We met in high school, and we'll be married for nine years this September."

Anita: "Church is a big part of our lives. My father is the minister at Greater St Mary Missionary Baptist Church, and we do a lot of community work in nursing homes and with church members. We teach the children about the older people in the church so we can plant a positive seed in their minds. We don't want them to become another statistic of black children, and the best way I can think of to do that is through the church.

This location is great, because there is a park two blocks away where we can take the kids to feed the ducks, and there is a recreation center nearby. We are near three major hospitals if anything should happen. This is good for me too, because this summer I am going to go back to school and finish my nursing degree. My daughter is in Girl Scouts and my son is in Cub Scouts, so between school and work and church it's pretty hectic—there's not a lot of time to sit and rest."

Son Jarvis had the final word. "You want to know what I like about Orchard Village? The peace and quiet!"

Name: Jose and Teresa Villafana
Location: Los Angeles, California
Children: Karen (16), Nadia (14),
  Nathalie (12), Erik (6)
Occupations:
  Jose: Construction worker
  Teresa: Homemaker/seamstress
HH Income Range: $12,600–35,100/yr
Rent: $525/mo
Unit Size: 4 BR/2 BA

Marvin Rand

Janet Delaney

Introduction: Jose and Teresa Villafana live with their four children in Villa Esperanza, a new apartment building on a quiet side street in South Central Los Angeles. The housing was developed by Esperanza Community Housing Corporation who, in partnership with the Los Angeles Community Design Center, purchased the site (originally slated for a sweat-shop) to build 33 affordable apartments, with childcare services, and a neighborhood center. The apartments face an interior courtyard where children play. We met the Villafanas after Jose came home from work, before the family went to a community meeting.

Jose is a construction worker, who often spends days away from home with his crew, building gas stations, car washes and convenience stores.

Jose: "It's hard work—recently I've had to get up at 4 am to drive to San Diego. I go wherever the job is.

We heard about Villa Esperanza at San Vicente Church one Sunday. There was also a banner up at the site. We were living in the neighborhood in a two-bedroom house—all the kids in one room. We applied and were accepted. I feel like we won the lottery!"

Teresa works at home. Her industrial sewing machine sits in a corner of the master bedroom.

Teresa: "Before Erik was born I worked in a sewing shop. Now I look after Erik, and take in sewing. Most of the shops pay 50 cents a skirt, so it's hard to earn more than $12–14/day. One lady pays $50 a day—I like to work for her. I prefer working at home, because I can be here for the children. Erik likes to run out and play in the courtyard with his friends. He also goes to the pre-school classes at the on-site daycare center."

Twelve-year-old Nathalie: "Sometimes I go to the center for after-school classes on the computer, and do my homework. I like it here. I have lots of friends, and my school is two blocks away. Where we lived before we were really crowded. I had to share a room with my two sisters. Now we have a lot more room. My mom is a lot happier and my dad is really proud."

Jose: "It's pretty safe here, although in the beginning people were jumping over the fences and stealing things. We had to make the fences higher. We have regular community meetings to discuss issues like security, or noise. There are a lot of rules here. They are very strict about keeping things clean, and we like that."

Nathalie: "Sometimes if the play areas are left messy they make the kids go out and clean them up. On holidays like Christmas we have parties in the courtyard. People here are from different countries like El Salvador, Guatemala, Ecuador and they bring dishes of the different food from their countries. Most of the people here are from the neighborhood, so many of them we knew before. But where we lived before we didn't go out much, because there were lots of gangs. Here I feel safe."

For Jose, the safety of the courtyard housing is a big plus. "I have to go away to work for days at a time, and I feel good that my family is safe here. We all feel very lucky to be able to live here."

Tomas Prosek

PART TWO: FACTORS INFLUENCING AFFORDABLE FAMILY HOUSING

CHAPTER THREE:
COMMUNITY NEEDS AND CONTEXT

Good affordable housing is closely related to good community planning. As part of their social mission to improve the livability of their community, non-profit and government housing agencies should become involved in long-term community planning in addition to single-project development.

PLAN PARTICIPATION

Effective and meaningful community plans require the participation of diverse people and groups. This can extend the timetable for achieving consensus. However, consensus reached through the community planning process hopefully builds political support for affordable housing as a featured element in a community plan.

Community planning requires the following components:
· Housing needs assessment
· Goals and strategies
· Evaluation of present context
· Community vision

Housing needs assessment

The community planning process begins with an assessment of community needs. Census information, demographic trend projections, evaluation of the existing housing stock, and the experiences of family service agencies all contribute toward the development of a needs assessment. The location, rent, and sales price of existing housing and its correspondence with the income of current or future residents establishes the type of "affordability gap" that exists.

Based on this analysis, the needs assessment then quantifies how many units of what size and what rent or sales level would best meet the community's present and future needs.

Goals and strategies

After agreeing on housing needs, short and long term goals and priorities must be set. For example, in response to a deteriorating building stock, a community could set as its primary goal the rehabilitation of 150 units of family housing over a ten-year period, targeting them for households below 60 per cent of median income. In response to projected population growth due to employment growth, a second priority goal might be the construction of 100 new units for sale to low- to moderate-income households over ten years.

Improving the overall quality of residential life requires more than just improving housing. A community plan should also include goals concerning local industry and small business, schools, employment opportunities, public safety, and cultural and recreational facilities.

Once goals and priorities are established, strategies for carrying out the goals should be identified. Meeting affordable housing goals in existing communities almost always requires strategies for finding funds and creating incentives for the improvement of the existing housing stock, and for indentifying sites and financing for new construction.

Evaluation of present context

A community plan represents an opportunity for participants to discuss and descibe their perceptions of the major assets and liabilities of their existing environment. This process begins with the documentation of the existing neighborhood context using photographs, maps, and narrative. This information than becomes the basis for

Local residents formed a planning group and worked with Michael Pyatok and architecture students at the University of Washington to study the Cascade neighborhood in Seattle, Washington.

Michael Pyatok

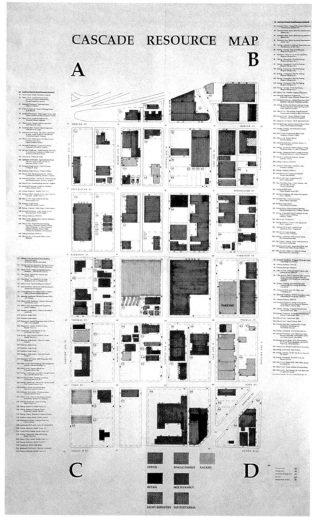

One product of the Cascade neighborhood study, a Community Resource Map.

New scattered site public housing fits in well with historic housing, Charleston, South Carolina. See p. 208

Richard Bradfield

Mission Bay in San Francisco is a largely abandoned industrial area. Many neighborhood plans have been created for this valuable property.

Tom Jones

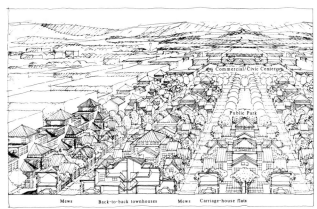

A vision of neighborhood with housing, civic, and commercial uses, one result of community planning workshops, Emeryville, California.

Michael Pyatok

community workshops focused on how the environment is currently serving the needs of the community.

Drawing on their own experiences, participants in the planning process can be very articulate with respect to the ways the buildings, streets, public spaces, institutions, traffic, transportation systems, and natural features affect life in the community. They can also express the social and cultural significance of places and buildings within the community which may not necessarily be evident to outsiders.

The analysis of the built environment of the community looks not just at the physical features and expression of the community, but also at underlying social and economic factors that affect the uses and appearances of buildings and places in the community. Sometimes the forms and conditions of structures in a community create the appearance of prosperity or security, while masking actual social and economic conditions. Conversely, the facades of buildings may appear weathered or undistinguished, but the economic health and vitality of the community may be strong.

Community vision

The final stage in the planning process is the generation of a comprehensive vision for the future of the community. The vision takes the form of a plan which uses maps, diagrams, and before-and-after sketches which convey the physical changes desired by the community. The text of the community plan should articulate how physical improvements are linked to social and economic improvements in achieving desired goals. The amount and type of resources and the required governmental actions necessary to implement the plan should be clearly delineated. A community vision and plan should illustrate and explain the interactive relationships between affordable housing preservation and development activities and other public and private improvements. Affordable housing activities undertaken within the framework of such a shared vision is more likely to be positively received by both its residents and the whole community.

The strong relationship between community planning and successful affordable housing has been recognized by groups across the political spectrum. This was demonstrated by the broad support HUD received for their 1994 requirement that communities who solicit HUD financial support must have a consolidated plan which establishes long range needs and identifies appropriate contexts for affordable housing.

COMMUNITY PLANNING IN DIVERSE CONTEXTS

The participatory, local community planning as outlined above is peculiarly North American. One significant result of this decentralized, locally initiated process is a diversity of plans and a related diversity of affordable housing design.

The diversity of architecture evident in the most recent generation of affordable housing also reveals a strong response to the diversity of climates, materials, building traditions, dwelling types, and street and open space patterns found throughout the nation.

At the same time, there are broad similarities in site planning approaches and housing typologies which are shared by affordable housing developments in similar types of communities. Many American communities face similar underlying social and economic conditions, and congruities of social and economic need unite communities that differ geographically and physically. For example, when considering the forces affecting a community and its potential strategy for improving itself, high-density Harlem and low-density Watts have more in common with one another than Harlem has in common with suburban New York or Watts has with rural California.

There are also congruities of physical forms and land-use patterns that broadly define communities as being either part of a city, a suburb, a town, or a rural area. In broad terms, the divisions that exist between city, suburb, and country town correspond to both social and land-use identities which heavily influence affordable housing activity. Community based architects, developers, and planners must be aware of the particular issues they may face that are specific to the communities in which they work.

The following sections examine in greater detail the common challenges and opportunities facing contemporary sponsors and designers of affordable housing based upon their work in one of the following three types of American communities:

• Older urban neighborhoods
• Suburbs and small towns
• Rural areas

OLDER URBAN NEIGHBORHOODS

Most American cities have residential and mixed-use neighborhoods that are facing decline. The loss of manufacturing jobs in or near these neighborhoods contributes to unemployment and lower incomes among residents. This loss is often coupled with general economic disinvestment and deferred maintenance or abandonment of privately held buildings. In various proportions, groups or blocks of housing require renovation, and small or large vacant tracts of land require redevelopment.

The effort to restore and revitalize older urban neighborhoods requires a strategy for one or more of the following types of housing activities:

• Renewal of older housing
• New housing infill
• Multiple development co-ordination
• New district development
• Urban design co-ordination

Single-family homes for first-time buyers at Lyton Park Place, Minneapolis, Minnesota.
See p. 152

Franz Hall

Duplex and triplex townhouses at Hyde Square Co-op, Dorchester, Massachusetts.
See p. 176

Peter Vanderwarker

Mixed-income high-density rental housing, Cascade Court, Seattle, Washington.
See p. 116

Yannis Paris

Dilapidated historic housing before renovation, Regent Terrace, Philadelphia, Pennsylvania. See p. 239

Howard Brunner

After renovation, Regent Terrace is a community of affordable family housing.   *Eric Mitchell*

Renewal of older housing

Community plans place a high priority on the rehabilitation of existing housing as a first step in halting physical and social decline. Housing preservation and restoration activities may range from upgrading building systems and repairing facades and roofs, to more drastic rehabilitation which involves the reconfiguration of the rooms.

The preservation and revitalization of architecturally significant, historic structures is another potential activity in older urban neighborhoods. Historic preservation is often eligible for financial resources that are not available for non-historic rehabilitation work. Historic preservation can also reinvigorate local pride and increase outside interest in the community.

New housing infill

When deterioration and abandonment become prevalent, there is a likely pattern of arson and vandalism that may lead to demolition activity. Razed structures are replaced by untended vacant lots that further degrade a community. Therefore, selective in-fill development of vacant parcels is a companion strategy in these types of communities.

Inserting new structures into the existing fabric to achieve a balance between the architectural character of the surrounding buildings and the contemporary spatial needs of families is a challenge. Attempting to insert developments that are at different densities to the adjacent structures requires design sensitivity.

Occasionally there is an opportunity or an economic necessity to develop several scattered sites within the community simultaneously. Balancing the architectural goal to develop each site in response to its surroundings with the economic goal for efficient, replicable unit plans raises another set of challenges.

Multiple development co-ordination

New affordable housing, public amenities, and complementary non-residential uses may all be necessary to attract the general reinvestment and resettlement that are desired for older urban neighborhoods. Determining which sites and facilities should be developed first may be crucial to generate momentum toward the final development goals. Affordable housing is often chosen to play the initiating role for community improvements because it may require less public investment and lead time to develop than other public improvements.

Attempts to reinvigorate older urban neighborhoods by attracting new residents can create tension regarding the appropriate balance between affordable housing and market-rate housing and between the needs of existing residents and the expected benefits and impact of new residents. Plans for these types of neighborhoods must resolve this tension in order to proceed.

New district development

In addition to declining neighborhoods, many cities contain large tracts of under-utilized land which offer an opportunity to plan and develop new neighborhoods. Such tracts may have been industrial or railyard districts or former military bases, which have been ignored by market-rate developers. These potential new urban districts typically contain environmental hazards, insufficient infrastructure, inadequate access, or other impediments to development that require a substantial commitment of initial financing to mitigate or overcome.

Characteristically, the development or redevelopment of new districts requires pioneers; affordable housing developers and their residents may be more willing than market-rate developers in such urban areas.

City officials or citizens often expect new neighborhoods to provide a range of housing types and affordability. This imperative may derive from a goal to balance housing affordability and jobs. Environmentalists and housing advocates have a common interest in maximizing affordable housing in new urban districts served by existing mass transit and infrastructure as an alternative to regional sprawl, and freeway dependency.

Urban design co-ordination
Multiple urban sites and new districts represent unusual opportunities for creating diverse public and private realms and for integrating many building types and sizes within a unifying plan.

Within an overall urban design plan for a revitalized new neighborhood, there are alternate approaches to the incorporation of affordable housing. One strategy for incorporation is the prior designation of certain sites coupled with site-specific financing. A second strategy is the requirement that each site or phase in the plan set aside a certain percentage of the units in each building as affordable units. Under this strategy, market-rate and below-market-rate units are constructed and financed together.

Under either approach overall planning and design guidelines can be adopted, which make affordable housing indistinguishable from market-rate housing.

Infill housing matches the local context, Field Street, Detroit, Michigan. See p. 154
Kadushin

SUBURBS AND SMALL TOWNS

Suburbs and small towns have been homes to more North Americans than center cities since the early 1960s. Seen once as a solution to urban housing ills, suburbs in particular have existed long enough to generate their own housing problems.

Although suburbs and small towns mirror some of the same social and physical problems as many center cities, they often lack the political or financial resources to address them. Unlike cities, they also tend to lack a wide range of housing types, and they often lack inhabitants with widely varying incomes and cultural backgrounds.

In suburbs and small towns, affordable housing sponsors face the following challenges:

· Predominance of the single-family house
· Lack of good multi-family models
· Reduced public realm
· Neighborhood acceptance

Predominance of the single-family house
In post-war suburbs, development was largely predicated on the idea that the single-family detached house on a generous lot was the most acceptable model for residential life. The strict separation of residential districts from other uses was another norm for this period of suburban settlement. Although initially touted as an economical way to house America's returning veterans, this settlement model has become increasingly costly both to the consumer and to the environment.

Lack of multi-family models
The movement to provide new and less expensive models for suburban and small town residential development originated among market-rate developers. Many of them

Field Street is part of a neighborhood plan called Island View, Detroit, Michigan. See p. 154
Kadushin

A mix of new construction, rehab, market-rate and affordable housing helps make the Randolph Neighborhood in Richmond, Virginia a diverse and balanced community. See p. 210

Tom Bernard

The American Dream—a single-family detached home in the suburbs.

The American reality—the sameness and anonymity of suburbia.

Less costly, higher density alternatives to single-family homes can be designed to appear friendly and less dense in suburban communities. Townhouses at 25 units per acre, Tower Apartments, Rohnert Park, California. See p. 90

Michael Pyatok

recognized that the cost of constructing new homes under the old pattern was increasing more rapidly than household income.

Many towns and suburbs have responded to pressure from developers to reduce housing costs by allowing greater housing density, smaller lots, and attached or clustered housing units in some areas. Unfortunately, much of the higher-density housing constructed between 1950 and the present is seen as unattractive and undesirable. Bulky buildings, motel layouts, and cheap materials contributed to this problem, as did the fact that many communities allowed this type of housing in less desirable areas such as near industrial areas, freeways, and fringe areas.

This post-war multi-family housing stock often has none of the architectural character or locational advantages of older apartments built for the Depression-era middle class. As a result, a primary task for suburban and small town affordable housing sponsors has been to create a new model for higher-density housing.

REDUCED PUBLIC REALM

The suburban and romantic small town ideal derives from a largely upper-class concept of a community as a picturesque enclave of individual residences existing within nature. This ideal manifested itself in the characteristic front lawns, which in older, more affluent suburbs appear to merge together to form a park-like setting between the street and the individual homes. The front lawns originally defined a new kind of expansive, soft public realm that contrasted with the more contained, harder public realm of city streets and plazas.

Over time this idealized public realm has shrunk in size and diminished in landscaping. This is especially true in high growth areas with soaring land prices where individual homes have grown as lots and front yards have shrunk, and where the expanses of concrete paving and garage doors have become the dominant visual features.

The emergence of gated communities and the popularity of cul-de-sac street patterns has also led to more fragmentation and social isolation within newer suburbs, and further reduced the pleasure and efficacy of pedestrian life.

The physical and social isolation characteristic of many residential suburbs and their sprawl has spawned a movement to create an alternative model. Calling itself "the new urbanism", this movement harks back to 19th and early 20th century small towns and suburbs. The new urbanists are united in a desire to develop new residential community models that contain greater housing variety and a vital public realm. A few privately developed communities such as Seaside, Florida, and The Kentlands, Maryland, demonstrate some of the new urbanists' planning and design concepts. The aesthetic results and market successes of these communities have attracted positive media attention.

If more market-rate developers adopt some of the new urbanist approaches, the physical character of new developments will improve. But on their own, market-rate developers will still need public financial subsidies if they are to create significant numbers of affordable housing units in these new communities.

NEIGHBORHOOD ACCEPTANCE

Affordable housing sponsors value social connections and strive to promote a positive sense of community among their residents. In this regard they are pro-community. But the housing they construct or the people who will live in it are often seen as a threat to a community. Trying to develop affordable housing in a multi-family development poses a significant challenge to suburban and small town sponsors. People who live in conventional detached housing often view those who live in other types of residential structures as less desirable neighbors.

Homeowners often view renters as less stable neighbors who will bring crime and lower property values to their neighborhood. These stereotypes can be challenged by developers and public officials through focused public education efforts that illustrate the profiles of potential qualifying residents of affordable housing. As existing residents actually meet people in the neighborhood who need affordable housing, and understand their income levels, job descriptions, and the schools their children attend they realize that these people are their neighbors. Some homeowners forget that they once were renters, or that they too once struggled to find a downpayment.

"Subsidized housing" raises strong negative connotations about poorly designed, poorly managed "projects" filled with people who don't work. Developers and managers of well-designed and well-managed affordable housing often must take community members on tours of their existing developments to see the quality of the environment, meet residents, and talk to neighbors who are willing to testify that living next to such affordable housing does not lower property values.

In some regions, organizations that advocate on behalf of non-profit developers (such as Non-profit Housing Development of Northern California) are developing community acceptance campaigns that strive to educate people in the ways described above.

Good design cannot completely eliminate fears of other kinds of people, but the promotion of high quality design standards in these communities should at least remove design as a contentious issue and allow other opinions and concerns to be aired.

RURAL AREAS

A new wave of American residential settlement is occurring in some rural areas. The 1990 census projects faster growth in rural areas than in cities, towns, and suburbs. Some of this growth is spurred on by new manufacturing concerns locating in these areas where land and labor are cheaper. At the same time, changes in grazing, mining, forestry, and

Six-unit buildings house mixed-income condominiums at Battle Road Farm, Lincoln, Massachusetts. See p. 166

Lucy Chen

agricultural operations are leading to job losses and lower wages for existing rural residents. Rural areas contain some of the greatest extremes of wealth and poverty in America.

The challenges for rural affordable housing developers include:

• Restrictions on density
• Providing appropriate models

Restrictions on density
Separated both by income and often by great spaces, rural residents and the rural housing market share the primacy of the house on its own plot of land, with its own front and back door. This housing type is promoted by land-use regulations which often require very large lots, from one unit per acre to 40 or more acres per unit, in an attempt to preserve rural character. Although these regulations may have originally been intended to protect and promote small farmsteads, in many cases small farms are not viable and the large plots are used as retreats for wealthy households.

Rural requirements for large lots derive in part from notions of rural livelihood which do not reflect the reality of existence for large sectors of the rural population. They may also relate to the dependency on ground water and the requirement for septic fields, which are restraints that may vary widely within the same region.

Providing appropriate models
The predominance of detached buildings suggests a need for affordable housing in many rural areas. Yet the pressure for detached buildings must be reconciled with the pressure for economy of construction. Since rural housing development will usually stand out against a natural or agrarian landscape, the image of the housing as seen from a distance will be of substantial concern. One alternative rural site plan model is buildings which appear to be single residences but actually contain several units. This model is particularly appropriate

Affordable family rental apartments are woven into a pecan orchard at Dermott Villas, Dermott, Arkansas. See p. 247

Timothy Hursley

OPAL Commons, a rural mixed-income co-housing community on Orcas Island, Washington, See p. 68

Ron Glasset

in locations where large, older homes and agricultural buildings are common, and can provide sources of architectural context.

A second rural model is clustered housing, which is not a prevalent rural model but which is common in other parts of the world. Clustered housing conveys a strong social as well as physical cohesion by defining exterior common spaces and creating a recognizable form much like a village in the larger landscape. Clustering achieves more economical housing and closer social ties; it also accomplishes the preservation of large tracts of agricultural land or open space that might otherwise be subdivided.

Under either model, rural developments should be linked to open space preservation as an alternative to large-lot subdivisions. The co-existence of affordable housing with agricultural, recreational, and even wildlife preserve uses is possible with careful community planning and site design.

COMMON GOALS IN ALL COMMUNITIES

Common to all three categories of communities is a uniform goal for affordable family housing to be integral to the larger vision and plan for the community. In some instances it will be expected to stand out as a symbol of change and an image of a better future. In other instances it will be expected to fit in, as a complement to the present and bridge to the past. Each community has the right and obligation to help define the role that affordable housing should play within a community plan.

Other factors shape the final design of the development, but the ultimate measure of the success of the design for the community will be the degree to which it fulfills its expectations. Outsiders may appreciate architectural quality and value design awards, but true design excellence comes from meeting the community's needs and enhancing the neighborhood in the eyes and hearts of its residents.

Tomas Prosek

CHAPTER FOUR:
POLICY, FINANCE, AND REGULATIONS

Grand community plans may excite the imagination,
but making them become real depends upon the
co-ordinated support of public policy, financial
practices, and local land-use regulations.

DESIGN QUALITY AND REGULATIONS

Where local and state agencies have co-ordinated their programs, resources, and approval procedures to promote and reward good design, project sponsors have a positive environment in which to create their residential development. By contrast, talented architects and experienced non-profit sponsors have been frustrated, if not defeated, when they have undertaken projects in communities that have no public policy support for good design, limited or capped financial resources, and planning and zoning rules that promote inappropriate housing models.

Taken together, the rules, restrictions, and criteria of each agency or institution involved become major determinants of the design of affordable housing. The challenge to committed architects and sponsors is to have an impact on the regulators long before they have to comply with the regulations.

PUBLIC POLICY AGENCIES

Public affordable housing policies adopted by federal, state, and local governments and agencies are the legal basis for all housing programs. Housing programs are then fashioned and implemented in response to general policies. Both at the level of the general policy, and in the details of funding programs, there are opportunities to include language and procedures that would promote higher construction quality and better design.

One or more of the following entities may be involved in generating policies and programs which govern affordable housing developments:

• HUD
• State and local governments
• Tax credit allocation committees

HUD
The agency with the greatest influence on affordable housing design is the federal Department of Housing and Urban Development, HUD, which is responsible for carrying out the housing programs that are enacted and approved by the Congress and the President. Affordable housing funding programs are constantly being added, modified, and deleted as part of the political process in Washington, DC, a situation of primary concern to affordable housing sponsors and advocates.

HUD oversees the Community Development Block Grant (CDBG) program which allocates yearly grants based on a congressional formula. CDBG awards to communities are a major though shrinking source of affordable housing funds. HUD also operates its own programs which make direct project grants in response to competitive individual applications by a project sponsor, or by a locality. Cuts in these programs projected over the next several years are a result of a shift in policy made by the President and Congress and carried out by HUD.

San Francisco City Hall, one source of political and financial support for affordable family housing.

Tom Jones

HUD family housing built in the 1950s to minimum standards, Oakland, California.

Willie Pettus

**CONSOLIDATED PLAN
for
Housing & Community Development**

July 1, 1995 - June 30, 2000

May 16, 1995

City of Oakland
Office of Housing and
Neighborhood Development

A consolidated plan, an essential strategy for local government to support affordable family housing.

When making direct grants, HUD administers both policy and funds; costs and designs are controlled through their formulas and regulations. These regulations have always been a challenge for designers to decipher and to apply.

Housing for formerly homeless single mothers and children, developed with state funding assistance, West HELP, Greenburgh, NY. See p. 172

Jock Pottle

New community room and library at 555 Ellis Street, San Francisco, California. See p. 108

John F. Martin

HUD has lifted some of its strict cost control measures for housing, which were based on sometimes erroneous assumptions regarding the cost-effectiveness of standardized, box-like buildings. At the level of the district offices, HUD now appears to be more concerned with design than in the past. HUD and some other federal agencies like the Federal National Mortgage Agency (FNMA) conduct design awards programs. However, some project sponsors and their architects affirm that considerable energy is still required to get better buildings when working with federal policy guidelines.

State and local governments

Most states require localities to adopt some form of local housing policy that identifies affordable housing needs and indicates how their fair share of those housing needs will be met. The policy should address both unit production and rehabilitation goals, and should indicate how the local zoning and the availability of sites will accommodate these goals. Any locality that is seeking federal funds to support its affordable housing programs must now generate a local consolidated plan which contains this information plus financial strategies for achieving affordable housing goals. These policies should reinforce or complement one another.

At the local and state level, project sponsors have a better opportunity to influence policies and their related programs so that they recognize and support well-designed buildings. For example, when state agencies and local government make financial awards, they can require or recognize the inclusion of supportive services and amenities in affordable housing, the provision of a variety of housing unit types, and a commitment to high quality materials and design.

Municipalities and states can create higher design standards than federal ones. When both federal and non-federal funds are used, HUD may accept the higher standards as a legal basis for raising cost allowances. In one case HUD told a project sponsor that an elevator was not needed for a two-story senior development. When the locality showed HUD that its own housing policy required elevators for any seniors living above grade, HUD relented and funded the elevator.

Tax credit allocation committees

The federal government has codified the Federal Tax Credit for Low Income Housing, a funding program which gives investors in affordable housing an attractive tax break. Although the financial program is an adjunct to the federal tax code, state tax credit allocation committees select which developments are awarded funds. Many of the better state tax credit allocation agencies make their awards based upon some form of a scoring, or point system for evaluating projects which are applying at the same time. Several states have had very successful experiences by giving extra points to family housing which contains features that contribute to better quality, livability, and design.

For example, in California, the point system rewards developments with bigger units and more bedrooms for families, ample resident community rooms, and designated children's play space and equipment. Since sponsors competing for tax credits know that the inclusion of these features will enhance their chances to receive funding, the state supports better design through its program.

At all levels of public policy, incentives and requirements for more durable and more livable family housing improve the general level of project applications for funding and affordable housing design quality.

FINANCIAL AGENCIES

With supportive public policy in place, adequate and timely public financial assistance is the next critical factor in obtaining good design. Public agencies which are the primary source of affordable housing funds have an opportunity and a responsibility to support good local design at several points in the development of a project.

Other funders should share and support high design standards as well. Since most affordable housing depends upon multiple sources of funds, the interaction among the following potential funders is important:

Playground at Tuscany Villas, Davis, California. See p. 78

Jane Lidz

- Local government agencies
- Redevelopment agencies
- Private foundations
- Private lenders

Local government agencies
Local finance agencies which administer CDBG and HOME funds can incorporate criteria reflecting design quality into their standards for lending or granting local funds, and they should be committed to supplement state and federal financing to provide adequate development budgets for superior design.

Their on-going public financial support for good design should also include local programs that give local housing producers grants or deferred loans for retaining architects in the predevelopment stage of a project. These same agencies can assist non-profits by financing site feasibility studies so that several alternative sites or schemes can be evaluated before a project site is selected.

Some local public funds should also be committed to support affordable housing education programs for both sponsors and citizens. Evaluating and illustrating the positive benefits of good design, and examining the effect of the local codes and approval process on cost and design are important research and discussion components of public education.

Redevelopment agencies
In this era, the source of local funds is severely limited. In many jurisdictions the sole or primary source of local financing is the local redevelopment agency. Redevelopment agencies use tax exempt revenue from existing properties combined with bonds and other public debt to raise housing funds.

In addition to being a source of project funds, redevelopment agencies also have the statutory authority to acquire and set aside sites, adopt urban design guidelines, conduct architectural review and make final project approvals. The integration of all this activity in one agency creates an opportunity and a responsibility to support good design consistently throughout its programs.

In some cities, additional funds have been raised for affordable housing through programs in which developers of hotels, high-rise offices, and other private facilities pay a housing mitigation fee linked to the demand for affordable housing created by their anticipated workforce. The decline of office construction and the economic downturn of the 1990s has weakened community's ability to enact such provisions, but they should be considered for the future. Such programs may be part of the activities of a redevelopment agency, or may be centered in some other agency.

The constant need to stabilize and expand sources of local revenue for housing requires advocacy and creative thinking. Those concerned about design quality should participate in or support these efforts.

Private foundations
While most affordable housing is primarily dependent on low interest loans or grants provided by public agencies, private financing of some kind is typically needed as well. Private financial resources must be available and committed to augment public funds in achieving good design.

Private foundation grants have played a valuable role in providing such additional funds, which project sponsors have used to improve building quality and to finance specific

Daycare center at Sarah P. Huntington House, New York City. See p. 244   *Rody Jean-Luis*

Bankers, funders, and elected officials at a grand opening for new affordable housing, San Francisco, California.
A.N.D.

amenities that would not have been achieved with only public funds. The commitment on the part of some investors to good design has led them to mount their own education campaigns directed to other financial investors and government agencies.

National equity investors and funders such as the Local Initiatives Support Corporation (LISC) and the Enterprise Foundation have also undertaken programs to help local officials and non-profit sponsors learn how to get better quality developments, through workshops, conferences, and continuing education programs. Housing advocates hope that other regional and local foundations will become involved in this type of support.

Private lenders
Most family affordable housing also depends on private banks or savings and loans to provide construction financing or permanent financing. Private banks and savings and loans develop their own risk criteria for lending, but some recognize and factor into their evaluations the long-term value of affordable housing which includes beneficial amenities and is well designed.

One example of a lender's program that recognizes the value of design quality is the AHP (Affordable Housing Program) sponsored by the Federal Home Loan Bank. This program offers deferred grants and loans to applicants through periodic competitive rounds. While their primary criteria for participating in developments is to help reduce debt burdens that would otherwise make projects infeasible, they make their awards using criteria which also include other factors. They are explicitly interested in assisting developments which provide amenities and other features and resident programs that increase livability, contribute to a stronger sense of community, and promote opportunities for individual and family development.

PLANNING REGULATIONS AND PROCEDURES

The next and perhaps most complex hurdle that project sponsors face is their own local planning code and planning approval process. In the US, each city, town, or county adopts its own planning code. Planning codes are co-ordinated to land-use maps, which subdivide the jurisdiction into zones designated by what types of uses are allowed within each zone (residential, commercial, manufacturing). Planning includes the on-going act of designating zones and determining what uses, heights, densities, parking, and other requirements pertain to them.

Prior to the early 1900s, there was no zoning as we know it today; market forces dictated what was built where. In one of the earliest legal tests of zoning, the courts determined that communities did have the right to regulate land use for the common welfare, and to protect the rights of each property owner against the possibility of deleterious uses on adjacent properties.

Court decisions in the 1920s supported the legal rights of communities to adopt zoning restrictions, and explictly supported the separation of single-family housing from other uses. The formal separation of single-family from multi-family housing, freestanding houses from row houses and apartments began with that decision, and, combined with automobile use, accelerated the development of the suburban landscape we have inherited today.

The influences of zoning districts and other planning conditions on any development are enormous, and affordable housing in particular will be subject to or dependent on one or more of the following:

• Conventional planning code regulations
• Planned unit development regulations
• Inclusionary zoning
• Affordable housing incentives
• Planning approval process

Conventional planning code regulations
Since the 1920s, local zoning ordinances have evolved under the influence of planning theory, lobbying, and advocacy to become elaborate regulations. Many residential zoning ordinances and planning codes now regulate: the dimensions of building lots, the number and type of units

A new single-family housing development built with reduced street widths, setbacks, and parking regulations, setting new standards. Benson Glen, Renton, Washington. See p. 70

Dick Springgate

on the lots, the amount of land covered by any building, the height of buildings, the spaces between buildings and adjacent structures or lot lines, the minimum amount of open space per unit, and the minimum number of parking spaces.

Although planning codes are ostensibly established to promote new development that reflects community standards, planning codes are often a patchwork of regulations designed more to prevent the bad than to encourage the good. Regulations such as the placement of buildings on their sites with equal setbacks from neighboring structures were intended to produce compatibility, but they actually promoted the boxlike, motel-type apartment buildings typical of the 1950s through 1970s, when applied to large lots.

These types of buildings have contributed to a negative perception of higher density housing in many communities as well as a distrust of planning and zoning documents and procedures.

Planned unit development regulations

Partially in response to the need for a more flexible approach to planning, and to get more control over architectural design features, many communities adopted planned unit development (PUD) zoning in the 1960s. Under the PUD approach, larger sites could be developed at higher densities and conventional setback and other location regulations might be reduced, in exchange for a better overall design.

The PUD process depends on project sponsors, professional planners, and community groups being clear and reasonable about the various tradeoffs that can and should be made. When PUD zoning is used developers are encouraged to

identify natural or historical features that should be preserved as part of a development. They may also be encouraged to achieve greater affordability than conventional detached construction might allow, while still producing a desirable residential environment.

Implicit in much of PUD zoning are two assumptions. One is that developers need to be given an incentive such as a density bonus so they will elect to use the PUD approach. The cost savings and superior design that may result from PUD zoning should motivate the sponsor to expend the often higher design fees and longer approval process associated with the PUD approach.

The second assumption is that the community will get some public benefit from the resulting design, with the possibility that the lower development costs per unit of many PUD plans will be passed on to the housing consumer.

While many PUD developments have produced good design, and the approach is favored by many planners, their housing prices and rents have not been substantially lower unless required to be so by law.

Inclusionary zoning

In the 1980s beginning in New Jersey and then Southern California, communities were legally or morally challenged to be more proactive in obtaining affordable housing as a part of new market-rate development. This led to the adoption of inclusionary zoning, by which communities required a certain percentage of all new units to be affordable, often in exchange for an incentive such as a density bonus. This affordable housing overlay was most successfully adopted in communities undergoing strong market-rate growth pressures.

A reduction in required parking was granted in exchange for a parking management plan that included future parking expansion potential. The Farm, Soquel, California. See p. 74
Alex Seidl

A Celebration of
Affordable Housing in the
East Bay

"YES! In My Back Yard", a booklet documenting affordable housing in the East Bay of the San Francisco Area, by the American Institute of Architects, East Bay Chapter Housing Committee.

The financial and social success of many developments with mixed incomes does prove the compatibility of market-rate and affordable housing.

Affordable housing incentives

In addtion to PUD and inclusionary zoning, other provisions and incentives in local planning and zoning codes are also valuable in promoting housing affordability, and in responding to the daily living requirements and spatial priorities of lower income families.

Many affordable housing developments have relied upon one or more of the following zoning provisions in their community planning code to support the combination of better design and more economical development:

- Abundant sites zoned for multi-family housing
- Reduced minimum lot sizes
- Reduced street widths
- Density bonuses
- Greater building coverage allowances, in exchange for interior amenities
- Reduced open space requirements, with criteria for demonstrated usability
- Lower parking requirements
- Acceptance of tandem (one car behind the other) parking arrangements and common open lots
- Acceptance of shared pedestrian/auto courts and cul-de-sacs as secondary play space (bike riding, etc.)

Planning approval process

The planning code and professional planning staff of a community may promote good models of affordable housing, but the neighbors adjacent to any proposed development will have their own perceptions regarding appropriate new housing. Differences between the allowances and provisions of the planning codes, and the preferences of neighbors must be resolved through the planning approval process. This process usually culminates in a public hearing before an appointed planning commission, planning board, or architectural review board.

The planning process itself can have a major impact on a design as various participants attempt to shape the project based on their attitudes regarding higher density or affordable housing. Opponents of affordable housing typically assert that affordable housing is not compatible with their neighborhood because of its density and scale as well as its impact on parking, traffic, and open space use. The success of a project in obtaining approvals as designed and financed depends on its sponsor's ability to show how these issues are addressed, and consequently how the density and design will be compatible with existing patterns or may enhance livability for both the residents and the community.

Many affordable housing sponsors must undertake various studies to prove the compatibility of their development or determine what, if any, mitigation is required. This is a major burden on a project sponsor, and requires a commitment of time, funds, and creativity beyond what is required for other types of projects. Failure to anticipate and respond to the issues raised by the public may seriously affect a proposal, and may lead to a shift in design emphasis away from meeting residents' needs and toward meeting the demands of a few outspoken critics.

Even when public policy, financial agencies, and planning code regulations are fully supportive of affordable housing, the public participation and the approval process is the final determinant of affordable housing design excellence.

Tomas Prosek

CHAPTER FIVE:
THE DESIGN PROCESS

The design of affordable family housing is a complex and challenging process that requires the participation and co-operation of the developer, neighbors, potential residents, local officials, and the architect. The architect must help guide this team with great sensitivity and patience to a design solution that resolves physical, social, and cost issues, and produces a building that the entire community can be proud of for generations.

WHO DESIGNS AND DEVELOPS HOUSING IN THE US?

Historically, few Americans had an architect design their home. Even today, fewer than 5 per cent of the population shapes their individual homes with the help of their personal architect; the rest buy or rent their homes or apartments, choosing from among the options provided by others. Real estate developers and builders instruct their architects, if they have one, to create generalized responses for specific markets. Today, about 60 per cent of this new housing is single-family and detached, and mainly built in suburbs. About 40 per cent of new housing is in multi-family units, developed in both cities and suburbs. For the last decade most of this housing has been built by private developers, although an increasingly significant portion has been built by private non-profit development corporations or community development corporations (CDCs), partly with government subsidies. Due to massive funding cutbacks by past administrations, public housing authorities, which used to account for about 10 per cent of new family housing, have, since 1982, built less than one-half of 1 per cent of new family units annually.

Although in a minority, some innovative developers and their architects are trying to reshape community form. In reaction to the wastefulness of the American lifestyle they seek to develop new communities by more environmentally responsible means. These developers are attempting to design more sustainable communities by: limiting the role of the automobile in laying out new communities; increasing density to conserve land, natural resources, materials, and energy consumption (both embodied in the construction and during its operation); combining land uses and community functions to reduce travel time and expand the possibilities for walking; and experimenting with health-conscious and environmentally-sound building materials and methods. These experiments are taking place in middle- to upper-income communities, mainly suburbs, where developers operating in a market of educated customers are enlisting architects to help them develop a new niche in the competitive world of housing development.

In contrast to most private developers, CDCs often develop housing with the participation of potential residents and surrounding neighbors. Although some private developers use focus groups to test their market, they often do not ask the opinions of neighbors. Participation in the design process has been practiced by CDCs out of necessity. Providing families of modest means with decent housing has always required a thoughtful use of land and resources to succeed with tight budgets. Recently, the political controversies around community acceptance of affordable housing have made broad-based input common in the development process.

Historically, this is a relatively new process because it incorporates in a painstaking manner multiple viewpoints of real people for making design decisions instead of the interpretation of abstract market concepts. In many countries, and until recently in the US, government subsidized housing included little or no input from potential users, neighbors, or property managers. There are examples from around the world of housing developed as ideal housing types by well-intentioned architects, planners, and social reformers that served residents badly, was unsympathetic to the larger neighborhood, and often led to social and physical decay.

A typical single-family suburban street. *Willie Pettus*

A new street in a traditional pattern, Randolph Neighborhood, Richmond, Virginia. See p. 210
Tom Bernard

Pruitt Igoe Homes, St Louis, Missouri. *Public Domain*

Chatham Village, affordable rental housing, 1930, Pittsburgh, Pennsylvania. *Tom Jones*

High-rise family housing built in the 1960s, San Francisco, California. *Tom Jones*

St Francis Square, affordable family housing, 1963, San Francisco, California. *Peter Aaron/Esto*

Examples of historic non-profit sponsors of affordable housing

Labor unions, churches, and other benevolent organizations have a history of building thoughtfully designed housing for those whose interests they served. In some large cities such as New York and Pittsburgh, local public housing authorities (PHAs) and charitable organizations began building model affordable housing in the early 1900s. Some of this housing is in use and attractively maintained today. However, until 1937 when the first federal housing programs were enacted, the country's low-income populations were not served directly by government assistance, for the most part. Though initially committed to good design and site planning, PHAs were rapidly pressured by the late 1940s to emphasize quantity over quality. Especially after World War II, when the Depression-era sympathy with the poor abated, many PHAs were beset with deteriorated projects. However, there have been some exceptional PHAs, which committed themselves from the beginning to scattered-site, small project development and designs that were compatible with the neighborhoods.

In the 1960s there was an attempt to create government incentives for the private sector to produce affordable housing. Although some good housing was built under these programs by the end of the 1970s corruption, poor design, and other failures led to a major reduction in reliance on the private sector. Rigid and minimal standards often governed the design of federally-assisted housing; the idea of using market-oriented focus groups to guide design was rarely considered. Only very recently have local PHAs begun to enlist the participation of residents in the renovation of their housing. Even this change in the process of designing public housing fades to insignificance in comparison to the enormous need. After more than 50 years, housing owned and managed by PHAs still comprise only a tiny percentage US housing stock.

More recent models of private and non-profit sponsored affordable housing

Since their emergence in the late 1960s and early 1970s non-profit or community development corporations (CDCs) have become the key providers of housing affordable to those whose income puts them in the lower one-third of US families. Funded by federal programs begun in the Kennedy, Johnson, and Nixon eras, CDCs have been providing people with lower incomes access to the design services of architects in a manner not unlike what has always been available to home buyers and renters with higher incomes. Although construction budgets are often smaller, these developers and their architects give as much or more attention to housing built for families with low incomes as is given to multi-family housing built for higher-income households.

COMMUNITY-BASED DESIGN

In comparison with most for-profit developers, many CDCs make a greater effort to please all those who may be affected by their housing developments. It is common for CDCs to contact neighborhood leaders when they see a need and an opportunity to provide housing for people whose incomes are below 80 per cent of the area's median. CDCs are also formed by local community leaders and residents as the result of a specific issue or opportunity relating to their housing needs. When preparing plans for a new development, the experienced CDC seeks information from neighbors, from their own board members and staff, and from residents of its own developments. Increasingly neighborhoods require this kind of input from both for-profit and non-profit developers as a condition of acceptance of a project before the design process begins. Some CDCs now assemble a short list of architects known for designing high quality affordable housing and invite representatives from a neighborhood to participate with them in the final process of interviewing and selecting their architect.

Neighborhoods are affirming their right to be concerned about any change in the life they have grown accustomed to, regardless of the good intentions of outsiders or new-comers. This concern moves people beyond simply being protective of their private property to being concerned about the quality of life of their whole community. Like the neighborhood watch concept, this reaction demonstrates that all actions affecting private property, whether for private profit or for the larger public good, are a matter for public scrutiny. Hence, people see themselves as having a right to participate in the design of a new housing development in their neighborhood.

People earning below 80 per cent of a region's median income should be able to live where they wish. Those who wish to foster security for the community as a whole should recognize that this security depends on stability in the lives of people of all income levels. Many of the most important providers of service in the community—firemen, police officers, teachers, health-care workers, bank clerks, restaurant workers—often earn less than 80 per cent of the community's median income but cannot afford to live in the community they serve because home prices and rents are beyond their means. Neighborhood watchdogs should think twice about excluding affordable housing, they could be excluding the very people who safeguard their community.

Through thoughtful design and intelligent planning non-profit developers and their architects are assisting the cause of fair housing practices. They both protect the rights of newcomers, regardless of their income, and satisfy the concerns of a neighborhood's existing residents. The architect must then demonstrate a sensitivity to the needs of those to be housed in the new development and of those who already live in the area.

ORGANIZING COMMUNITY PARTICIPATION IN THE DESIGN PROCESS

Experience demonstrates that a design committee (DC) representing the following groups should be established at the beginning of any housing development process:

· The board of directors of the CDC
· Neighborhood residents
· Representatives of users
· Property managers

The board of directors
Since the CDC is responsible for the long-term ownership and operation of a rental property, a design committee assigned to work with an architect should include members of the CDC's board of directors along with representatives of the host neighborhood. Boards of CDCs can be very diverse, composed of professionals, business people, clergy, architects, concerned citizens and activists from low-income communities. Some board members usually come from similar social and economic backgrounds to those of the future residents and will know their concerns.

Northtown Housing Board members at a planning meeting, Rancho Cucamonga, 1994.
Michael Pyatok

Neighborhood residents
The processes of real estate development and housing design can strengthen lower income communities if the CDCs and their consultants orchestrate the process in a way that encourages members of the community to become advocates for affordable housing. Architects who participate in a community design process learn more about the specific cultural and social needs of the families to be housed. On the other hand, participating members from the community will not always share values. Church leaders, business persons, advocates, and neighborhood associations may have different ideas about how the housing and the residents will fit into the community. To identify and address all the different community concerns requires sincerity, patience, and creativity on everyone's part. Under the leadership of a good team the process can lead to both design and political consensus. This process creates a body of supporters who can advocate at planning commissions, city councils and before the loan boards of lending institutions. The expertise gained by people in

low-income communities in developing housing gives them the confidence to fight established institutions for economic justice in other areas as well.

Representatives of users

If a CDC has completed other family housing developments, their residents can participate helpfully in the design of a new one. Because of their income level they may share lifestyles with those being served. They know what it is like to live as a tenant sharing common facilities like open space, laundries, tot-lots, etc. To the surprise of participating neighbors, who very often are owners of single-family, detached homes, the tenants of multi-family, attached housing share many of their concerns and aspire to the same goals, regardless of difference in incomes.

Oakland Community Organizations Board members at a groundbreaking.

Property managers

The design committee should also include a representative of the company who will manage the development. Since renters are perceived to be transient and to have little stake in their neighborhood, neighbors are usually more concerned about rental housing than they are about housing for new homeowners. Property managers are a valuable source of information about how to design durable environments; their input is a great help to both the design of housing and its performance in a neighborhood. Some CDCs send their property managers to annual seminars to gather information about their experiences and to share it with the development teams. Some CDCs include representatives from their property management in the design process, to learn from previous experiences. If this practice was customary, more lessons would be learned and housing design would be improved.

Because most non-profit housing is well studied during the design process and carefully monitored during operation, the property managers and non-profit sponsors of government-assisted affordable housing are often more sensitive to the needs of tenants and neighbors of their housing than are developers and absentee owners of market-rate housing or public housing authorities. Good management in non-profit housing, along with affordable rents, has encouraged families in such housing to be more stable than typical homeowners. It is not uncommon for families living in non-profit rental housing to reside in the same apartment or house until their children have fully grown and left home.

A neighborhood may ask the CDC and the property managers to allow their representatives to participate in creating the selection criteria for prospective tenants. Although the income level of tenants is set in advance, CDCs have some flexibility in deciding who their future tenants will be. Their selection criteria are always as strict as any proposed by neighbors themselves. CDCs will undertake a credit check, a review of previous landlord references, a visit to the prospective tenants' present homes, a check of previous police records, etc.

The number of applicants for rental housing developed by CDCs typically exceeds the number of available units by as much as twenty times. It is not uncommon for a 20-unit development to have over 400 applicants. After eliminating some applicants because their income exceeds the limit, CDCs use their screening criteria to reduce the list to a smaller number who then participate in an open lottery. Because of this process, the CDC will often have less troublesome tenants than for-profit landlords in the same neighborhood.

THE DESIGN PROCESS

Lessons learned from the case studies

Although the case studies that follow represent diverse communities, certain elements of the design process are common to most of them. The typical design process is described below; it starts with the selection of an architect, which should happen as early in the process as possible. The goal of the community design process is to establish a productive two-way communication between the development team and the community; the architect plays a critical role in this process, which has several goals:

• To learn how the community feels about itself.
• To help it become aware of specific issues that affect it.
• To develop design solutions that address community concerns without compromising the needs of the eventual residents or the basic feasibility of the project.
• To create a supportive constituency for the development to help gain land-use and funding approvals for the project.
• To provide a model process and product for future community-based development efforts.

Choosing an architect

Architects differ significantly in their style of working with clients. When interviewing architects the design committee should evaluate several aspects of their past performance:

• Ability to work with people: Their capacity to listen and work well with people whose opinions may differ from theirs.
• Knowledge of the problem: Their sensitivity to the special needs of households for whom they are designing, and their awareness of the social and architectural history of the neighborhood.
• Demonstrated history of similar projects: Their experience in designing attractive developments with similar construction budgets for similar household types.

• Technical knowledge: Their ability to manage the project from the initial planning through the construction phase.

Ability to work with people
Developments may take 3 to 5 years depending on the degree of difficulty encountered during its critical phases. Issues include:

• Addressing the concerns of local neighbors
• Obtaining approvals from local planning and building departments
• Supporting the sponsor while it acquires financing and satisfies the requirements of private and public funding sources
• Working with the contractor, subcontractors, and building officials to build the development

Many people are involved in each of these phases. People disagree; nerves become frayed. The architect is a critical player and must be a patient, tolerant listener who can turn many diverse opinions into consensus without sacrificing the quality of the final product.

The architect should be able to explain how s/he involves others in the process of making design decisions. Rather than portray his/her solution as the best and only one worth considering, or provide token participation with a few, preselected options, architects should assist the design committee's hands-on process of shaping all key decisions. This approach often uses three-dimensional, alterable scale models to help the DC explore many alternatives in the search for neighborhood design values that are compatible with the needs of future occupants.

Besides creating a product more sympathetic to neighbors and future users, another important consequence of the hands-on approach is the sense of co-authorship and cohesion that develops in the participating group. The group who participates in this process will be more likely to defend the development in the public forums of planning commissions and city councils who may fear misinformed opponents, and meetings of loan officers of lending institutions, who may fear lending to such developments.

Knowledge of the problem
Whether by designing such developments on their own or while working for others, architects accumulate both the technical and the intuitive knowledge necessary to solve a problem. Until architects complete five to seven such projects under the direction of more experienced architects, or have accumulated at least 10 to 15 years experience, they are not really ready to take one on their own. An architect's travel experience and knowledge of housing design in other countries and cultures, coupled with an awareness of the social and physical history of housing issues in the US, indicate a level of sophistication that will benefit both the eventual users of the development and its neighbors.

Demonstrated history of similar work
Architects must be able to show well-designed housing, which they have completed for similar budgets, by arranging site visits to similar developments they have designed and by providing a list of previous satisfied CDC and for-profit clients.

Technical knowledge
Although it is impossible to rank the many services supplied by the architect, among the most important are the careful attention to planning and building codes during the design process and the monitoring of the contractor's performance during construction to insure the development is being built according to the plans and specifications and within the original budget. No other member of the development team can provide these services. Given their tight budgets, CDCs cannot afford endless changes during construction because of inadequate drawings or instructions from the architect, or because of ignorance of a detail in local, state, or national codes and regulations. The committee which selects an architect must be certain that the full team of architect and engineers has a proven track record completing similar developments on budget.

Pyatok explaining some principles of good site planning in a participatory workshop.

A traditional small-town streetscape.   *Willie Pettus*

A typical mixed-use street in Oakland, California.   *Michael Pyatok*

A lively street in the "Chinatown" district, Oakland, California.   *Michael Pyatok*

NEIGHBORHOOD CONTEXT ISSUES WHICH A DESIGN COMMITTEE SHOULD CONSIDER

Architects should show their understanding of the role that housing can play in shaping a community and its physical fabric. Depending upon the existing context, architects must either recognize its value or perceive the lack of valuable forms and structure—a lack which a new development could rectify by establishing new patterns for others to emulate. When a neighborhood has a combination of physical conditions and social memories that the local population cherishes, architects must recognize these as worth respecting. Such settings may include a wide variety of characteristics. Some important ones are:

• Traditional residential streetscapes
• Traditional mixed-use streetscapes
• Architectural scale and detail
• Neighborhood vitality
• Historic context

Traditional residential streetscapes
A well-tended public domain with streets of an intimate width lined with front porches, street trees, and well-kept front yards facing sidewalks where people stroll and children play. Garages, if they exist, are tucked away to the rear of the homes. Such neighborhoods were probably designed prior to World War II and the massive increase in automobile usage. The DC should become familiar with the historic development patterns and elements of buildings particular to its neighborhood. They should be certain that new developments have roads, parking and dwelling entries carefully designed to respect these street patterns, even if densities must be significantly higher to reflect the reality of today's housing development costs.

Traditional mixed-use streetscapes
Another successful traditional streetscape has buildings without landscaped setbacks abutting the sidewalk. The buildings have ground floor shops or offices topped by housing with balconies or bay windows that overlook the street below. This is a traditional way of life for people in towns and cities around the world, many of whom work in the businesses below the housing. The vital activity on the street at most hours of the day, the easy access to goods and services, and the sense of community often found on such streets makes mixed-use developments key to rebuilding US neighborhoods. However, in low-income neighborhoods it is often difficult to finance commercial space due to high vacancy rates in the area and lack of disposable income in the surrounding community. In spite of these difficulties, a growing number of CDCs have recognized the importance of building new mixed-use developments on such streets to revitalize the neighborhood with new businesses, services and jobs. The DC must be certain that its proposal respects the design characteristics of such streets.

Architectural scale and detail

To give higher-density housing a friendly appearance in the eyes of neighbors and visitors, buildings should have exterior forms that fit in with or interpret the character of the better buildings in the immediate neighborhood. Attention should be paid to:

· Articulation (expressing individual dwelling units).
· Roof shapes (enhancing the silhouette of a building against the sky).
· Room-sized elements, all of which relate dwellings to the street (porches, bay windows, dormers, room projections, porticos, arcades).
· Architectural detail (brackets, railings, chimneys, entry columns, sunscreens, roof vents).
· User enrichments (opportunities for residents to decorate their exteriors with planting, garden structures, sculptures, windchimes, birdfeeders, etc).

If the architecture of an existing neighborhood has traditional responses to all of these design issues, a new development should be sensitive to but not mimic them. If a neighborhood is lacking in these elements, new affordable housing can re-establish them and become a model or standard to be equaled by future developments in the neighborhood.

Neighborhood vitality

A thriving neighborhood may not always be tidy. Working neighborhoods in which people live and operate family businesses understandably give priority to the success of their businesses. Although the display of wares, the manufacture of goods, or the signage that advertises a business activity may appear untidy, these are signs of hope, industry, and entrepreneurship that may not be compatible with aesthetic standards that impose financial burdens on fledgling businesses. If a neighborhood has these characteristics, a new development should reflect them and encourage new residents to add their own layers of economic diversity and cultural display.

Historic context

Researching a region's architectural and planning history should be the first assignment for any design team. Sometimes new developments are sited in historic districts and are subject to strict design review guidelines that regulate massing, materials and setbacks. In other cases, new developments are in a position to restore a part of a context that has been tattered by poor judgment or the ravages of disinvestment, disrepair, abandonment, or fire. For example, to name just a few such restoration strategies, new housing may need to:

· Reinforce the street frontage between existing buildings
· Permit passage through a development for neighbors needing a shortcut to other places (when security allows).
· Provide open space useable by neighbors and residents.

· Respect the shape of a neighborhood's existing topography
· Provide public parking for the neighborhood

By adopting these measures a new development can complement its physical context. Its social context may be supplemented by bringing in needed services such as childcare, adult education, community facilities and recreational programs which neighbors identify as essential to rebuilding the social infrastructure of the neighborhood.

Tower Apartments, Rohnert Park, California. See p. 90   *Michael Pyatok*

Langham Court, Boston, Massachusetts. See p. 198   *Steve Rosenthal*

Safe courtyard at Southside Co-Housing, Sacramento, California. See p. 84   *James Kline*

Shared auto-pedestrian court, Fulton Mews,   *Tom Jones*
San Francisco, California.

Tuck-under parking at Tower Apartments, Rohnert Park, California.   *Michael Pyatok*
See p. 90

Taming the auto

All developments face the same difficult questions about the automobile. Parking placed in clustered lots or in garages at the outer edges of a development permits open spaces within the development to be safer for pedestrians and children. But remote parking areas are hard to supervise. Also, residents and visitors are likely to arrive by car unless good transit is available. They feel as though they are entering the back door when they arrive in a large parking lot at the outer edge of a housing development. On the other hand, if parking is brought into the heart of a development in order to place each resident's vehicle as close to home as possible, the development suffocates from too much pavement. If making room for the automobile and its driveways results in a noticeable separation between pedestrian open spaces and dwellings and consequently between front porches and sidewalks, the social potential of a pedestrian environment is diminished. An alternative to the large, remote parking lot or a-car-in-every-house are small parking areas that bring the automobile relatively close to home and allow a comfortable network of pedestrian open spaces undisturbed by driveways and parking lots.

No matter how the automobile and pedestrian open spaces are defined, the number of parking spaces required for a site is the most critical factor for any site plan. As long as land use policies and development patterns force Americans to be addicted to the automobile, and more than two parking spaces are required per dwelling to accommodate residents and guests, the pedestrian environment will be compromised.

One way to economize on space is to combine automobiles and pedestrians in the same courtyards or plazas for a limited number of households with an emphasis on the presence of pedestrians. In order to convey the feeling of a pedestrian space, asphalt paving associated with driveways should be avoided, and pavement associated with pedestrian use such as stamped and colored concrete should be encouraged. Abundant landscaping, an intimate scale in outdoor spaces, front porches, patios and other pedestrian-friendly uses facing the public realm will reinforce pedestrian over automobile use. Speed bumps and driveways that use bollards instead of curbs convey the impression that the automobile is a guest in a place that pedestrians also use.

If a development spends more money on pavement and landscape to create automobile/pedestrian courts that soften the vehicular presence, the local planning authorities should reduce the landscaped open space requirements or permit a slightly higher density of units to compensate for the added expense of the enhanced driveway surfaces. In effect, pedestrian use of the vehicular areas will increase because the cars must move more slowly through such spaces, and hence the need for landscaped open spaces for pedestrians is lessened.

Public and private open spaces

Family housing developments must always provide adequate open space for residents. Although zoning codes mandate minimum requirements for both public and private open space, the design team must consider the actual needs of the residents. Property managers are responsible for maintenance and security of public and, to some degree, private open space; their participation in designing these spaces is critical.

Public open space

A hierarchy of public spaces must be considered for family housing. In many cases central spaces or courtyards that can be used by groups for gatherings and parties, also serve as access to individual homes. There may be room for a barbecue drum, picnic tables, and larger trees. Although courtyards are generally defined by surrounding buildings, planting must be carefully chosen to help soften the edges of a space, to create interest and delight, to provide shade in warm climates, and to keep people back from ground floor windows.

Where there are families with children, the needs of different age groups must be addressed as well as is possible. Young children (4 to 12) will use play areas with a play structure that should be visible from the homes and public rooms such as common laundries. When older children play on the site, they will prefer private places to gather in groups, or more active games such as basketball. If it is possible to provide half-court basketball, care must be taken to separate it adequately from living areas so conflict is minimized. On the other hand, such areas should be well supervised by the housing, secured from the outside and well lit to prevent crime.

The art of locating planting includes ensuring that it will survive the active play of children. All right angle turns in pathways need wide turning curves to accommodate children making short cuts. All vertical planting—trees, shrubs and vines—need to be out of the way of running children, preferably near fences, buildings, and other obstacles that children will avoid.

Security

In both inner city and suburban neighborhoods, security is a first priority of residents, owners, and property managers. Stable community life is best served not by prison-like enclaves, but by socially active settings where neighbors are clustered into smaller groups so they can watch over each other's children and keep out unwanted visitors. Contrary to site-planning norms for housing of the last three or four decades, nothing is gained in a social sense, other than trouble, by connecting rear yard areas for shared use beyond about thirty families. If people need to visit friends living in an adjacent cluster, they can walk down the street to their neighbor's front door and ring the doorbell. This adds activity to the street and limits unsupervised roaming in rear courts.

Private open space

No matter how densely a neighborhood is developed, residents deserve private patios, porches, and small front yards to provide welcome relief from efficient interior living quarters. These spaces can serve a number of purposes, including:

- A secure place for small children to play, that is visible from the kitchen or living room
- A place to store bicycles, barbecues, and patio furniture, and to grow flowers and vegetables
- A place to sit outdoors, eat, or enjoy the fresh air
- A place from which to observe and, if desired, engage in life in the neighborhood
- A transitional space between the public realm and the privacy of the home in which residents can greet neighbors, put down groceries before entering the house, and keep strangers at a distance from the edge of the house

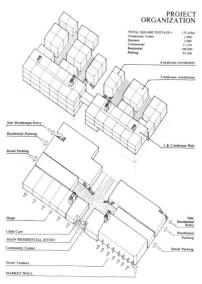

Main secure entry leads to multiple secured entries to both upper terraces and flats, Hismen Hin-nu Terrace, Oakland, California. See p. 100

Front porch at Woodlands, housing for single mothers, Boulder, Colorado. See p. 130

Jerry Butts

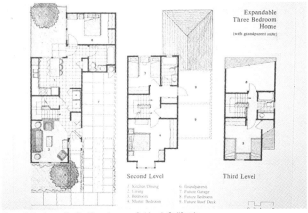

Expandable home for first-time buyers, Oakland, California.

Kitchen–dining room looking through to back porch, Battle Road Farm, Lincoln, Massachusetts. See p. 166   *Lucy Chen*

Rear patio at Tower Apartments, Rohnert Park, California. See p. 90   *Michael Pyatok*

Planning the home or apartment

Throughout this country's history, the organization of domestic space has responded to the cultural and social factors of the time. This period of US history is no different. Current household types differ from the past in that more than half of all households have no children, and about 24 per cent are single persons living alone. Of those families with children, more than a quarter have only one adult living in the household. Several cultural groups include in-laws or grandparents as part of the household. Because of the recent recession, grown children, who formerly would have left home, are still living with their parents. Each of these household types warrants special design considerations. The current population is better served by housing that provides small studios or separate in-law units, shared living arrangements, multi-generational homes, live–work combinations, and transitional or temporary housing as well as conventional family homes.

Many of us live in smaller quarters compared to previous generations for several reasons, among them the growing scarcity of resources, which has raised the costs of land, wood, metals, and other materials. The cost of borrowed money for construction as a percentage of total costs is much higher than it was just after World War II when suburban expansion exploded. Environmental concerns about wetlands, air and water quality, and non-toxic building materials have added costs to new developments. One way to ease these problems is to consume less of everything, including the amount of housing we inhabit.

Smaller units require a greater attention to floor plans to avoid wasted space and to maximize the residents' ability to place furniture. Private outdoor spaces are important additional rooms to a home; all shared public spaces become active extensions of a household's living space. Placement and size of windows are critical because they enhance views and make small spaces feel larger.

Personal identity

Owners and managers of rental housing worry about what tenants may do to the interiors of their dwellings and therefore discourage most alterations that respond to immediate household needs. Also, remodeling a dwelling unit is an expensive process that has not been facilitated by technical innovations. However, private outdoor space, while also controlled by management, is an opportunity for residents to display their personal identity. Since this multi-purpose buffer space lends itself to inexpensive decoration, it is a logical place for residents to be creative in shaping their living environment.

The opportunity to personalize should occur both in front and in back of a dwelling unit. The front space is usually the place where guests are welcomed and neighbors are greeted and engaged in conversation. The back space offers relaxation and more informal social interchange between neighbors; possessions that residents consider inappropriate for display in the front space may be kept here. Both these places need some definition in the form of fencing and landscape. However, fences should not separate residents from the public realm. Neither side of a fence is secure if people on both sides cannot greet each other in some way and protect each others' property.

Public art and neighborhood value

Every effort should be made to enlist the contributions of artists to the design of affordable rental housing. Culturally appropriate art produced by an interactive process between artists and residents is a tenant-organizing tool. A strong tenant organization inspired by its own cultural creations instills pride and encourages long-term upkeep and neighborly vigilance against unwanted activities.

Economic development

Even if built in a neighborhood without supportive services, well-designed family rental housing may deteriorate rapidly, and the physical planning strategies used to exclude crime will not be successful. To support lower-income families in a crime-free setting, neighborhoods must also offer jobs, good schools, easily available services, retail shopping, and access to mass transit.

CDCs should not shy away from mixed-use areas. Not only do developments in such areas provide needed housing, they also bring back services and commercial ventures that have fled the neighborhood. Thus they rebuild the urban fabric that has been destroyed by years of disinvestment or limited investment by outside retail chains. Street life prompted by lively business activity supervised by people living on the floors above the businesses is an important deterrent to street crime.

Families who need affordable housing also need affordable shopping. When non-profit developers are successful in meeting this dual challenge, they also serve the larger urban design goal of creating compact, pedestrian communities with a reduced dependency on vehicular transportation. The combination of housing and shopping also supports local businesses who employ local residents.

It is often financially very difficult to include retail space because the expected rents must be lower than what will be needed to support the mortgage and operating expenses. The CDC must find additional sources of subsidy to fund this space, just as it must do so to write down the residential rents. But since for-profit developers often cannot get access to such forms of assistance, only CDCs can be expected to revitalize a retail district with their housing programs.

In the absence of an industrial base to provide decent blue collar jobs, housing design should respect the fact that many families must earn additional income from home-based businesses. Non-profit developers and property managers should permit home and apartment designs which can include home-based businesses operated by their residents. Homeowners and tenants living in market-rate developments are often given this freedom. Other options include allowing

tenants to sub-lease a room to grandparents for social and economic stability or to a sub-tenant to recapture income lost when a working child leaves home.

Ultimately, the best way to make households independent of government assistance is through economic development that provides local employment. This is no easy task for, while most neighborhoods with lower income households readily accept well-designed affordable housing, these same areas often have a hard time attracting successful or new businesses unless retail and commercial rents are also subsidized to absorb some of the risk due to the lack of start-up capital by small businesses.

Children with public art statue, University City Townhomes, Philadelphia, Pennsylvania. See p. 236

Don Matzkin

Townhouses over streetfront retail, Frank Mar Housing, Oakland, California. See p. 112

Willie Pettus

Daycare center at 201 Turk Street, San Francisco, California. See p. 120   *John Sutton*

On-grade court and main entry at Hismen Hin-nu Terrace, Oakland, California.
See p. 100

Michael Pyatok

Simple forms and bold tones at Daybreak Grove,
Escondido, California. See p. 130
Loisos/Ubbelohede

SOCIAL SERVICES

As noted elsewhere, an individual's or household's inability to afford housing is a combination of lack of earning capacity and a speculative private market that forces up the price of housing when people need it the most. The market responds well to those who have high incomes; apartment rents or home prices meet their income level or willingness to pay. But a limited earning capacity insures a struggle to meet housing expenses. Other services required to help people maintain or increase their ability to work are now being included by CDCs who traditionally supplied only subsidized housing. These services may include: childcare to give parents time to work or to train themselves to improve their earning capacity; child-rearing classes to improve the next generation's chances of avoiding the problems of poverty; educational services to encourage prudent shopping, wise nutrition practices, and better management of limited household finances; and counseling to help people to break dysfunctional behavior patterns and to find jobs.

THE IMAGE OF HOUSING

Reusing existing housing stock and making sure that new housing respects the character of surrounding buildings is very important to today's neighborhoods. Whether in small towns, big cities, suburbs, or rural areas, each neighborhood has accumulated some sense of history in the buildings and landscaping of previous generations. The present generation will also leave its mark; in this way neighborhoods are constantly changing. But the more architecture that previous generations have left behind, the more accustomed people are to these familiar images. Particularly now with diminishing resources and a lagging economy it is harder to restructure our neighborhoods. The instability and insecurity of life caused by global and national economic changes also cause people to want to hold on to the stable images of the past. New housing must both respect these concerns and create images that inspire hope for a better life.

Successful multi-family residential architecture must please the host neighborhood as well as its new residents. In much of the US, adventurous, avant-garde design may not be appropriate for affordable housing. An exception may be parts of the Southern California region where an emphasis on new and unusual design has created a context of its own. Many older cities have residential neighborhoods emerging within districts such as industrial zones that may never have been used for residential purposes. These places offer fertile ground for architectural experimentation where there is less chance of irritating conventional neighbors. Such choices may be driven by either the lifestyle of the inhabitants or the many design possibilities of relating to non-residential forms. When design committees and architects are choosing the architectural character of a new development, whether it is avant-garde, neo-traditional, or a rehabilitation of a historically valuable structure, they should remember that people who live in affordable family housing are, regardless of income, typical of families around this country. They deserve to fit into a neighborhood with a sense of quality and quiet dignity.

Steve Rosenthal

Michael Pyatok

Eric Mitchell

Marvin Rand

Brian Clements

PART THREE: CASE STUDIES OF AFFORDABLE FAMILY HOUSING

CHAPTER SIX:
GUIDE TO THE CASE STUDIES

- Introduction to the Case Studies
- The Costs of Affordable Housing
- American Dwelling Types

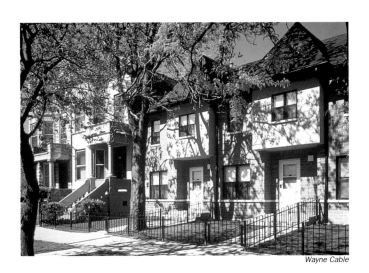

Wayne Cable

INTRODUCTION TO THE CASE STUDIES

Background

The case studies represent a wide cross-section of recent affordable family housing developments from around the country. The focus of the book is *new* construction of affordable *family* housing, either for-sale, co-op, or rental. Representation from each region was important to demonstrate both regional variation in design and threads of continuity across the country. However, in a few cases we chose to bend the rules. In New York City, although there is little new construction of affordable housing, there is a tremendous amount of rehabilitation of older structures. From the southwest, a region where we had difficulty finding examples of affordable family housing, we selected some senior housing that responds well to the hot climate. In each case, the evaluation of the development was based on both its design excellence and the importance of the community development issues it illustrated. The length of the case study was also partly determined by the amount of high-quality artwork submitted, and the ease of access to information about the development. We recognize that we probably omitted some affordable housing developments that deserved to be included—if so, we did not hear about

them in time for publication. We hope that there will be a sequel to this book. Certainly, the companion slide library will be updated periodically with new developments that demonstrate design excellence in affordable family housing.

The Special Characteristics Guide identifies a wide range of categories by which the case studies can be analyzed and lists which developments fall into which grouping (for example, infill housing, mixed-use, or historic structures rehabilitation). This assists the reader to focus on a specific interest area, and turn immediately to the relevant case study.

The Case Studies

Each case study tells the story of an affordable family housing development from its conception through the design and development process to its culmination as a living community. Interviews with architects, sponsors, project managers, residents, neighbors and property managers reveal insights into important issues. The images are chosen to match the text and to best explain the design as it relates to both the residents and the neighborhood. The project summaries give a synopsis of technical information, including the names of key players in each development process.

MAP OF THE UNITED STATES AND REGIONS REPRESENTED IN THE CASE STUDIES

THE COSTS OF AFFORDABLE HOUSING

The term "affordable" refers to the financial capability of residents, not necessarily to the development cost of housing. The costs of designing and developing affordable family housing depend largely on the location, the size, and the design itself. Allegedly high development costs are sometimes cited by critics of affordable housing as a reason to curtail funding programs and somehow let the market provide affordable housing at a lower cost.

An extensive study was undertaken by the Local Initiative Support Corporation (LISC) and the California Tax Credit Allocation Committee of 35 housing developments built by both types of developers in urban and suburban areas in California to determine whether there is any basis for these concerns.

The study found that there were no differences in cost, once the methodology of comparison took into account the different regulatory, financial and programmatic environments within which these two different types of developers work. In fact, the non-profit developers often proved to be less expensive. The study is especially significant since California's non-profit sector has produced many nationally recognized, award-winning designs for affordable housing during the past decade.

The study revealed the following conclusions.

1. Non-profits generally build housing for larger families with a higher percentage of three- and four-bedroom units. Private developers build housing primarily with one- and two-bedroom units. Comparisons based on cost-per-unit ignore the differences in size of units built by these two types of developers.

2. Non-profit developers often include service facilities such as childcare centers and counseling offices not included by private developers. These costs are often wrongly combined with the cost-per-unit when comparing developments.

3. Non-profit developers typically assemble financing from three to six sources, greatly contributing to staff and consultant costs and adding considerably more time to the development process. By comparison, private developers often get financing from one or two sources.

4. Non-profit developers, because of their funding sources, often must abide by Davis-Bacon regulations, paying prevailing wages during construction. For-profit developers escape these requirements and save from 15 to 30 per cent on construction labor costs.

5. Non-profits include developer fees as part of their costs up front. For-profit developers often make most of their profit after the development stage (cash flow, project sale, management fees) and, therefore, these do not appear as development costs, yet they are clearly passed on to tenants or buyers at some point, with major impacts on affordability.

6. Non-profit developers often build projects that are smaller in scale than those executed by for-profit developers. Economies of scale during construction are not the same for 20–50 unit developments versus 100–200 unit developments. Also, administrative costs are often the same for different size projects, appearing as a higher per-unit cost for smaller developments.

7. Non-profit developers often select sites which for-profit developers would reject because they are too costly to develop. Yet, once the sites are developed the buildings fulfill important community needs.

8. Non-profit developers often choose to develop housing at higher densities in inner city locations to lower the cost of land per unit and to serve more families in need. This decision adds to the cost of the parking, elevators, structure (for three-story buildings instead of two-story), sprinkler systems for attached dwellings, etc. For-profit developers often choose lower-density suburban edge conditions where regulations and costs are lower.

9. Non-profit developers of rental housing often plan to manage their properties afterwards and design with an eye to longevity, spending more up-front to lower long-term expenses. Merchant developers who sell their developments five years after completion often overlook long-term costs for short-term returns and spend less on good quality materials and design.

10. Non-profit developers sometimes must overcome stereotypes held by neighbors about people with lower incomes and spend more to create attractive developments to help dispel these misconceptions. For-profit developers more often serve populations who do not rouse fears in the neighborhood, and they have less incentive to put extra creativity and resources into the design of the buildings.

The study shows that when non-profit and for-profit developments are compared taking into account these factors, there are no systematic differences in costs. The cost figures shown in the development summaries of each case study is the developer's best estimate of the costs at the end of construction. They are intended to give the reader a sense of the comparative costs of different densities of affordable family housing in different regions. However, because of the differences in completion dates and many of the factors mentioned above, direct cost comparisons are not always appropriate.

AFFORDABLE HOUSING AS DERIVATIONS OF TRADITIONAL AMERICAN DWELLING TYPES

Although the single-family house, freestanding on its own lot, is often characterized as the typical American dwelling, as a nation we have always lived in a diversity of dwelling types. Even in small communities, there may be a mixture of different dwelling types, including freestanding houses, attached houses, units above one another as "walk-ups" or flats and housing over stores.

Well-designed affordable housing strives to use a dwelling type that has some relationship to the historic or adjacent types in a community, but is adapted or updated to the family needs of contemporary life. Affordable housing need not mimic the type of dwelling next door, but it should include appropriate dwelling types.

The diversity of American traditional dwelling types, often designed to be affordable when they were built, shows a pragmatic and creative response through our history often by unknown architects and builders to accommodate more people on less land within the reach of family incomes.

For purposes of the case studies, developments have been categorized according to the following list of dwelling types. Several projects represent hybrids of traditional dwelling types, or mixtures of more than one type on the same lot or in the same district. In such cases, they have been shown as combinations of more than one type of dwelling.

The adjacent drawing illustrates the range of potential dwelling types as they might occur within a hypothetical town block pattern. Lot size, building coverage, and rear or courtyard open space will vary in actual towns.

American dwelling types

Group 1—Freestanding buildings, outside entrance to each unit from a street or a shared courtyard

A	Single-family house	
B	Single-family + secondary unit	
C	Single-family + cottage	(SF+C)
D	Two-family "house"	(Duplex)
E	Three-family "house"	(Triplex)
F	Multiple-family dwellings in large "house"	(Multiplex)
G	Clustered detached houses/cottages on single lot	(SF Clus)

Group 2—Attached buildings, outside entrance to each unit from street or courtyard

H	Row houses	(Row House)
I	Two to four (or more) vertically stacked units	(Flats)
J	Courtyard housing	(Court)
K	Alley housing over garages	(Alley)

Group 3—Multiple unit buildings, entry to each dwelling from common stair or interior hall

L	Walk-up apartments	(Apt-walk)
M	Low-rise apartment (max. 5 stories)	(Apt-low)
N	Mid-rise apartment (6–15 stories)	(Apt-mid)
O	High-rise apartment (16+ stories)	(Apt-high)

Group 4—Residential use above other uses. Usually Group 2 or Group 3 dwelling type over commercial premises

P	Mixed-use	(Mix)

A list of national organizations, and a list of state coalitions that support design excellence in affordable housing are listed in the Resource Guide at the back of the book to give the reader access to a wide range of resources in this and other community development activities.

American Dwelling Types:

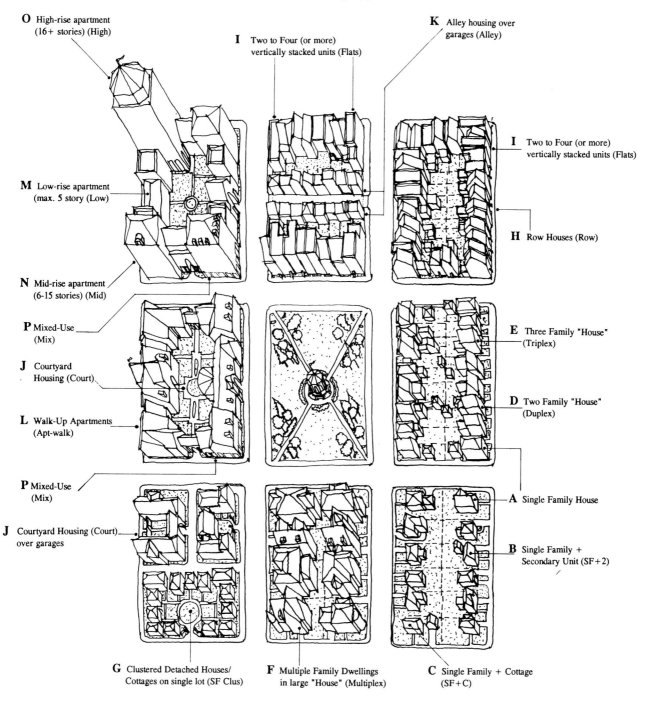

O High-rise apartment (16+ stories) (High)

I Two to Four (or more) vertically stacked units (Flats)

K Alley housing over garages (Alley)

M Low-rise apartment (max. 5 story (Low)

I Two to Four (or more) vertically stacked units (Flats)

N Mid-rise apartment (6-15 stories) (Mid)

H Row Houses (Row)

P Mixed-Use (Mix)

J Courtyard Housing (Court)

E Three Family "House" (Triplex)

L Walk-Up Apartments (Apt-walk)

D Two Family "House" (Duplex)

P Mixed-Use (Mix)

J Courtyard Housing (Court) over garages

A Single Family House

B Single Family + Secondary Unit (SF+2)

G Clustered Detached Houses/ Cottages on single lot (SF Clus)

F Multiple Family Dwellings in large "House" (Multiplex)

C Single Family + Cottage (SF+C)

Michael Pyatok

CHAPTER SEVEN:
THE NORTHWEST AND NORTHERN CALIFORNIA

Twenty developments in the northwest and northern California region were selected for review as two- and four-page case studies:

OPAL Commons, Orcas, Washington
Benson Glen, Seattle, Washington
Nuevo Amanecer Apartments, Woodburn, Oregon
The Farm, Soquel, California
Tuscany Villas/Villa Calabria, Davis, California
Stoney Creek Apartments, Livermore, California
Southside Park Co-housing, Sacramento, California
YWCA Family Village, Redmond, Washington
Tower Apartments, Rohnert Park, California
Matsusaka Townhomes, Tacoma, Washington
Parkview Commons, San Francisco, California
Lorin Station, Berkeley, California
Hismen Hin-nu Terrace, Oakland, California
Del Carlo Court, San Francisco, California
YWCA Villa Nueva, San Jose, California
555 Ellis Street, San Francisco, California
Frank G. Mar Community Housing, Oakland, California
Cascade Court Apartments, Seattle, Washington
201 Turk Street, San Francisco, California
111 Jones Street, San Francisco, California

OPAL Commons is the OPAL Community Land Trust's (CLT) first development on Orcas Island, a ferry's ride from the coast of Washington. The 18 houses are arranged in four clusters on 7 acres of open, rural land. Separated from automobile routes, parking areas at the site perimeter serve the clusters, which are connected by footpaths. A community center is planned on the commons and a community garden is convenient to the housing.

The architect, Fred R. Klein, himself a resident of the island, found resident/homeowner participation in the design process yielded a richer result than that which would have occurred had the architect been in total control. "By allowing the participatory design process to unfold, residents had to take some responsibility for the outcome," he said. "The project was truly theirs; they felt an ownership of the design that kept them from throwing darts at me—and they seem to love their homes." The homes themselves are simple, two-story gabled structures with front porches and side sheds. Board-and-batten or horizontal siding completes the vernacular, Victorian farmhouse image common in the northwest.

Although Orcas Island is mainly zoned for one house per 5 acres, this site lay within the village sub-area plan, which allowed six detached or eight attached homes per acre. When density was addressed in Klein's first meeting with the future homeowners, the comments ranged from: "Since the site is only 7 acres, why would you want to put more than one house on it?" to, "OPAL's mission is to serve the most in need. Since we have a critical shortage of affordable housing, and our zoning allows for 56 units if we do attached homes, I think we should go for the maximum."

At the end of the meeting 16–20 detached homes was the accepted unit count. Comments solicited from the county planning department, the commissioner representing the island, and the head of the village planning advisory board influenced the discussion. Still, according to the architect, the site plan and many aspects of the home design—there are four types—were a direct response to the owners' quality-of-life preferences. With coaching from the architect, the residents' participation in the planning process determined the density, lot selection, and location and orientation of homes on the lots.

Both Jeanne Beck, former Executive Director of OPAL CLT and project manager of OPAL Commons, and Fred Klein agreed that inflexible rules and regulations were problematic during the development process. Said Beck, "Meshing the rules and regulations of both the Farmers' Home Administration and the Housing Assistance Program with the tenets of community land trusts was a major obstacle." In the absence of a local ordinance covering stormwater management the development had to comply with one in Seattle that was overly rigorous and cost more than it should have." Beck reflected, "Community participation, both pro and con, had the biggest impact by bringing to the forefront the shortage of housing in San Juan County, an issue previously ignored."

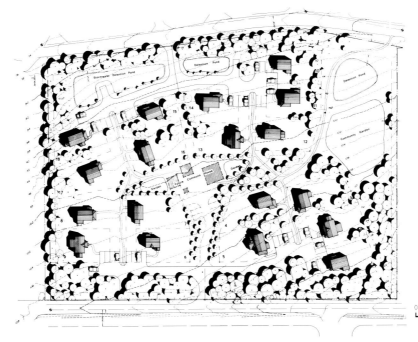

0 30 feet   N

Site plan

Courtyard with homes around Ron Glassett

Four-bedroom house with entry porch Ron Glassett

OWNER/DEVELOPER
OPAL Community Land Trust

ARCHITECT
Fred R. Klein AIA

CONTRACTOR
Sound Construction

FUNDERS	**TYPE**
FMHA 502 Demonstration Loan	Loan
Washington State Housing Trust Fund	Grant
CDBG Funds	Grant
ProBono legal and planning fees	

DEVELOPMENT TYPE
New construction for-sale single-family homes.

RESIDENT PROFILE
Low- and moderate-income first-time homebuyers, incomes $14,200–37,700.

DENSITY
5 units/acre

DEVELOPMENT PROFILE

Type	N°/Units	Size (sf)	Sale Prices
1 BR	6	832	$77,500
2 BR	3	1,008	$85,000
3 BR	8	1,008–1,108	$85,000–93,000
4 BR	1	1,250	$93,000
TOTAL	18		

Common house: (future)
Parking: 44 surface
Total site area: 7 acres

CONSTRUCTION TYPE
Two-stories woodframe, board-and-batten siding, comp. shingle roofs, septic tanks.

COSTS
Land Cost: $78,172; Constr. Costs: $1,396,581; Other Costs: $120,880; **Total Development Cost: $1,595,633.** (Completed January 1995)

Interior Ron Glassett

Located in Renton, a working-class suburb of Seattle, Benson Glen is an unusual single-family development. Near a Boeing factory, the neighborhood is racially mixed with a range of entry-level buyers. Although the houses have all sold and are well liked, Architect William Kraeger, vice president of Mithun Partners, concluded that, "The greatest innovation and community benefit is the potential now being realized for permanent changes and improvements to the codes, planning, and design review processes." The Benson Glen Report, published after completion of the development, has recommended changes which, if implemented, would greatly improve the production of housing in King County. For example, at Benson Glen required parking spaces were reduced from four to two, with one car in the driveway. This saved about $3,000 per unit, and reduced stormwater drainage from the hardscape. The width of the lots was reduced so that the garages could be placed at one side of the site and recessed to reduce their visual impact. Setbacks were also reduced to 15 feet, and the lot size was reduced to 3,600 square feet, which significantly lowered the developer's land costs. However, the restored wetlands adjacent to the site added a significant cost to the housing, and reduced the developable land area. A quarter-acre park was built as part of the development and is an amenity for the whole neighborhood.

The 43 houses were built in four models. These ranged from a two-bedroom home designed for single parents with children to a three-bedroom house with separate eating areas for adults and older children. In many of the homes the garages could be expanded for two cars, or converted to family rooms; a second floor can, in most cases, be extended over the garage by reusing garage roof trusses. Although buyers had to earn no more than 80 per cent of the area median income to qualify, they preferred the homes with larger, more flexible plans. In fact, one model proved so popular that the architect had to design a second exterior elevation to keep all the houses from looking alike.

Unlike many of these case studies, Benson Glen had no initial participation by the community in the design process. Market preference, purchasing power, and demographic information came from existing demographic data, and was refined by the non-profit's board, made up of bankers, an attorney, a builder, an architect/planner, and a marketing specialist. Simplicity and efficiency were crucial to keeping building costs low. The contractor worked on a cost and materials basis, constructing the buildings from one side of the site to the other in an orderly sequence. Although the houses are varied in respect to the character of the elevation facing the street, they were designed as simply detailed boxes of standard materials. The site is surrounded by a variety of building types, including a three-story condominium building and older single-family houses. The Benson Glen houses face the street in a similar manner to the older homes, creating a neighborhood with the character of a traditional American neighborhood.

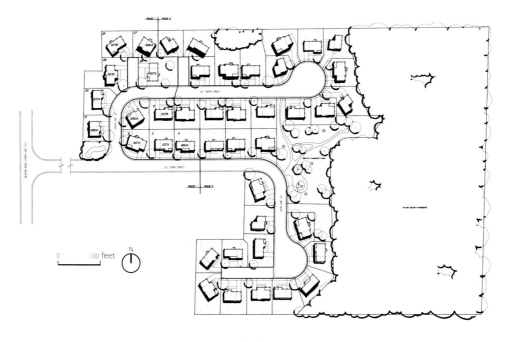

Site plan

Exterior view of The Cedar Dick Springgate

Entrance view of Benson Glen Dick Springgate

Exterior view of The Poplar Dick Springgate

DEVELOPER
Threshold Housing

ARCHITECT
Mithun Partners, Inc.

:

CONTRACTOR
Conner Development

FUNDERS	**TYPE**
Local Initiatives Support Corp.	Recoverable grant
Washington State	Recoverable grant
Local Banks	Mortgages

DEVELOPMENT TYPE
New construction for-sale single-family homes.

RESIDENT PROFILE
Moderate-income families at 75–80% of AMI.

DENSITY
7.2 units/acre

DEVELOPMENT PROFILE

Type	Nº/Units	Size (sf)	Sale Prices
2 BR	1	960	$112,000
3 BR	42	1,147–1,342	$123,000–134,000
TOTAL	**43**		

Parking: 43 garages
Total site area: 11.62 acres, including wetlands

CONSTRUCTION TYPE
Two-story woodframe, horiz./board-and-batten siding, comp. shingle roofs.

COSTS
Land Costs: $75,000; Constr. Costs: $4,085,000; Other Costs: $530,000; **Total Development Cost: $5,090,000 ($118,375/unit).** (Completed 1993)

Nuevo Amanecer Apartments Woodburn, Oregon

10 units/acre

Nuevo Amanecer, "New Dawn", is a 90-unit, multi-phase housing development intended for non-migrant farm workers engaged in nursery work, field work, and Christmas tree harvesting in the heart of the Willamette Valley, Oregon's primary agricultural region. Housing for these essential workers is in very short supply. The Nuevo Amanecer housing was developed by the Farmworker Housing Development Corporation (FHDC), a private non-profit corporation formed by concerned citizens. FHDC and the architects organized design workshops with farmworkers, service providers, and local business people to help shape the physical and cultural aspects of the development. The first phase was completed in March 1994 and included 50 apartments, a laundry, and a meeting room.

The design of Nuevo Amanecer is based on the creation of neighborhoods within the development that consist of 20–30 units around each plaza or park area. The generous site made it possible to create distinct exterior spaces for the community to use and to give each of the neighborhoods a special character. Plans for phase two call for each open space to be developed for use by a different age group, an approach inspired by the small local parks in older parts of Woodburn. Sensitivity to balancing cultural issues of the predominantly Hispanic residents with those of the larger community prompted the design of a network of paths connecting neighborhoods, public plazas, and playgrounds for an evening promenade or *paseo*; the floorplans feature large kitchens.

To incorporate elements of both the Anglo and the Hispanic traditions, the architects designed a building type that is a hybrid between the courtyard and row house. To provide maximum natural light as well as increase both acoustic separation and spatial variety, the one- and two-story units are connected only along their short sides. Nancy Merryman, partner in the architectural firm of Robertson, Merryman, Barnes, said, "Our favorite idea was the use of scissor trusses. They are fast and easy to erect, cost no more than conventional flat-bottom trusses and provide an amazing volumetric benefit inside the units. Small bedrooms feel special and living areas feel much more spacious and light. The only added cost is some extra sheetrock and finishing. Our best cost-saving strategy was having a contractor work with us through the entire design and construction document phase. Walsh Construction, who is experienced in building affordable housing, who believed in the same goals, and who was excited about doing some interesting housing was absolutely instrumental for success."

In the second phase, FHDC is planning to build 40 more living units, a daycare facility, and a larger community building useable for English classes, medical, and legal clinics. The architect reported, "We were complimented by the Planning Commission on the design. All the members of the public who came to speak against the development changed into supporters after seeing the presentations and drawings. During construction, people living in adjacent market-rate apartments called to ask if they could rent apartments." Nuevo Amanecer shows that housing for working families who are essential to the local economy can be an asset to the whole community.

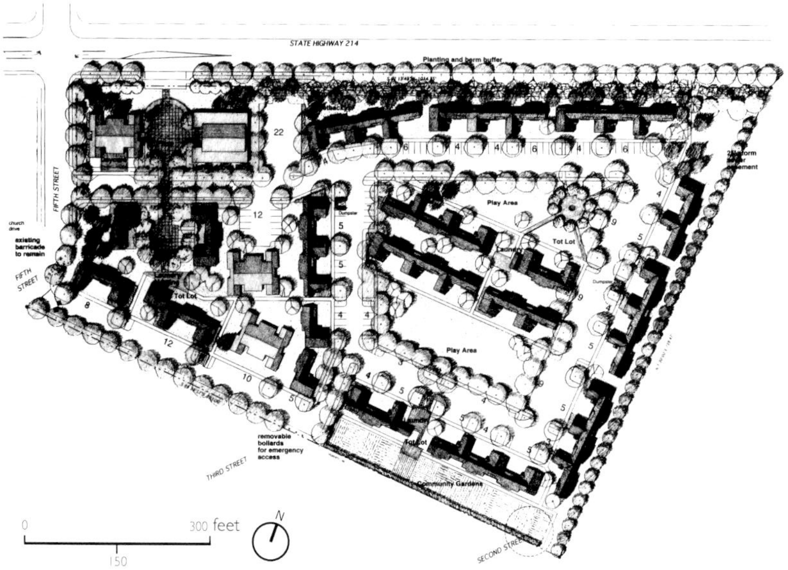

Site plan

Three-bedroom unit Laurie Black Photography

Plaza with laundry and meeting room at the end Stephen Cridland

Detail of a courtyard Laurie Black Photography

OWNER/DEVELOPER
Farmworker Housing Development Corp.

ARCHITECT
Robertson, Merryman, Barnes

LANDSCAPE ARCHITECT
Carol Mayer-Reed

CONTRACTOR
Walsh Construction

MANAGEMENT
Princeton Property Management

FUNDERS	TYPE
US Bancorp, Portland, OR , State tax credits	Equity
NOAH	Perm. loan
Oregon Housing & Community Development	Loan/grant
Enterprise Social Investment Corp./FNMA	Equity
Federal Low Income Housing	Tax credits
Oregon Dept. of Economic Development	Grant
Federal Home Loan Bank of Seattle	Grant
West One Bank	Constr. loan
Housing Assistance Council	Loan
CASA of Oregon	Loan
State Farmworker Housing Tax Credit	Equity

DEVELOPMENT TYPE
New construction rental attached townhouses.

RESIDENT PROFILE
Very-low-income families, incomes at 40% of AMI.

DENSITY
10 units/acre

DEVELOPMENT PROFILE

Type	N°/Units	Size (sf)	Rents
2 BR	15	770	$310
3 BR	25	1,050	$350
4 BR	10	1,200	$380
TOTAL	50		

Community/laundry: 1,275 sf
Parking: 220 surface
Courtyard/play area: 8,500 sf (plaza); 20,800 sf (park)
Total site area: 5.81 acres (phase I)

CONSTRUCTION TYPE
Two-story woodframe, painted wood comp. & stucco siding, comp. shingle roofs.

COSTS
Land Costs: $200,000; Constr. Costs: $2,249,412; Other Costs: $1,324, 025; **Total Development Cost: $3,773,437 ($73.84/sf).** (Completed March 15, 1994)

The Farm is the fortunate result of a compromise that matched community goals with those of a private developer and a non-profit sponsor of affordable housing. What began as a proposal by the owner/developer of an 11.5-acre former farmstead to develop the property into single-family houses and a limited number of affordable rental apartments, ended with a development that provided the same amount of housing with 87 per cent of it affordable, a new park, a childcare center, and lots for single-family houses that were built for sale at market rate to help fund the affordable housing.

The original proposal failed to gain approval because it did not preserve the character of the area or the rural setting with its grasslands, views of oak woodlands, and riparian vegetation along a creek. As an alternative, the Mid-Peninsula Housing Coalition (MPHC), working with Green Farm Limited Partners, the owners of the 11.5-acre site, and the Santa Cruz County Redevelopment Agency proposed a master plan for the property. The redevelopment agency purchased most of the site; the Lion's Club provided funds for a childcare center and construction; and other agencies assisted in various ways. The old farmhouse stands across the street from the new white-painted, wooden buildings with gable roofs and front porches that reflect its architecture character.

This was the first major new rental housing development for families with low incomes in the area since 1989. Applicants living or working in Santa Cruz County were given preference, and all those now living at The Farm were already residents of the county. The 39 units are mainly in two- and three-bedroom townhouses with separate entrances leading to semi-private yards and/or to front porches. The common open space was configured to provide a view corridor to the riparian landscape east of the development. Smaller buildings with two-bedroom units occupy sites visible from Cunnison Lane and Soquel Drive; larger apartment buildings with six units are located toward the back of the development area where they are less visible from the streets. Differences in building size are minimized visually by articulating their forms in similar ways.

Parking is located on private streets behind the buildings with two entrance points off Cunnison Lane. The original number of parking spaces required by the county was reduced because automobile ownership is not only lower than in the average residential tract but the MPHC management has also developed a parking management plan through experience in other developments, which controls parking needs through screening of applicants and strict enforcement, aided by resident stickers.

A childcare center, located at the intersection of Cunnison Lane and Soquel Drive, is operated by a local non-profit organization, Growth and Opportunity, Inc. The center receives state and federal subsidies as well as funds from the development to ensure that fees are affordable for residents of The Farm and the surrounding community who need childcare. Housed in a one-story building, the center shares

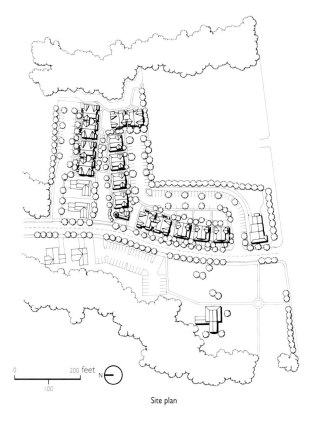

0   200 feet   N
100

Site plan

Lower floor plan—six-unit building   0   20 feet   Upper floor plan—six-unit building

Six-unit buildings Alex Seidel

DEVELOPER
Mid-Peninsula Housing Coalition

ARCHITECT
Seidel/Holzman

CONSULTANTS
Landscape Architect: Anthony Guzzardo and Assoc.
Development Consultant: Community Economics

CONTRACTOR
Lyntrak Construction Co., Inc.

PROPERTY MANAGEMENT
Mid-Peninsula Housing Management Corp.

FUNDERS	TYPE
SAMCO	Perm. loan
Union Bank	Constr. loan
Federal Low Income Hsg	
Tax Credits Mission First Financial	Equity
Santa Cruz County Redev. Agency	Grant
American Red Cross	Loan
California Department of HCD	Loan
Santa Cruz Co. Human	
Resources Agency	Childcare grant
Santa Cruz Co. Sanitation District	Loan
The Lions Club International	Predev. funds
Northern California Community	
Loan Fund	Predev. loan

DEVELOPMENT TYPE
Two-story rental townhouses and stacked flats. for-sale SF homes (mkt rate).

RESIDENT PROFILE
Very-low- and low-income families, incomes less than $31,200 (60% AMI).
Ave. income is $16,720. Families, incomes at or above median (SF homes).

DENSITY
13 units/acre

DEVELOPMENT PROFILE

Type	N°/Units	Size (sf)	Rents/Sale Prices
Single-family	6	1,670–2,200	$245,000–345,000
1 BR	1	716	$520
2 BR	16	906	$344–625
3 BR	22	1,180	$372–695
TOTAL	**45**		

Childcare center: 2,016 sf
Parking : 99 surface (9 for daycare)
Total site area: 4.2 acres

CONSTRUCTION TYPE
Two-story woodframe, painted wood siding, comp. shingle roof.

COSTS
Land Cost: $1,413,335; Constr. Costs: $2,880,935; Other Costs: $1,955,397; **Total Development Cost: $6,249,667 ($138,881/unit).** (Completed June 1993)

parking and vehicle access with the adjacent housing. During evenings and on weekends the building serves as a community meeting place.

The architects held meetings with interested neighbors and members of the community to address their concerns. The initial opposition to the development vanished when people saw and liked the design. Since its completion The Farm has won several awards for design excellence and is perceived by neighbors as being attractive and well managed. The single-family houses that were built as part of the master plan sold easily for good prices, demonstrating that the prospect of affordable rental housing did not devalue the neighborhood. One neighbor commented that her attitude toward housing for people with low incomes had changed because of her experience with the development:

"Before we moved into the neighborhood we wanted to consider the potential effect of The Farm on property values, crime, and so forth. Mid-Peninsula Housing arranged for us to visit five of their similar housing developments. We met with residents and property managers and got a very good idea of the way the housing was managed and the type of people they housed. I also worked closely with my realtor to research recent sales in the areas around those developments. We discovered that in all cases property values remained the same or increased—the situations were no different to those in areas without affordable housing. So we felt very comfortable purchasing a house next to The Farm."

Management building with one-bedroom unit above Alex Seidel

Six-unit building from garden plots Alex Seidel

Six-unit buildings from courtyard Alex Seidel

Front of six-unit buildings Alex Seidel

Two-unit buildings from Cunnison Lane Alex Seidel

Elevations of two-unit buildings

Tuscany Villas/Villa Calabria Davis, California

In designing Tuscany Villas/Villa Calabria, architects Davis and Joyce confronted the familiar problem of creating an identifiable place in a nondescript setting. The site has single story duplexes on one side, a very large three-story apartment complex on another side, and open fields on the other two sides. To bridge the gaps in scale and massing between the existing buildings, the architects designed two-story buildings with three-story sections either in the middle or at the corners and placed them well back from the property line of the area of single-story buildings. The three-story sections provide a visual link with the larger apartment complex, but, as a whole, the new buildings do not overpower the smaller duplexes. As the names imply, the buildings' massing refers to the Italian villa, a residential building type that was imported long ago into California because of its similar Mediterranean climate. In Davis, as in Tuscany, simple, rectangular forms and earth colors look appropriate.

A large utility easement and a road divided the site into three areas. The architects took advantage of this division to create separate identities for each parcel's use. Two groups of family dwellings surround outdoor areas; the building for seniors has its own parcel. The six senior units are organized around a two-story, open-air atrium. This sheltered space provides protection from summer heat or rain for those who wish to sit outside and more security for the entries to units. The 30 family units have two and three stories to allow for some separation of activities and a degree of privacy. When possible the dining area is separate from the living area, mainly so that children could be doing homework or some other activity without being distracted by the television-viewing or talk of occupants of the living room. Most of the units have private patios at grade. On the family side, many of the patios are adjacent to one of the two large common areas. Senior residents have a community garden area. For most units there are individual entries in shared entry areas marked by a trellis or hedge. Although this area of suburban Davis is quite safe, site lighting was provided, and tall shrubbery was not used near entryways.

Scattered throughout the site, the parking is placed near each building but oriented and landscaped to have minimal visual impact on the neighbors. Multi-family zoning in Davis allows for a relatively low density—about 15 units per acre—but requires two parking spaces per unit. Keith Bloom, project manager for the developer remarked, "We were able to obtain a variance from the City to reduce the amount to 1.75 spaces per unit, but even this amount of parking exceeds what residents need. The result is an under-utilization of land." Two large areas of common open space are provided for residents, an active space with play equipment and one with benches and trellises. An exercise "par course" and a barbecue and picnic area are other community amenities.

Community participation in the design process was important but limited in scope. Members of the community contributed to the selection of colors for the buildings, facade treatments, and street landscaping. Design review of the plans by the City staff did not change the initial design to any great degree. Reflecting on the lessons learned from this and other

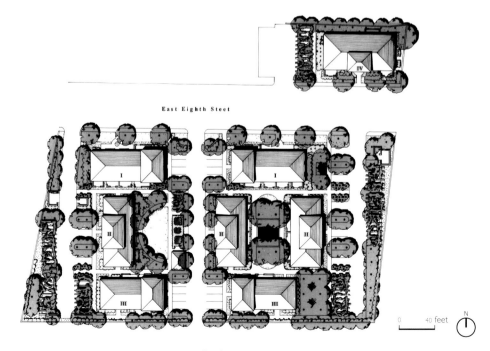

East Eighth Steet

Site plan

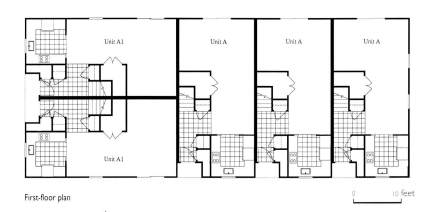

First-floor plan

0   10 feet

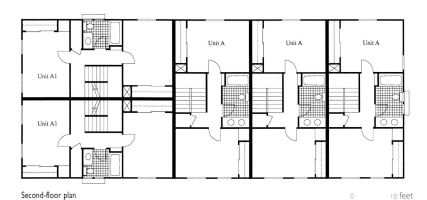

Second-floor plan

0   10 feet

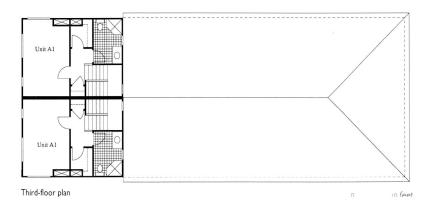

Third-floor plan

0   10 feet

OWNER/DEVELOPER
Community Housing Opportunities Corporation

ARCHITECT
Davis and Joyce Architects

LANDSCAPE ARCHITECT
Keller, Mitchell, Caronna

CONTRACTOR
Camray Construction

PROPERTY MANAGEMENT
Linda Nelson

FUNDERS

	TYPE
Wells Fargo Bank	Constr. loan
State Dept. of Hsg and Comm'ty Dev.	Loan
Savings Assoc. Mortgage Company	Perm. loan
Fed. Low Income Hsg Tax Credits	Equity
Private donor	Donated land

DEVELOPMENT TYPE
New construction rental flats and townhouses.

RESIDENT PROFILE
Very-low- and low-income families, incomes below $30,000;
very-low- and low-income seniors, incomes below $16,000.

DENSITY
Families: 15 units/acre; seniors: 28 units/acre

DEVELOPMENT PROFILE

Type	Nº/Units	Size (sf)	Rents
1 BR	2	850	$275–445
2 BR	12	915–980	$300–550
3 BR	22	1,260–1,300	$325–600
TOTAL	36		

Laundry: 300 sf
Parking: 69 surface with carports
Courtyard/play: 3,200 sf
Total site area: 2.2 acres

CONSTRUCTION TYPE
Two- and three-story woodframe, stucco exterior,
comp. shingle roofs.

COSTS
Land Cost: $0 (donated); Constr. Costs $2.6m ($56/sf);
Other Costs: $1.8 m.; **Total Development Cost: $4.4m.
($122,000/unit).** (Completed December 1993)

Tuscany Villas/Villa Calabria Continued

developments, the architects acknowledged that even though each community and resident group is different, it is important to listen to feedback from occupied buildings and to make changes based on that feedback. Yet after a certain point, Joyce says, "We have learned that further compromise is actually harmful to the design. It is our job to put together a design that is a unified, cohesive whole. That sometimes means telling people that what they think they want will end up being something they won't like—not an easy job!"

From the perspective of Keith Bloom, both the residents and the neighborhood were happy with the housing. However, Bloom stated that, "The greatest lesson I have learned is that regardless of how many buildings one has developed in the past and regardless of how well designed and—once built—how well managed these developments are, the developers of affordable housing must always be prepared to address NIMBY issues in the next project. Many neighbors and politicians choose to ignore your track record and instead focus on their fears of the stereotypical public housing project, slum, welfare housing, etc. The developer's ability to use rational arguments with these groups is nearly impossible given their emotional assessment of your development. However, I would hope that over time, as more groups like mine continue to develop high quality affordable housing, communities will come to recognize this and thus will be less of a hindrance to this kind of development."

Although the occupancy of Tuscany Villas and Villa Calabria is recent, residents are generally enthusiastic about living there. One tenant of the family complex expressed a commonly held opinion, "The most successful point about the housing is that by living in a clean, safe, and non-stereotypical low-income environment you don't feel so down and out about your situation, which allows for more motivation toward success."

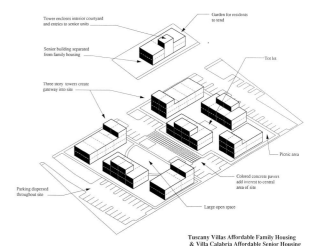

Tuscany Villas Affordable Family Housing & Villa Calabria Affordable Senior Housing

Analytic site axonometric

Patios adjacent to play area courtyard Jane Lidz

Trellised entry to townhouses Jane Lidz

Entry to site Jane Lidz

Trellised mailbox at garden courtyard Jane Lidz

Garden courtyard Jane Lidz

Stoney Creek Apartments Livermore, California

The city of Livermore, 40 miles from San Francisco, has seen tremendous growth in recent years as people move further into suburban and rural areas due to the high cost of housing in the Bay Area. Most new housing has been single-family detached, but recently home prices and apartment rents have become unaffordable for many local workers. The city of Livermore and the local housing authority have been developing affordable housing and assisting local developers to address this need. Working closely with the non-profit developer, Eden Housing, Inc., and the redevelopment agency, architect Chris Lamen approached the design of Stoney Creek Apartments with the goals of creating a safe, durable environment that would not appear as a "project". The development team had to compete in a city-controlled design competition for a limited number of development permits. Stoney Creek was awarded a permit in recognition of the high design quality. The planning staff commented, "The architecture provides a distinct identity as well as a very pedestrian oriented environment."

The housing combines 70 stacked flats and townhouses in 10 detached buildings clustered around five courtyards. Given the long, narrow site with limited street frontage, the architects had to design a circulation system that would allow access for automobiles to the back of the site and also create a family-oriented environment. The traditional single-family neighborhood with sidewalks lined with trees backed by houses with front porches was the model. To achieve this image a private street was created along the full length of one side of the site that provided efficient circulation while freeing most of the site from vehicular traffic.

The driveway also permitted the buildings to be set around courtyards with a neighborhood scale where children could play safely. The transition from the public courts to the private homes is softened through the use of on-grade front porches, fenced patios, and planting. Kitchens and breakfast rooms open onto private patios adjacent to the courtyards, creating opportunities for residents to visit with their neighbors while watching their children.

An important addition to the attractive landscaping was created by Martha Heavenston, a local artist, who made cement and tile animal sculptures in the courtyards for toddlers to enjoy. Each courtyard has a different theme. A system of paths weaves through the complex linking the courts to one another, and to the play structures and basketball court for the older children.

Designed with varied geometry and massing, the buildings have the character of larger, individual homes. Large windows, which bring generous daylighting to the living rooms, are shaded by deep overhangs during the hot summer days. A wall along the street frontage is made of river rock from the nearby river; the rock is also used to face the fireplace in the community room. The designers carefully considered the long-term social life of the development. According to the architect, "We have learned that developing the opportunity for the residents' possession of exterior space and for personal identification of the individual unit creates a tie between the residents and their homes. This feeling of ownership is in direct correlation with the way the resident takes care of the housing."

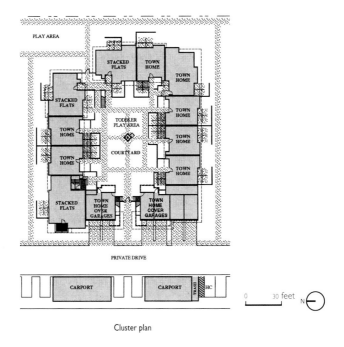

Cluster plan

Interior view of community room Jay Graham

Typical courtyard neighborhood Jay Graham

Entry to courtyard as seen from private drive Jay Graham

OWNER/DEVELOPER
Eden Housing, Inc.

ARCHITECT
Chris Lamen and Associates

LANDSCAPE ARCHITECT
Cottong & Taniguchi

CONTRACTOR
Ross Construction

PROPERTY MANAGEMENT
Eden Housing Management, Inc.

FUNDERS	TYPE
City of Livermore	Loan
Livermore Redevelopment Agency	Loan
State Department of Housing and Community Development	Loan
Wells Fargo Bank	Constr. Loan
California Community Reinvestment Corp.	Loan
S.H. Cowell Foundation	Grant
Federal Low Income Housing Tax Credits purchased by Mission First Financial	Equity

DEVELOPMENT TYPE
New construction rental flats and townhouses.

RESIDENT PROFILE
38% very-low-income families; 62% low-income families.

DENSITY
16 units/acre

DEVELOPMENT PROFILE

Type	N°/Units	Size (sf)	Rents
2 BR	36	938–1,100	$347–608
3 BR	34	117–1,274	$386–702
TOTAL	**70**		

Community/laundry: 520 sf
Courtyard/play: 10,000 sf
Parking: 131 surface/carport
Total site area: 5 acres

CONSTRUCTION TYPE
Two- and three-story woodframe, resawn plywood and battens, horizontal siding, comp. shingle roofs.

COSTS
Land Cost: na; Constr. Costs: $6.5m.; Other Costs: $3.4m;
Total Development Costs: $9.9m. ($90/sf).
(Completed February 1993)

Southside Park Co-housing Sacramento, California

This 25-unit housing development is located in a neighborhood that had declined drastically while speculative developers waited to replace the houses with office buildings. It uses the co-housing model imported from Denmark and advocated by architects Charles Durrett and Kathryn McCamant, which requires the residents to co-operate in designing their homes and to agree to share in such activities as the preparation of dinners for the community. Southside Park residents' homes are grouped around shared facilities for dining, recreation, laundry, and gardening. Low-income families or individuals occupy five of the units, six houses are for people with moderate incomes, and 14 were sold at market rates. Some of the people who bought houses had been renters in the neighborhood.

Although the homes sold for moderate prices, they had such amenities as hardwood floors, wood siding, and porches which, because they were agreed upon well in advance, cost less to provide. According to David Mogavero of Mogavero Notestine Associates, the project architects, co-housing costs less because most of the units are pre-sold; thus the developer's risk is minimized and the need for a brokerage firm is eliminated. Co-housing also enables residents to economize by using the community-owned dishwashers, laundry machines, and gardening tools instead of buying them.

Despite the economic benefits, co-housing's main attraction is social. Southside Park's advantages for working parents and their children are so significant that residents compare the community to an extended family. Owner Laurisa Elhai said, "Most of us came into the group because we wanted to live in a real community, not a neighborhood where you don't know anyone. The kids look out for each other, and adults take an interest in all the children, not just their own." Speaking about the community dinners held in the common house Elhai said, "It's such a luxury to come home after work and have someone else cook and clean up, and I can just sit around afterwards and talk because my children go and play with other children."

As an infill development Southside Park also demonstrates that automobile-dependent suburbs are not the only option for those who want an attractive and safe place to live. Another resident and founding member, Dale Crandall-Bear, stated, "We wanted to reduce our dependence on driving everywhere, and we didn't want to run away from reality to the suburbs. We knew that raising children in the inner-city would be a challenge, but there is security in being in a group." The design promotes security through owner involvement instead of using fences, gates or alarm systems. In fact, security was another issue that helped residents engage the community. Car vandalism was the main problem, and when kids from across the street confessed to doing some of it, the Southside Park residents put up a basketball hoop to provide other outlets for their time and energy. Resident David Mandel explained, "We are trying to get to know the neighbors and revive the dormant neighborhood association. This is the way we are dealing with security issues."

Motivation toward community notwithstanding, co-housing has its caveats. American are perhaps less inclined toward

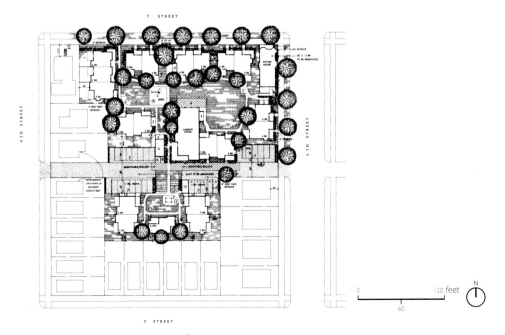

Site plan

1	FRONT PORCH
2	LIVING ROOM
3	DINING ROOM
4	KITCHEN
5	BATH
6	WASHER/DRYER
7	BEDROOM
8	STORAGE

First floor plan   Second floor plan

2 bedroom and 4 bedroom floor plans

Dining room viewed from living room James Kline

Entry porch provides layered, defensible space James Kline

OWNER/DEVELOPER
Owner: Southside Park Co-housing
Developer: Ergos Developments

ARCHITECT
Mogavero Notestine Associates

CONSULTANTS
Development Managers: Mogavero Notestine Associates
Landscape Architect: Doug Strayer
Programming Consultant: The Co-Housing Company

CONTRACTOR
Ergos Development

FUNDERS

FUNDERS	TYPE
Sacramento Redevelopment Agency note/delayed 2nd	Land
Sacramento Svgs. (now) First Interstate Bank	Perm. loan
Northern California Loan Fund	Predev. loan
Sacramento Community Dev. Partnership	Predev. loan

DEVELOPMENT TYPE
New construction for-sale flats and townhouses.

RESIDENT PROFILE
Families with low-, moderate- and market-rate incomes.

DENSITY
20 units/acre

DEVELOPMENT PROFILE

Type	N°/Units	Size (sf)	Sale Prices
I BR	4	640	$ 88,743
2 BR	7	1,025	$121,501–124,307
2 BR	2	1,189	$134,382
3 BR	8	1,302	$138,614–143,306
4 BR	4	1,423	$150,102–151,927
TOTAL	25		

Community/laundry: 3,682 sf (includes storage)
Courtyard/play: 8,000 sf
Parking: 27 surface/carport
Site area: 55,147 sf (1.27 acres)

CONSTRUCTION TYPE
Two-story woodframe, masonite lap-wood siding, comp. shingle roofs.

COSTS
Land Cost: $425,000; Constr. Costs $1,960,000 ($78,400/unit); Other Costs: $815,000 ($32,640/unit); **Total Development Cost: $3,200,000.** (Completed September 1993)

consensus in all community decisions than the Danes, who live in a very small country and have a tradition of co-operative living. Planning co-housing usually takes more time than conventional housing—Southside Park took over four years to plan—and prospective buyers must understand this and set their expectations accordingly. Bureaucratic hurdles cause major problems as, for example, when the redevelopment agency would not give the Southside Park group title to the land until they had the money to purchase the property, and the banks would not lend money without proof of a title. At the same time the group, which now had 11 families, faced major expenses such as hiring consultants and architects. All was resolved after a long and difficult process.

David Mandel described the site planning process, which consisted of workshops run by McCamant and Durrett, "For the site planning, we broke into two groups and used modeling kits to explore alternatives. Each group presented their alternatives, and when it became clear that one of the plans was better, it was more or less the final design concept." The architectural design was developed by Mogavero Notestine Architects with gabled roofs, front porches, and horizontal siding to fit in with the turn of the century houses in the neighborhood. Southside Park is located in an historic district. The 100-year-old Potter house was restored and integrated into the development in one corner of the site; two units were put into it. George Branson, a neighbor who helped build support for the co-housing observed that, "This development has taken a blighted corner of the city and transformed it into something really nice. There is hope for the older buildings, some of which are being rehabilitated. I would like to encourage other neighborhoods that are reluctant about this sort of housing to visit Southside."

4 BDRM   2 BDRM   2 BDRM

4/2/2   COMMONS ELEVATION

2 BDRM   2 BDRM   4 BDRM

4/2/2   REAR ELEVATION

Wrap around porch at entry from street James Kline

Partial T Street elevation James Kline

POTTER HOUSE   4 BDRM   2 BDRM   2 BDRM   4 BDRM   4 BDRM   2 BDRM   2 BDRM

"T" STREET ELEVATION

0   16 feet

Trellised patio extends Common House dining room into common space James Kline

YWCA Family Village Redmond, Washington

A recent study of the demographics of homelessness found that the Eastside of King County, Washington, which has been developing rapidly over the last decade, was particularly lacking in services for the fastest growing population of homeless people, women with children (over 6,000 in 1993). According to Sue Sherbrooke, Finance and Property Director for the Young Women's Christian Association (YWCA), "Many of these families are victims of job loss, loss of a partner, or domestic violence." The YWCA has an innovative program designed to help families stabilize their lives and develop the skills to live independently. In 1994, 100 per cent of the families leaving the program secured permanent housing.

Besides transitional housing, the residents need job counseling and childcare. To increase their understanding of the daily needs of women and children in transition, architects Michael Pyatok and Ron Hopper met early in the design process with YWCA program staff. The result is a safe and functional apartment building with ground-floor YWCA offices and social services wrapping around south-facing recreation facilities. Screened porches off the upper story corridors become play areas on rainy days.

Although the Family Village is among the tallest buildings in Redmond it fits in well both physically and socially. The architects saved tall trees in the front and designed the exterior to resemble a comfortable old northwest lodge, giving it a welcoming appearance. The building's height and placement near the corner of the lot also made possible greater open space for use as play areas for the childcare center and parking.

Sue Sherbrooke noted, "The Redmond community has enthusiastically supported this program. The adjacent school has welcomed the children; Boy Scouts have built furniture for the childcare center; clothing donations have overwhelmed the Working Wardrobe (a program to help women with clothing for job interviews); and church groups have furnished the apartments."

A crucial factor in this success, according to the architects, was the reputation of the sponsor. "The stature and presence of the YWCA in this community shows at every turn in fund-raising, in obtaining approvals from neighborhood groups and public officials, and in their ability to operate the program."

Since most people have been living on the streets with little or no income the YWCA works every year with corporate sponsors to underwrite operating costs. This is possible, according to Sue Sherbrooke, because, "We have been in King County for 101 years, and when we tell people we have a commitment to this development, they know we mean it."

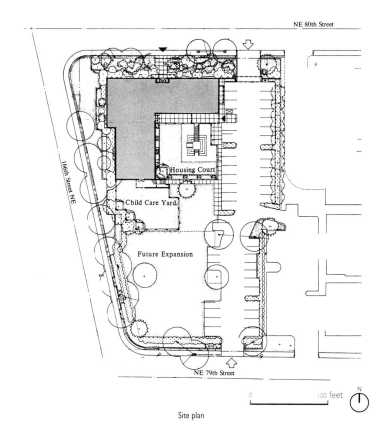

Site plan

Screened play porches from play yard Michael Pyatok

View from 166th Street NE Michael Pyatok

OWNER / DEVELOPER
YWCA of Seattle-King County

ARCHITECT
Design Architect: Pyatok Associates
Architect of Record: Stickney and Murphy Architects

LANDSCAPE ARCHITECT
Jane Garrison

CONTRACTOR
Walsh Construction

PROPERTY MANAGEMENT
YWCA of Seattle-King County

FUNDERS	TYPE
State of Washington Housing Trust Fund	na
King County CDBG	na
City of Bellevue CDBG	na
City of Redmond CDBG	na
City of Kirkland CDBG	na
City of Mercer Island CDBG	na
City of Issaquah CDBG	na
King County Housing Opportunity Fund	na
Individuals, Corporations, Foundations	na

DEVELOPMENT TYPE
New construction rental stacked flats with services,
& YWCA offices.

RESIDENT PROFILE
Very-low-income, homeless families with children.

DENSITY
21 units/acre + offices and childcare

DEVELOPMENT PROFILE

Type	N°/Units	Size (sf)	Rents
2 BR	17	650	$100 (ave.)
3 BR	3	800	$100 (ave.)
TOTAL	20		

Client services: 4,000 sf
Childcare center: 3,000 sf
Parking: 45 surface
Site area 42,086 sf (.96 acres) (phase 1)

CONSTRUCTION TYPE
Four-story woodframe, wood shingle siding,
comp. shingle roof.

COSTS
Land Cost: $703,000, Constr. Costs $2,264,839
($72/sf); Other Costs: $327,891; **Total Development
Cost: $3,295,730.** (Completed March 1993)

Tower Apartments Rohnert Park, California

The Tower Apartments straddles the boundary between the two northern California cities of Rohnert Park and Cotati that are located in a rapidly expanding rural–suburban area characterized by low-density development. At 25 dwelling units per acre, Tower Apartments is three times the density of its surroundings, yet feels comfortable both from the street and inside the complex. Composed of two- and three-story buildings framing two courtyards, the site plan makes use of virtually every foot of space. The frontage on the main street has two-story townhouses; three-story buildings with townhouses over flats line the courts, and a combination of surface and "tuck-under" parking occupies the edges of the site. A service street separates the courtyards, one of which has a play structure and a building with a community room and a management office. Painted in light pastel colors and enlivened by roof dormers, pergolas, and porches, the buildings project a lively and appealing image; their style reflects the older architecture in the area.

The architects led participatory design workshops to incorporate suggestions from neighbors and public officials. Although the City of Rohnert Park was very supportive of the development, Cotati was concerned that the housing conflicted with its image of a rural community. The buildings along the main street were built at two stories and set back an extra 5 feet to address their concerns; this response made the apartments and open spaces smaller. Among the features

designed to encourage residents to personalize their homes are trellises with hooks for hanging plants on the front and rear patios. Architect Michael Pyatok noted, "When people settle into their housing, they are more likely to treat it as their own."

In addition to making birdhouses on a pro bono basis to decorate the residents' front porches, Pyatok applied for and won a grant from the National Endowment for the Arts to create artworks for the building. Two well-known local artists were hired and worked with residents in a series of workshops to create a visual imagery that would express their aspirations and memories. Beyond creating eight mural panels and landscape elements, the workshops fulfilled the goal of giving residents the opportunity to exercise cultural responsibility for their new community.

Nichols Stewart, project manager for Burbank Housing, commended the design for raising the community's opinion of affordable housing. "We intended Tower to showcase the possibilities of urban design in a suburban environment. Many people, including public officials, have been impressed." At the grand opening County Supervisor Tim Smith commented, "If you had told me two years ago that you could design affordable housing at 25 units per acre in Rohnert Park, I would have said you were crazy. This housing proves you can do it and do it well."

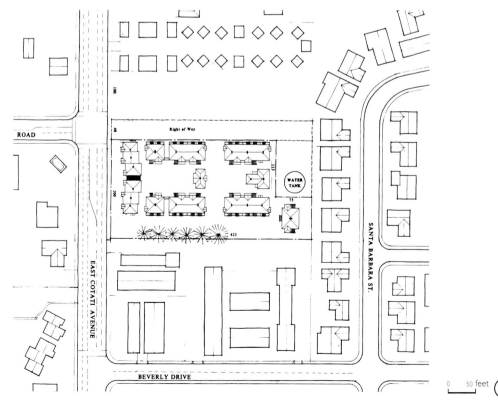

Site plan

3 BR and 4 BR Townhouses, E. Cotati Boulevard Michael Pyatok

Front porch, looking past parking Douglas Kahn

Courtyard with stoops to townhouses over flats Michael Pyatok

OWNER/DEVELOPER
Burbank Housing Development Corp.

ARCHITECT
Pyatok Associates

LANDSCAPE ARCHITECT
Rich Seyfarth

CONTRACTOR
J.M. Hershey Construction

PROPERTY MANAGEMENT
Burbank Housing Management Corp.

FUNDERS	TYPE
Low Income Housing Tax Credits purchased by Mission Housing Investment	Equity
State of California RCHP (Bond Issue)	Loan
Citibank	Loan
AHP, Federal Home Loan Bank	Grant
Rohnert Park Redevelopment Agency	Loan
Sonoma County CDBG	Loan
Low-Income Housing Fund, San Francisco	Predev. Loan

DEVELOPMENT TYPE
New construction rental attached townhouses and flats.

RESIDENT PROFILE
Low-income families, incomes $13,500–28,000.

DENSITY
25 units/acre

DEVELOPMENT PROFILE

Type	N°/Units	Size (sf)	Rents
1 BR	8	500	$270–375
2 BR	14	825	$300–445
3 BR	24	1,150	$335–520
4 BR	4	1,350	$390–580
TOTAL	50		

Community/storage/laundry: 1,800 sf
Courtyard/play: 20,000 sf
Parking: 104 surface/tuck-under
Total site area: 87,120 sf (2 acres)

CONSTRUCTION TYPE
Two- and three-stories woodframe, hardboard siding, comp. shingle roofs.

COSTS
Land Cost: $550,000; Constr. Costs: $3,792,690 ($76/sf);
Other Costs: $1,909,654 ($38/sf); **Total Development Cost:**
$6,252,344. (Completed August 1993)

Matsusaka Townhomes Tacoma, Washington

Catholic Community Services of Western Washington (CCS-WW) formed the Archdiocesan Housing Authority (AHA) in 1979 to develop, build, own, and manage affordable housing for people with low incomes. According to Paul Purcell, the vice president for community development, AHA decided to build family housing with two-, three-, and four-bedroom apartments on a site across from a lot on which they were developing office space. The new 26-unit development is home to nearly 100 people, including 60 children. Purcell remarked, "We wanted to bring a concern for families to the design process. We made a play area in the back accessible by two small sidewalks from the street, and there is a large job-training program as well as childcare and a social service agency across the street. We remodeled the old school into our office building and moved about 100 jobs into the community. We have also increased pedestrian activity in the neighborhood."

Working with Tonkin Hoyne Architects, CCS-WW initiated a community design process. Purcell noted, "We set up a committee of neighbors and possible users, and met in the parish across the street. We had a community vote on the different schemes for the building. The community was very supportive of the process and the project." The design of the buildings and their colors were derived from the other homes and buildings in the neighborhood. The massing on the main street matches that of the commercial and institutional buildings; the building steps down in the back to match the single-family houses behind. "The townhomes design with the distinctive colors and individual entrances from the street reinforces a sense of ownership for the residents," noted architect Les Tonkin. The townhouses wrap around the courtyard and have front and back yards; windows in the rear walls permit parents to watch the play area. Resident manager Minerva Ilarra-Casado remarked, "All the back doors face the courtyard, so we can all see one another. People interact a lot because of this." The night-lighting is good, and residents have joined a block watch.

Commenting on the effect of Matsusaka Townhomes Paul Purcell said, "This development has been used as a statewide example to showcase how to do affordable housing well. If sponsors recognize the dignity of the residents in the design and construction, the place becomes a source of pride, rather than a source of problems. If you build cheaply you create an eyesore. The residents know you don't care, so they don't care. If you build quality, you get respect. We believe every individual and family deserves the opportunity to live in affordable and respectable housing."

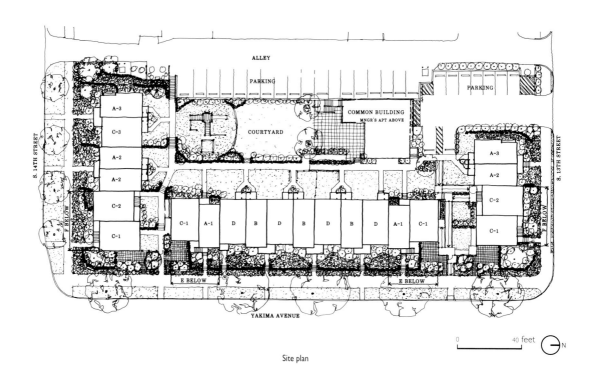

Site plan

View from across Yakoma Street John McLaren

Courtyard looking north John McLaren

View north along Yakoma Street John McLaren

OWNER/DEVELOPER
Archdiocesan Housing Authority
Hilltop Housing

ARCHITECT
Tonkin/Hoyne Architects and Planners

CONSULTANTS
Landscape Architect: Edward Watanabe
Development/Marketing: Low Income Housing Institute

CONTRACTOR
Lugo Construction

PROPERTY MANAGEMENT
Archdiocesan Housing Authority

FUNDERS	TYPE
State of Washington Housing Trust Fund	Loan
Tax Credits purchased by Seafirst Bank,	Equity
Key Bank, and Washington Mutual with the	
WA Community Reinvestment Alliance	Loan
Federal Home Loan Bank	Loan

DEVELOPMENT TYPE
New construction rental flats and townhouses.

RESIDENT PROFILE
Very-low- and low-income families, incomes $0–26,520, below 60% of AMI.

DENSITY
29 units/acre

DEVELOPMENT PROFILE

Type	No/Units	Size (sf)	Rents
2 BR TH	7	780	$276–558
3 BR Flat	4	1,036	$319–622
3 Br TH	11	975	$319–622
4 BR TH	4	1,188	$356–719
TOTAL	26		

Community/laundry: 750 sf
Courtyard/play: 6,400 sf
Parking: 27 surface
Total site area: 39,000 sf (.89 acres)

CONSTRUCTION TYPE
Two- and three-story woodframe, hardboard siding, comp. shingle roofs.

COSTS
Land Cost: $226,000; Constr. Costs: $2,400,000; Other Costs: $900,000; **Total Development Cost: $3,526,000.** (Completed December 1994)

Parkview Commons San Francisco, California

Parkview Commons, condominiums for low- to moderate-income first-time homebuyers occupies the former site of the San Francisco Polytechnical High School. After four years of trying to sell the site, which is located across the street from Golden Gate Park, the school district gave the city a 75-year lease to the land to develop affordable housing. In 1984 a coalition of neighborhood groups began a community based planning process to develop an affordable family housing program for the site. A proposal by a developer/architect team, BRIDGE, Pacific Union, and David Baker + Associates, was selected. In 1987, opponents of the development succeeded in putting a referendum on the ballot in a special election, which was defeated. Mayor Art Agnos mediated a settlement by creating a forum, as he put it, "where the neighborhood opposition was free to vent their feelings. We listened and tried to address people's concerns. It is important to sort out the legitimate concerns from NIMBYism. Once this point has been reached, it is time for the public official to act in a supportive and proactive role." That the community opposition was not able to stop the development is a testament to the tenacity of local decision-makers and the many dedicated people who devoted years to making it happen.

The 114 affordable housing units range from studios to four-bedroom units and are divided into three-story flats facing the streets and two-story, mid-block cottages. Automobile access is restricted to parking mews accessed from Carl and Frederick Streets. The flats at the street edges have individual tandem garages in raised basements, and the townhouses have garages off parking courts. Because the garages are connected to fire stairs the flats have direct internal access—a very popular feature for security reasons. The cottages are accessible from three pedestrian walks bordered by gardens that traverse the block and negotiate the nearly 50-foot difference in grade. The change in grade contributes to the image of a Mediterranean hilltown also suggested by the eclectic style of the new buildings. Two former Art Deco-style gymnasiums were saved from demolition and serve as a community center and a circus school.

Residents of Parkview Commons purchase their dwellings but lease the land under them for a nominal amount. To offset this subsidy, the city in turn holds a second mortgage on the property with a lien in the amount of the difference between the sale price and the market value. To ensure long-term affordability and to eliminate speculation and windfall profits, the city obtained the right to purchase the property under an option for 4 years and a right of refusal for as long as the owners have the home.

Homeowner Julie Carpenter likes the design and the spaciousness of her home. She remarked, "It fits in with the neighborhood, and I feel safe walking to my house at night as the paths are well lit. I wish there was a little more open

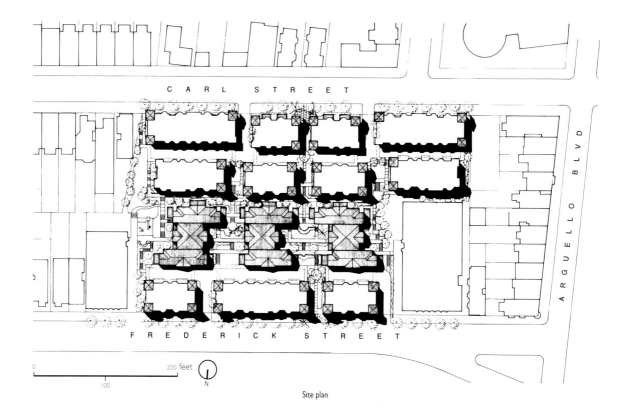

Site plan

Buildings with flats which line interior walkways feature tiled-roof towers at corners John Sutton

OWNER/DEVELOPER
BRIDGE Housing Corporation
Pacific Union Development Company

ARCHITECT
David Baker·Associates, Architects

LANDSCAPE ARCHITECT
Omi Lang Associates

CONTRACTOR
Hunter & Moffet Contractors

MANAGEMENT
Urban Pacific Properties

FUNDERS   **TYPE**
Wells Fargo Bank   Constr. loan
City and County of San Francisco   Perm. loan/grants/
                                         land lease
FHA funded PMI for low-inc. units

DEVELOPMENT TYPE
New construction for-sale attached townhouses and flats.

RESIDENT PROFILE
Low- and moderate-income households, incomes
$19,500–52,800.

DENSITY
44 units/acre

DEVELOPMENT PROFILE

Type	N°/Units	Size (sf)	Sale Prices
1 BR	16	590	$99,000
2 BR	26	790–950	$99,000–127,000
3 BR	38	1,090–1,270	$99,000–138,000
4 BR	34	1,410–1,490	$99,000–147,000
TOTAL	114		

Parking: 186 114 garages + 72 tandem spaces
Total site area: 2.57 acres

CONSTRUCTION TYPE
Three-story woodframe, wood siding, flat and tiled roofs.

COSTS
Land Cost: $2,500,000; Constr. Costs $9,988,000; Other
Costs: $4,522,000; **Total Development Cost: $14,510,000
+ land.** (Completed 1990)

View of internal townhouse cottages with tot-lot in foreground John Sutton

Parkview Commons Continued

space for the kids to play—it gets pretty noisy. It would also be nice to have a community room. Moving into a house this affordable is an opportunity I would never have had. Many of us are now active in the larger community and the neighborhood."

Architect David Baker praised the San Francisco Planning Department for its creative and flexible attitude about the city zoning code. The department was also very supportive of affordable housing and of community involvement in the planning process. Baker said that, "The project was permitted as a planned unit development, which allowed us to modify the zoning codes as we saw fit. Still, we developed our design to follow the spirit, if not the letter, of the San Francisco Planning Code and the Residential Design Guidelines, particularly in having compatible street edge setbacks, heights, and bay modulations."

This affordable housing development has set a standard not only for design but also for the political stamina of affordable housing advocates. People have said to Don Terner, president of BRIDGE Housing, "You can build affordable housing in our community if you build something as nice as Parkview Commons."

Cottages step uphill while facing the interior courtyards John Sutton

0   25 feet   N

Site section looking west

View of internal pathway leading toward Frederick Street John Sutton

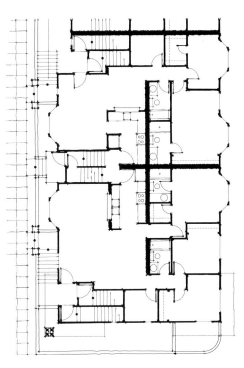

3 BR flat/Unit plan

Frederick Street elevation facing Golden Gate Park John Sutton

Interior of cottage townhouse John Sutton

Pedestrian path steps down from Carl Street to Frederick Street John Sutton

Lorin Station Berkeley, California

Lorin Station is a successful mixed-use development on a struggling commercial corridor. For years the neighborhood has tried to support businesses in spite of crime and disinvestment. According to Director Duane DeJoie, "The South Berkeley Community Development Corporation is interested in helping shape and steer social and economic development in the community. We did a survey to see what type of businesses people would like to see—they wanted a cafe, a produce market, and a laundromat." The City of Berkeley also hoped the development would act as a catalyst for the area. However, mixed-use is not so simple to develop. "We found that the type of funding available was for housing," said John Orevicz, the development consultant. "Once the funding was obtained, the lenders were very concerned about the leasing of the commercial space—the developer had to set aside five years worth of rent—$225,000—but in the end it only took 90 days to lease the space. The occupants are organizations, not retail as intended."

The neighborhood, represented by the Harmon Street Neighborhood Association, was concerned about parking, open space, building height, and the character of the future residents. After many meetings, the development team was able to resolve these issues and the project went forward. Security was a major issue throughout. As architect Steven Kodama stated, "When the building was first conceived the area was in transition, and security was the primary concern. The design of the commercial storefront was carefully looked at to provide security without creating a fortress or the appearance of distress. Roll-down security doors were installed to give the openness needed during daytime hours and security in the evenings." The apartments are entered from the residential side street through a security gate; the parking is secured with an automatic gate.

Lorin Station was designed to fit into the scale and character of Berkeley's older Alcatraz-Adeline business area with commercial on the ground floor and housing above. But the small size of the building made it inefficient from a development point of view. "The soft costs for a 14-unit building are not a whole lot less than for a 100-unit building," noted Orevicz. The small site has minimal open space, but it is well landscaped and has a playground for small children. Six-foot wide hallways which allow children more room to run and play compensate for the limited outdoor space. A community room on the ground floor provides a space for parties and other communal activities. The third-floor apartments have balconies, and all units have large bay windows to maximize natural light.

John Orevicz commented, "A lot of people thought that this building would never be built. The local business owners were thrilled when it began construction—they felt it was a wonderful addition to the neighborhood." DeJoie added, "Lorin Station feels like a quality apartment building. The residents say it doesn't look like a 'project', and they don't feel as if they live in a 'project'."

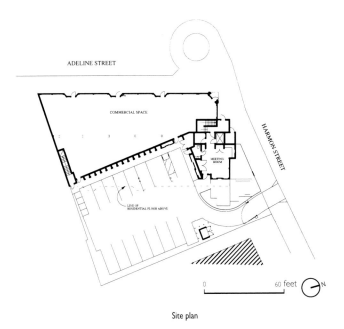

Site plan

2 BR flat unit plan

View of Adeline Street facade Russell Abraham

View of Harmon Steet elevation Russell Abraham

View of entry at corner of Adeline and Harmon Russell Abraham

OWNER/DEVELOPER
South Berkeley Community Development Corp.

ARCHITECT
Kodama Associates

CONSULTANTS
Construction Manager: John Orevicz
Development Consultant: Community Economics
Landscape Architect: Gradjansky & Catz

CONTRACTOR
J.R. Roberts-Ohbayashi Corp.

PROPERTY MANAGEMENT
Alton Management Corporation

FUNDERS	TYPE
City of Berkeley Redevelopment Agency	Loan
Wells Fargo Bank	Constr. loan
CCRC Loan	Perm. loan
State of California RHCP Bond Issue	Loan
Low Income Housing Tax Credits syndicated by the California Equity Fund	Equity

DEVELOPMENT TYPE
New construction rental mixed-use stacked flats with elevator.

RESIDENT PROFILE
Low-income families with incomes $11,480–25,440.

DENSITY
47 units/acre

DEVELOPMENT PROFILE

Type	N°/Units	Size (sf)	Rents
1 BR	4	540	$287
2 BR	8	800	$316–580
3 BR	2	1,340	$636
TOTAL	**14**		

Community/laundry: 1,000 sf
Retail/commercial: 4,500 sf
Parking: 16 surface
Site area: 13,000 sf (.3 acres)

CONSTRUCTION TYPE
Three-story woodframe, stucco exterior, flat roof.

COSTS
Land Cost: $177,375; Constr. Costs: $1,570,160; Other Costs: $633,234; **Total Development Cost: $2,280,769.** (Completed March 1995)

Hismen Hin-nu Terrace Oakland, California

These 92 townhomes and apartments for families and seniors with low and very low incomes mend a deteriorating neighborhood by restoring its main boulevard with housing over shops. Family housing with a childcare center around quiet courtyards is built behind a ground-floor market, niches for street vendors, and a community center with job training, all of which contribute to economic development in the neighborhood. A multi-ethnic mix of tenants is depicted in exterior murals, frieze panels, decorative tiles, and steel entry gates in the form of a burst of sunshine. In the language of the local Native American Ohlones, Hismen Hin-nu means 'Sungate'.

Assisted by a grant from the City of Oakland in 1989, Pyatok Associates studied development scenarios for housing and neighborhood services on several underutilized sites along a major boulevard that runs through multi-ethnic neighborhoods. The San Antonio Community Development Council (SACDC), serving African-, Latino and Native-American residents, expressed interest in developing affordable housing for families and seniors on one of the sites and to expand opportunities for family-owned businesses. They joined the East Bay Asian Local Development Corporation (EBALDC), which serves the Asian-American community, to demonstrate solidarity during a period of racial unrest in the US. Architect Michael Pyatok recalled, "We organized a series of workshops using participatory modeling kits to help over thirty participants from the neighborhood to design their favorite plans for the site and to help them understand the implications of density. In the end, people voted to build four stories on the boulevard and three stories on the side streets in order to preserve a more accessible on-grade courtyard for the children."

The building, which faces the major east—west boulevard, is near the elevated tracks of the Bay Area Rapid Transit system (BART) that serves commuters. The diverse character of the street includes both underutilized lots reflecting a post-WWII suburban strip model and, closer to downtown, some older two- to three-story buildings with retail below and housing above.

The sponsors and architect wanted to recreate the older, denser pattern of mixed-use as an example of better planning for future developers along the boulevard, particularly with a BART station only a few blocks away.

The architecture is an interpretation of the Mission Revival Style, recalling graceful three- and four-story apartment buildings in the neighborhood. The Ratcliff Architects, with the contractor J.E. Roberts - Ohbayashi, worked hard to prepare construction documents and build this complex within the budget and time constraints typical of this type of project. The result is a successful building. Red tiled roofs, trellised balconies and warm colored stucco create a solid yet lively streetfront building along East 14th Street. Behind in the quieter courts, vivid colors define the entries to family townhomes clad in cool blue horizontal siding. Lush foliage overflows planters, softening the places where children play. The safety of the residents was a major consideration in the design process. As Joshua Simon, project manager for EBALDC remarked, "The artwork and degree of community surveillance created by the porches and windows on the street will have a big impact on safety and pride of building."

All family dwellings are designed as three- and four-bedroom townhouses, located in rear courtyards above parking, with no more than 20 families per court. Smaller units for people with fewer or no children are arranged as one- and two-bedroom flats in a four story elevator building facing the boulevard. The first floor along the boulevard contains: childcare center, community hall, market hall, and storefront retail. The residential entry, visible from the management office, is located at the central on-grade courtyard and has an intercom system. Once inside the central court, visitors must be buzzed in a second time to either one of the upper courts or one of the elevator-served buildings. Resident manager Manuel Guizar finds the intercom system is a significant help with security. Mail boxes and a slot through which to put rent checks after hours is adjacent to the office. The community hall and childcare are accessible from the street for the larger community, as well as from the on-grade courtyard.

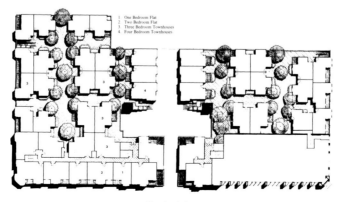

1. One Bedroom Flat
2. Two Bedroom Flat
3. Three Bedroom Townhouses
4. Four Bedroom Townhouses

Plaza level plan

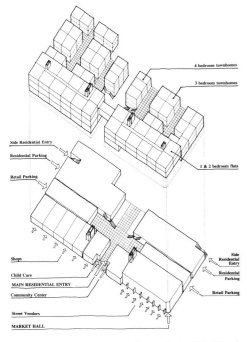

Project organization Michael Pyatok

Entry gate (Sungate design) Michael Pyatok

On-grade court showing entry gate Janet Delaney

View of upper courtyard with children Janet Delaney

DEVELOPERS/SPONSORS

The East Bay Asian Local Development Corporation
San Antonio Community Development Council

ARCHITECT

Design Architect: Pyatok Associates
Architect of Record: The Ratcliff Architects

LANDSCAPE ARCHITECT

Chris Patillo Associates

CONTRACTOR

J.E. Roberts - Ohbayashi Corporation

FUNDERS

	TYPE
City of Oakland RDA	Const./Perm. Loan
Calif. Department of HCD	Const./Perm. Loan
Calif. Comm. Reinvestment Corp.	Const./Perm. Loan
Wells Fargo Bank	Const. Loan
Bank of the West/Bank of Calif.	Bridge Loan
FNMA and CASH, Inc.	Syndication Partner
CDBG and NEA	Grant
The Ford Foundation and The James Irvine Foundation	Grant

RESIDENT PROFILE

Singles, couples and families with incomes $19,350–43,800
(family of 8)/year. Incomes between 50–60% of AMI.

DEVELOPMENT TYPE

New construction mixed-use rental housing, flats and
townhouses over parking and retail/commercial.

DENSITY

Apartments: 85 units/acre. Townhouses: 35 units/acre

DEVELOPMENT PROFILE

Type	Nº/Units	Size (sf)	Rent
1 BR	17	585	$332–$383
2 BR	35	800	$505
3 BR	30	1,050	$424–$653
4 BR	10	1.250	$699
TOTAL	92		

Circ/lobby/office: 3,292 sf
Commercial: 11,224 sf
Day care: 2,000 sf
Community room: 1,600 sf
Parking: 30 commercial, 89 residential 35,638 sf, 119 spaces
Total site area: 63,803 sf (1.46 acres)

CONSTRUCTION TYPE

Stucco and cement-fiber siding over two- to three-story
woodframe over concrete podium post-tensioned slab

DEVELOPMENT COSTS

Land Costs: $1,001,988; Constr. Costs: $10.47m.;
Other Costs: $4.83m.; **Total Development Cost:
$15.3m**; (Completed February 1995); Housing: $9.47m
($85/sf, $166,304/unit); Commercial: $1m ($36/sf)

A consortium of neighborhood vendors also participated in the design workshops, which resulted in the design of a two-story high market hall for them to continue their business. As a result, the developer was able to pre-lease the market, reducing the risk of retail in a low-income neighborhood. The market holds 14 small vendors inside and five vendors outside in niches along the building's facade. Not only does this contribute to local economic development, but it enlivens the street with people and contributes to a safer environment. The retail has its own parking garages primarily for the vendors and service entered from the side streets, with direct access to the stores.

Michael Pyatok convinced the sponsors to enhance the complex as a symbol of racial diversity and unity with artistic contributions from ethnic groups in the neighborhood. He applied to the National Endowment for the Arts (NEA) and was awarded $50,000 for public art. The coexistence of art from these diverse traditions inspires a spirit of co-operation not only among the tenants but in the community. Four artists (Horace Washington, Mia Kodani, Daniel Galvez, and Reynaldo Terrazas) interpreted their respective traditions in exterior art (e.g., the frieze panels contain geometric patterns from many cultures woven together). The artists will also document the cultural origins of their work in graphic displays permanently located in the lobby. The art and educational exhibit are intended to prove that America's cultural diversity is a source of energy for creating community, rather than a source of conflict. As Don 'Little Cloud' Davenport, Director of SACDC proudly exclaims, "This is the most beautiful building in all of Oakland!"

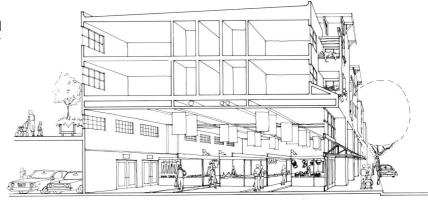

Section perspective through market hall

On-grade court with trellis Michael Pyatok

Art panel detail on East 14th Street Michael Pyatok

View along 26th Avenue Janet Delaney

View along East 14th Street Janet Delaney

Section perspective showing street vendors Michael Pyatok

Rear patio with trellis Janet Delaney

Street view showing retail stores Willie Pettus

Del Carlo Court San Francisco, California

Architects Daniel Solomon and Susan Haviland turned an irregular site with two street frontages, one exposed to the traffic of a very wide street and the other terminating in a residential lane, into a safe and sunny environment for families at Del Carlo Court. The Mission Housing Development Corporation (MHDC) and the San Francisco Mayor's Office of Housing assembled the initial financing utilizing a local housing trust funded through mandatory contributions made by developers of downtown office buildings. MHDC and their management company involved the architects in a constructive dialogue throughout the design process to develop a clear understanding of this working-class neighborhood and its households. Resident Mercedes Jirong, a home health-care worker whose daughter works part-time while studying choreography, loves the "...abundance of light and sunshine in the apartment. The neighbors are very friendly," she added. "We have a very good manager, and the whole place is kept nice and clean."

The courtyard, which is visible from two streets through large apertures in the buildings, provides a safe place for children to play and adults to gather. Resident Manager Margarita Pinate says, "It's a meeting and passing place. People cross the court to go to the laundry, to get their mail, visit with neighbors, and to get to the garage." The courtyard is paved with cobblestones, planted with sycamore trees, and secured from the street by beautifully crafted metal gates. Exterior wooden stairs evoke images of typical San Francisco back stairs and provide access from the court to the flats and townhouses. The two-story openings, flanked by 25 concealed parking spaces, safely serve as the entry for people and cars, and provide a glimpse into the intimate courtyard for passers-by.

The street and courtyard facades have wide roof overhangs supported on large brackets. Openings in the overhangs enliven the facades by allowing light and shadow to spill onto the walls and into the apartments. Del Carlo Court, which is consistent with the density of public and private housing in the immediate area, demonstrates the age-old urban wisdom of creating a secure courtyard behind a street-front building, with "eyes on the court" for child supervision and security.

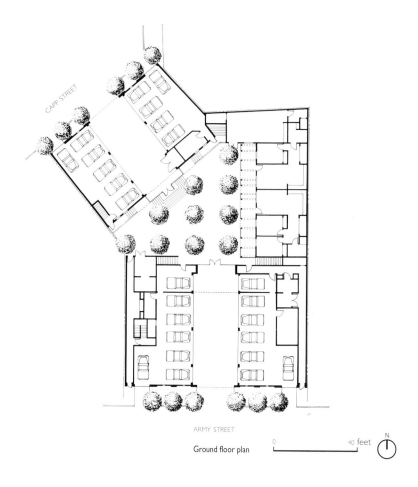

CAPP STREET

ARMY STREET

Ground floor plan
0   40 feet

N

Courtyard view of northeast corner Chris Irion

Courtyard from Army Street building entry Chris Irion

Capp Street building from Capp Street Chris Irion

OWNER/DEVELOPER
Mission Housing Development Corp.

ARCHITECT
SOLOMON Architecture and Urban Design

CONSULTANTS
Development Consultant: Community Economics
Landscape Architect: Gary Strang

CONTRACTOR
Nibbi-Lowe Construction

PROPERTY MANAGEMENT
Caritas Management Corp.

FUNDERS	TYPE
S.F. Mayor's Office of Housing	Perm. loan
S.F. Mayor's Office of Housing	Perm. loan
State of California RHCP (Bond Issue)	Constr./ perm. loan
Low Income Housing Tax Credits bought by Mission First Financial	Equity
Wells Fargo Bank	Constr. loan
Local Initiatives Support Corporation	Predev. loan
SF Redevelopment Agency	Predev. loan
Low Income Housing Fund	Predev. loan

DEVELOPMENT TYPE
New construction rental attached townhouses over flats, stacked flats.

RESIDENT PROFILE
Very-low- and low-income families, incomes 35–60% of AMI; AMI for family of four $58,800.

DENSITY
57 units/acre

DEVELOPMENT PROFILE
Type	Nº/Units	Size (sf)	Rents
1 BR	2	603	$361–599
2 BR	14	817	$393–708
3 BR	5	1,093	$426–777
4 BR	4	1,426	$496–902
TOTAL	25		

Parking : 25 garages
Courtyard/play area: 4,786 sf
Community/laundry: 1,000 sf
Total site area: 16,882 sf (.39 acres)

CONSTRUCTION TYPE
Three-story woodframe over reinforced concrete, horiz. and plywood/batten siding.

COSTS
Land Cost: $650,000; Constr. Costs: $3,878,869 ($79/sf); Other Costs: $708,815; **Total Development Cost: $5,237,684 ($120/sf).** (Completed 1992)

Villa Nueva is a successful solution to a complicated mixed-use program of secure affordable housing and accessible public facilities. The Young Women's Christian Association (YWCA) had been providing housing and services for poor women and their children in downtown San Jose since the early 1900s. The 1980s brought an increased demand. A steering committee headed by boardmember Mary Kelley developed a strategic plan and identified key partners whose expertise would be essential. These included Supervisor Susanne B. Wilson (who ultimately raised three million dollars in private donations for the development), the City of San Jose, and BRIDGE Housing. Kelley noted, "The City was very receptive to our ideas." Ben Golvin, project manager for BRIDGE, pointed out, "A key challenge was to convince the Redevelopment Agency that transitional housing in the downtown would be compatible with new commercial development."

Villa Nueva is a success, both architecturally and socially. The use of terra cotta roofs and a modern interpretation of the Mission-revival style allows the building to blend with surrounding structures. The structure fits gracefully into its urban setting, and acts as a transition from adjacent high-rises to residential areas at the edge of downtown. A compact five-story structure, the facility has 63 units of affordable housing on the upper three floors. The first two floors house a childcare center, a fitness center, a YWCA-administered career and personal counseling center, a women's crisis center, and a hostel for temporary housing. Two terraces serve the YWCA offices, while two smaller play areas serve the childcare center.

The provision of separate and secure access for the different uses and their parking on such a small site was a tremendous challenge for the development team. Architect Robert Steinberg noted, "Three stories of woodframe housing over levels of concrete public uses and parking was a creative structural and code-conforming solution for providing a dense facility at a reasonable cost." However, the building did have to be classified similarly to a high-rise structure, requiring costly exiting and life safety systems.

Although at the outset the YWCA had no development experience, Mary Kelley proudly pointed out that, "This development demonstrates that a group of women can conceive of, plan, and execute a $16 million development." Socially speaking, the building is a precedent-setting community resource. Although the YWCA has fulfilled its service and housing goals, both Golvin and Kelley note that it can be difficult to match your intended residents with the legal requirements of funding sources. Over half the resident children under 12 are now in the daycare program; the rest stay with relatives when parents are at work. The daycare and fitness centers meet critical needs of downtown office workers—since completion more than 1,000 applications have been received for the housing and more than 20,000 households have utilized the program services.

1. Apartment
2. Hallway
3. Lounge
4. Hostel
5. Childcare Center
6. Childcare Play Yard
7. Fitness Center Entry
8. Offices, Programs, and Counseling
9. Career Center
10. Plaza
11. Street Level Garage
12. Lower Level Garage

Elevation

Typical unit interior Robb Miller

Childcare play yard Robb Miller

Exterior view overall Robb Miller

OWNER/DEVELOPER
BRIDGE Housing Corporation
The Santa Clara County YWCA

ARCHITECT
The Steinberg Group

CONSULTANTS
Development Consultant: Community Economics
Landscape Architect: David Gates Assoc.

CONTRACTOR
L&D Construction

PROPERTY MANAGEMENT
BRIDGE (Housing)
YWCA (Facilities)

FUNDERS	TYPE
San Jose Housing Dept.	Loans
San Jose Redevelopment Agency	Grants
Bank of America	Constr. loan
First Nationwide Bank	Perm. loan
Private and Corporate Funders	Grants (YWCA only)
Low-Income Housing Tax Credits bought by Mission First Financial	Equity

DEVELOPMENT TYPE
New construction family rental apartments with services,
fitness center, day care center, hostel, and YWCA offices.

RESIDENT PROFILE
Very-low-income singles, and families with children,
incomes $11,240–28,935; general public; YWCA staff.

DENSITY
77 units/acre

DEVELOPMENT PROFILE

Type	N°/Units	Size (sf)	Rents
Studio	12	480	$345
1 BR	45	640–705	$395
2 BR	6	805	$445
TOTAL	63		

Community: Fitness center, on-site services, childcare center.
Parking: 100 spaces, 67 for housing
YWCA offices: 23,804 sf
Site area: 35,692 sf (.89 acres)

CONSTRUCTION TYPE
Three-story woodframe over two-story concrete, plus one-story
underground parking; high-rise construction, stucco exterior
tiled roof.

COSTS
Land Cost: $1.44m; Constr. Costs $10,068,502; Other Costs:
$3,176,873; **Total Development Cost: $14,685,375 (housing
and YWCA).** (Completed March 1993)

The 555 Ellis Street Family Apartments is a new rental housing development in San Francisco's Tenderloin district, an ethnically mixed area with many recent immigrants from Asian countries. The housing is part of an on-going effort by local non-profit organizations to provide family housing in a neighborhood with few multiple-bedroom units and to reverse the long-standing negative image of the Tenderloin. The site has excellent public transportation and proximity to downtown. Across Ellis Street is a public park and the new Tenderloin Recreation Center, with a large outdoor children's play area and a building with spaces for athletics, and arts and crafts.

The building contains mostly two- and three-bedroom units for families. It also includes nine studio apartments for single adults or couples. The development was initiated by Glenda Hope, director of San Francisco Network Ministries (SFNM), and a Presbyterian minister who has spent 22 years in the Tenderloin. "Although SFNM had no previous development experience, we raised a half million dollars from the National Organization of Presbyterian Women to help fund the project and a planning study, which told us we needed an established non-profit development partner. We chose Asian Neighborhood Design (AND) because of their excellent record in both design and development in the Tenderloin."

From the many community meetings came suggestions that helped mold the project. Among them was one that led to designing the store fronts as lighted cases to display artworks by Tenderloin residents on a rotating basis. Bright but attractive night lighting, a room useable for community meetings, and ground floor commercial space were other community suggestions incorporated into the design. Tom Jones, development director of AND noted, "The site was one of the last undeveloped parcels in the Tenderloin and offered a rare opportunity to provide housing for families with low incomes with new construction, in contrast to the typical approach in the district, which is rehabilitating older structures." With 38 units, the building is both economically efficient to manage and small enough to foster a sense of

community. The ground floor contains a lobby, a commercial space occupied by SFNM, and 10 parking spaces on the street side. In addition, it contains several community and tenant spaces, and the manager's unit.

A central secured entry adjacent to the front office, leads along a curving pathway from the front community room past the elevator to a large community recreation room. Counseling offices and a large laundry overlook the rear garden. Above are three full floors of apartments, all with bay windows to maximize daylight. The fourth floor of apartments is set back from the street in response to the city sunlight access code, which requires that winter sun reach the park across the street. The setback zone contains the large terraces for the studio apartments; these units have sloped ceilings and lofts for storage or sleeping. A tutorial center with computer stations, study desks, and a resource library are also on the top floor.

The large garden behind the building was designed with separate areas for children's play equipment and other activities. A patio partially covered by the residential floors above provides outdoor space for social events. A smaller, separate courtyard is used for quieter activity. Both of these open spaces are bounded either by one-story structures or by the back yard areas of adjacent lots, a situation that guarantees them long hours of sunlight for much of the year. The building design recalls older apartment buildings with many different unit plans and many units with cross-ventilation. Like older apartments in San Francisco the streetfront has a strong symmetry, and the building mass is broken down by vertical bays. Although it occupies 75 per cent of its site and has a density of over 100 units per acre, the building feels spacious, and the public areas are light-filled and generous.

The Mayor's Office of Housing played a key role in supporting 555 Ellis providing both funding and administrative assistance throughout the development process. Project Manager Joel Lipsky remarked, "This development fits our budgetary

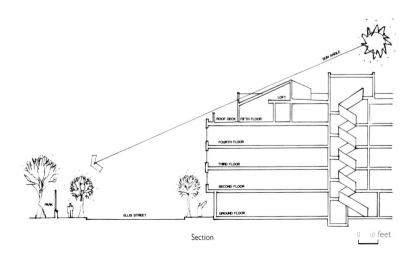

Section

0 10 feet

Typical living room furnished by residents John F. Martin

View along Ellis Street John F. Martin

OWNERS / DEVELOPERS
San Francisco Network Ministries Hsg. Corp.
Asian Neighborhood Design

ARCHITECT
Asian Neighborhood Design

LANDSCAPE ARCHITECT
Orsee Design

CONTRACTOR
Transworld Construction

PROPERTY MANAGEMENT
Caritas Management Corp.

FUNDERS	TYPE
S.F. Redev. Agency, Tax Increment Bonds	Deferred loan
San Francisco Mayor's Office of Housing	Deferred loan
Wells Fargo Bank	Constr. loan
First Nationwide Bank	Perm. loan
San Francisco Network Ministries and over 40 foundations and private contributions	Grants
Low Income Housing Tax Credits syndicated by the California Equity Fund	Equity
Fed. Home Loan Bank Aff. Hsg Program	Deferred loan

DEVELOPMENT TYPE
New construction rental stacked flats with elevator.

RESIDENT PROFILE
Very-low- and low-income families with
incomes $7,500–30,000.

DENSITY
122 units/acre

DEVELOPMENT PROFILE

Type	N°/Units	Size (sf)	Rents
Studio	3	500	$205–410
Studio+loft	6	420 + loft	$205–410
2 BR	10	800–850	$243–640
3 BR	19	1,000–1,120	$266–700
TOTAL	38		

Community: 1,875 sf (7 community rooms)
Courtyard: 4,280 + 1,200 sf roof deck
Parking: 10 spaces, garage
Commercial: 1,017 sf
Site area: 13,517 sf (.31 acres)

CONSTRUCTION TYPE
Four-story woodframe over one-story concrete, stucco
exterior, flat roof.

COSTS
Land Cost: $900,000; Constr. Costs: $4,567,853; Other
Costs: $1,582,447; **Total Development Cost: $7,050,300.**
(Completed March 1995)

guidelines. We realize that families with low incomes need educational services to remain stable in the community, and SFNM will be providing these with no on-going governmental subsidies." To minimize long-term maintenance and enhance the pride of residents, durable materials have been emphasized throughout the building. The facade has a concrete base with slate and glass-block infill; the upper stories are woodframe with painted stucco. Ground floor public spaces are finished with slate and cork flooring, with carpet in areas receiving less foot traffic. Partner AND, which also operates a furniture-manufacturing business and job-training program, provided the durable kitchen cabinets and custom tables designed for the community rooms.

The community was generally supportive of the development. Neighbor Jean White commented on the building, "It fits in well architecturally. I like the fact that it is not too big—we must have affordable housing, as long as we keep it from being over concentrated. We are worried about the crime element in this community, although I am confident that good management by people like Glenda Hope will make 555 Ellis successful." A perimeter and roof-top electronic sensing system and a double entry system augmented with surveillance cameras assures security, according to resident manager Hermy Almonte. As part of the application process Almonte made home visits to meet the families. "Many of these families used to live in one-bedroom apartments. Over 1,000 households applied for apartments here. For those who were selected, this is a miracle building!" Resident Merlin Willis agreed, "The screening of tenants helped security the most." He also expressed approval of the design, "The designers of this building should be congratulated—someone thought about how people really live! The kitchen is very large with lots of counter space, there is more than enough storage, and the hallways are large. Compared to where I was living before this is heaven."

View from rear yard to Loggia and community room Janet Delaney

Large community room looking through to terrace John F. Martin

Small community room/children's art room John F. Martin

Large community room showing library John F. Martin

Ellis Street elevation Janet Delaney

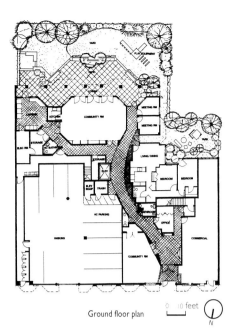

Ground floor plan

0 10 feet

N

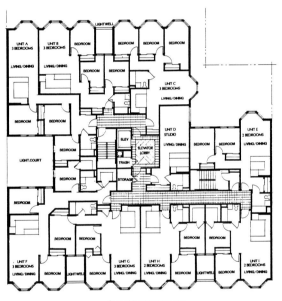

Second level building plan

View of housing from Tenderloin playground Janet Delaney

Frank G. Mar Community Housing Oakland, California

The Frank G. Mar Community Housing demonstrates the validity of high-density, mixed-use housing for inner city areas. It addresses the needs of Oakland's growing Asian community for three- and four-bedroom apartments to accommodate an influx of large families into the city's Chinatown neighborhood. The location of the Mar housing complex on a block-size former parking lot has helped revitalize the downtown commercial district by adding a resident population of about 300 adults and children. The proximity to shopping, transportation, work and the other services is a boon for the residents.

The 119 units are above street level commercial space and a two-level underground parking facility. Double rows of two-and-a-half-story units for families occupy buildings that line two streets and part of the interior of the block. Designed townhouses, each of these 54 units has an outdoor yard and a separate entry, eliminating the need for double-loaded corridors and enabling the front and rear of each unit to have natural light and cross ventilation. In fact, the townhouse units with high ceilings, skylights, and mezzanine bedrooms are full of light and belie their small size. A nine-story building contains the 65 apartments for the elderly.

At the center of the complex is a large open courtyard, which serves as a protected playground for the many children at certain times of the day and accommodates the elderly and other residents at quieter times. A laundry room and a community room also flank the courtyard. Property manager Bill Leung has observed that the courtyard is used in a variety of ways, "Sometimes meetings or celebrations are held there, and sometimes meetings held in the meeting room (adjacent to the courtyard) spill out into the courtyard. Children ranging in age from four to 18 play in the courtyard after school and before dinner. Seniors come out at dawn to practice tai-chi and jog, and then later in the day after the children have gone in for dinner."

According to Leung, the apartments, although generally liked, have received mixed reviews, "Some people like the high ceilings because they remind them of their old houses in China, while others find that they make too much space to heat. Some people like the open loft bedrooms for children, so that they can't lock themselves in, while others feel that there is not enough privacy in them to use as a master bedroom, making the unit less flexible. Some larger families say they would rather have extra floor area than the high ceiling."

The architects, MacDonald Architects, sought to give the development a sense of individuality, to keep it from projecting the image of a large housing project. Gable roofs signal the residential character of the complex; the different heights of the buildings and alternation of the roof forms contribute to a picturesque, village-like appearance. The architects have successfully integrated this large complex into the urban fabric by breaking up its massing so that the midrise block of apartments for the elderly faces a block-size former grand hotel of 1910 of the same height. The lowrise family units face buildings of comparable size; separate entries from the courtyard give them individual privacy. Front entrances that cluster on pedestrian lanes leading to the courtyard encourage neighborliness.

At first the architects wanted to incorporate ungated stairways leading from the street level into the central courtyard. However, the concerns of the property management over security resulted in a single pedestrian entrance controlled by an intercom. This control has effectively addressed the problem of access by non-residents. Although the division of the garage into resident and public parking prompted fears, security problems have not materialized. Security has proved to be so effective for the central courtyard that parents are willing to let their children play there unsupervised.

South elevation

Detail of housing over storefront retail Magnus Stark

OWNER/DEVELOPER
East Bay Asian Local Development Corporation

CO-SPONSOR: BRIDGE Housing

ARCHITECT
MacDonald Architects
Gee Architects-Assoc. Arch. for Constr. Observation

CONTRACTOR
J.E. Roberts-Ohbayashi Corporation

MANAGEMENT
East Bay Asian Local Development Corporation

FUNDERS	TYPE
Wells Fargo Bank	Constr. loan
City of Oakland RDA	Loan
Oakland Public Works Dept/	
Parking Authority	Loan
HUD (HODAG)	Grant
US Office of Community	
Services	Grant
Citibank	Loan
Federal Home Loan Bank	Grant
Mission Housing Investment	Tax Credits

RESIDENT PROFILE
Families with incomes below $30,000/year.
Seniors with incomes below $16,000/year.

DEVELOPMENT TYPE
New construction rental Housing, Family and Senior.

DENSITY: Family housing: 55 units/acre;
Senior housing: 270 units/acre

DEVELOPMENT PROFILE

Type	N°/Units	Size (sf)	Rents
1 BR	51	500	$443–$512
2 BR	35	800	$430–$563
3 BR	27	1,000	$494–$615
4 BR	6	1,200	$615
TOTAL	119		

Community laundry: 1,100 sf
Courtyard/play: 14,000 sf
Commercial: 12,500 sf
Parking: 310 (200 public) 94,700 sf
Total site area: 39,700 sf

CONSTRUCTION TYPE
Family housing: three-story stucco/woodframe;
Family/Snr housing: nine-story stucco/conc. bl. frame;
Both housing types built over two level concrete
underground garage and streetfront commercial space

COSTS
Land Costs: $2,284,681; Constr. Costs: $12.5m;
Other Costs: $4.78m; **Total Development Cost:**
(Hsg: **$13.8m**, Commercial: **$96k**, Garage: **$2.5m**).
Total: $17,281,215; (Completed 1990)

Family townhouses and senior apartments overlook courtyard and play area Magnus Stark

The original program projected 80 units of family housing to be constructed over commercial storefront space and grade-level parking for the residents. Thomas Lauderbach, who was the project manager for the East Bay Asian Local Development Corporation (EBALDC), reported that, in response to shortfalls in the funding, EBALDC sought and obtained a federal Housing Development Action Grant through the City of Oakland and offered to assume the development of a public parking facility. As a condition of approving the HoDAG loan application the City required additional units, which increased the total number to 119.

Lauderbach also stated that considerable negotiation took place with the City planners over many general and detailed issues. As an example he cited the change from typical iron balcony railings to translucent glass balcony walls which, though more costly, did address the planners' concern that the buildings' appearance would suffer if the belongings that residents would be likely to store on their balconies were visible. This solution addressed the problem and still allowed light to enter the dwellings.

The design and development process faced many hurdles that were overcome in inventive ways. With more than ten sources of financing the process was complex, to say the least. Subdividing the property into four parcels created a condominium with air rights and facilitated the commercial and public parking components. But this organization also added to the complexity and legal costs of the project. A very successful fund-raising effort permitted the debt-free development of the commercial portion of the project. As a result, an owner-subsidized childcare facility was given rent-free space in the project.

Reflecting on his experience with the Frank G. Mar Community Housing project, Thomas Lauderbach stated that, "User input is necessary to long-term success. The more opportunity those who are effected by the project have to comment on it, the better the facility will function. I am guaranteed of making a mistake if I assume instead of ask what will work for the future residents or the maintenance personnel."

Building section (East)

View of the courtyard with fenced private patios Magnus Stark

The massing of the building in relation to the double towers on the adjacent building Magnus Stark

Corner of 11th and Harrison showing mid-rise senior housing Willie Pettus

Passage between townhouse units Magnus Stark

View of the interior walkway showing planting and entry doors to the units Magnus Stark

The relationship of the green roofs to those nearby Magnus Stark

Overall view of the pedestrian street Magnus Stark

Cascade Court Apartments Seattle, Washington

Among the thorny challenges that architects face in designing housing for families with low incomes in historic neighborhoods is that of compatibility with older historically significant buildings. In the case of Cascade Court Apartments, GGLO architects met the challenge of designing a 100-unit apartment building next to a former single-family mansion with great success. If the architects had not been sensitive to the context, the much larger building might well have been an intrusion rather than a contribution to the neighborhood.

The adjacent building, the landmark Stimson-Green mansion built in 1900, was occupied by Priscilla Collins, who had grown up in the house. Concerned about the possibility of high rise condominiums being developed on the adjacent lot, she bought the parcel. Her desire that families be able to live in the neighborhood influenced her decision to sell the property at 25 per cent of the sales price to a non-profit development corporation, the Seattle Housing Resources Group (SHRG), which agreed to develop the site as housing for families with children.

When interviewed about the housing, Mrs Collins noted that the existence of an attractive building housing a diverse community had reduced crime in the neighborhood, particularly the drug traffic and prostitution that the formerly empty lot invited. "No one that I know of has complained about the residents," Mrs Collins affirmed, "instead planners and politicians show the development as a model." The building was planned to enable residents to observe people coming and going through the gated courtyard entrance. The manager's office has many windows, and is a central location of security. The entrance, lobby, mail area and laundry are visually connected to the office. Residents can view the lobby and screen their visitors from the units. Each of the two underground parking levels has a security camera as do the lobby and courtyard.

The massing of Cascade Court, which has three-story townhouses on the south side at the street front rising to five-story flats at the north side of the site, is also sympathetic to the view from the street of the Stimson-Green house. A central courtyard that divides the street frontage of the building into two facades also gives the building a scale more compatible with the mansion. The courtyard includes a play area for the children near the townhouses, which have the larger family units. Resident Manager Rosie Martinez mentions, "We have a program where the kids help pick up garbage in the courtyard in return for a pizza party at the end of the summer." The three-bedroom units are well lit by large square windows and come with dishwashers and laundries. Priscilla Collins' request for a variety of units to serve a diverse community of singles, couples, and families resulted in 39 studios, 35 one-bedroom, 14 two-bedroom, and 12 three-bedroom units arranged in various combinations of flats and townhouses.

Although the architects were not trying to emulate any regional architectural tradition, the Tudor revival style of the Stimson-Green house influenced their choice of materials, the patterned brick base with stuccoed walls above, and such features as the gabled parapets on dormers and bays capped with contrasting moldings and the pyramidal roofed towers. Taking advantage of an option allowed in the Seattle Land Use Code, the architects designed the building to mid-rise standards, which resulted in a lower structure with a larger footprint. In Seattle five-story wood-frame construction is allowed in the Uniform Building Code's type V-1 hour construction. This factor added to the regional economic advantage of wood and a competitive work force in wood-frame construction was important in determining the building's scale.

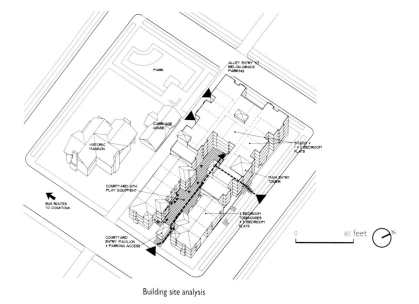

Building site analysis

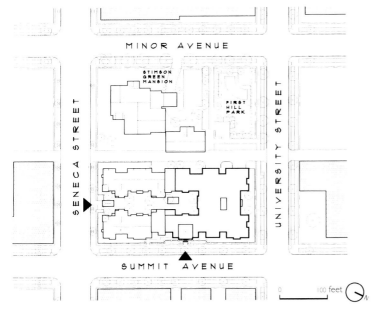

Site plan

Townhome facing courtyard with benches Yannis Paris

OWNER/DEVELOPER
Owner: Cascade Court Limited Partnership
Developer: Seattle Housing Resources Group

ARCHITECT
GGLO Architecture and Interior Design

CONTRACTOR
The Rafn Company

CONSULTANTS
Landscape Architect: Berger Partnership
Sales and Marketing: Ratti Swenson Perlux

MANAGEMENT
Seattle Housing Resource Group

FUNDERS

	TYPE
Nordstrom	Equity
State of Washington	Loan
Washington Mutual	Loan
Wash. State Hsg Finance Com.	Tax credit

RESIDENT PROFILE
Singles, couples and families with incomes ranging from $16,000–28,000 a year.

DEVELOPMENT TYPE
New construction rental housing, flats and townhouses over parking

DEVELOPMENT PROFILE

Type	Nº/Units	Size (sf)	Rents
Studio	39	400	$350–375
1 BR	35	600	$390–515
2 BR	14	740	$460–590
3 BR	12	1,200	$525–700
TOTAL	100		

Courtyard/play: 13,309 sf
Parking: 138 spaces
Office/lobby: 9,400 sf
Total site area: 28,827 sf (.66 acres)

DENSITY
151 units/acre

CONSTRUCTION
Five-story woodframe over two-story concrete below grade parking podium

COSTS
Land: $15.73/sf for land assessed at $75/sf; Construction Costs: $5,117,022 ($46.45/sf including parking; residential $60/sf); Other Costs: $1,943,945; **Total Development $7,060,967; $ 70,610 per unit.** (Completed March 1994)

Cascade Court Apartments Continued

The creative package of funding for Cascade Court from public and private sources demonstrates that alternative ways of financing housing for low income people can have exemplary results. In this case the package had a property owner committed to doing something positive for the neighborhood, a prominent Seattle retailer, Nordstrom, which contributed equity in exchange for tax credits, bank loans, a low interest loan from the State of Washington, and an energy conservation credit. Although no locally mandated design review existed, the architects worked through the design with Priscilla Collins and the staff of SHRG. Nancy F. Smith, Executive Director of SHRG, commented that the development was the result of an experienced team working together and the generous contribution of a valuable property.

First Hill, as its name suggests, was the first prime residential area developed in burgeoning Seattle around the turn-of-the-century. The hill's convenience to downtown employment and services was much prized by its affluent residents. The present residents, who earn no more than 40 per cent to 60 per cent of the area's median income, are also very pleased to have a home on First Hill. Cascade Court serves as an outstanding example of how to design affordable housing for families with low incomes in established neighborhoods.

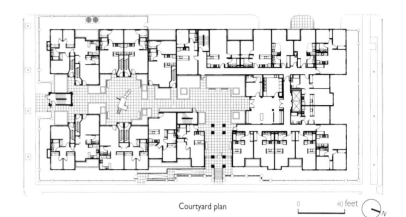

Courtyard plan

0   40 feet   N

Looking south from Seneca Street with Stimson Green mansion to the west Yannis Paris

Unit interior showing wood detailing Yannis Paris

Summit Avenue elevation Yannis Paris

Courtyard surrounded by townhouse units with play equipment Yannis Paris

Summit Avenue main entrance Yannis Paris

Typical kitchen Yannis Paris

The conventional wisdom in the US that high-density, high-rise affordable family housing is certain to have a negative effect on both residents and neighborhoods is not always correct. Two developments that encourage this revision are located adjacent to one another at 201 Turk Street and 111 Jones Street in San Francisco. At an average of 225 dwelling units per acre these two nine-story buildings have a very high density, yet they do not appear out of scale in the dense inner city Tenderloin District. A spacious yet intimate courtyard behind the buildings relieves the density and provides secure play areas for children and relaxation areas for seniors. According to Merle Malakoff of Mercy Charities, project manager for 111 Jones, HKIT Architects, who designed both buildings simultaneously, were successful in meeting the major challenge of reducing the impact of the buildings' height and density. On the street, the complex presents a formal, continuous facade of projecting bays. From the courtyard, three differently colored, horizontal divisions help the structures feel more villagelike. Larger family units on the second, third, and fourth floors of both buildings, have access to the courtyard via stairs and key-operated elevators and form clusters to facilitate the management of large numbers of children. These units overlook the courtyard to permit parents to supervise their children. Elderly residents live in smaller units on the upper floors.

Because Tenderloin parks are notorious for drug dealing and other dangers, a safe outdoor area was one of the main concerns expressed during community meetings held during the design process. Approximately 5,000 children live in the Tenderloin; most of them are from families of recent immigrants crowded into single-room occupancy hotels and studio apartments. Sherine Ta, a resident of 201 Turk Street expressed her happiness and relief at being able to live with the seven members of her family in a three-bedroom apartment instead of the studio they had shared for 12 years after arriving from a Hong Kong refugee camp, "Like many families with low incomes, we could not find affordable housing. Today my family is extremely happy...the change has been like a dream."

Residents are representative of the ethnic diversity of the Tenderloin; about half are from Southeast Asia, and the others are a mixture of Russian, African-American, Hispanic, and Caucasian ancestries. To effectively respond to these various cultures, management provides new residents with a personalized manual written in English and their native language, with tips for social services, safety, and other local issues. An independently managed childcare center located in 201 Turk operates two daily sessions that serve over 100 children from the neighborhood as well as the complex. The childcare facility is an integral part of this new community. It

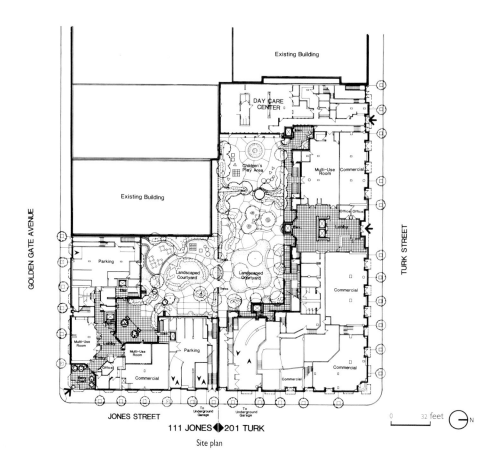

111 JONES ◆▶ 201 TURK

Site plan

201 Turk Street, detail John Sutton

Daycare center and play area, 201 Turk Street John Sutton

201 TURK STREET

OWNER/DEVELOPER
Joint venture partner: A.F. Evans Co.
Joint venture partner: Chinese Community Housing Corp.

ARCHITECT
Hardison Komatsu Ivelich and Tucker

CONSULTANTS
Landscape Architect: David Heldt
Financial Consultant: L. B. Share

CONTRACTOR
J. E. Roberts-Ohbayashi Corporation

PROPERTY MANAGEMENT
Evans Property Management

FUNDERS	TYPE
San Francisco Redevelopment Agency	Loan
Mayor's Office of Housing	Loan
Federal Home Loan Bank Affdbl. Hsg. Prog.	Grant
State of California RHCP Prog. (Bond Issue)	Loan
Wells Fargo Bank	Constr. loan
Citibank	Perm.loan
PG&E	Equity
Philip Morris Capital Corp.	Equity
Prudential Insurance Co. of America	Equity

DEVELOPMENT TYPE
New construction mixed-use, rental stacked flats, walk-up and elevator-served.

RESIDENT PROFILE
Very-low- and low-income singles, couples and families, incomes $8,800–43,440.

DENSITY
201 units/acre

DEVELOPMENT PROFILE

Type	N°/Units	Size (sf)	Rents
Studios	12	435–475	$332–490
1 BR	81	575–645	$376–610
2 BR	45	805–1,005	$409–701
3 BR	37	1,050–1,420	$440–728
TOTAL	175		

Community: 2,160 sf multi-use space
Retail/commercial: 6,300 sf
Courtyard: 10,440 sf
Parking: 56 spaces, underground garage
Total site area: 37,810 sf (.87 acres)

CONSTRUCTION TYPE
Nine-story reinforced concrete (post-tensioned slabs/1 level parking).

COSTS
Land Cost: $5,728,000; Constr. Costs: $18,654,766 ($86.66/sf, incl. garage); Other Costs: $10,913,025;
Total Development Cost: $35,295,791.
(Completed April 1994)

201 Turk and 111 Jones Continued

was sited to take full advantage of the open space within the protected courtyard. Multi-purpose spaces for cultural, recreational, and educational forums (computer training, for example) have proven their value by being completely reserved each weekend.

As with many such endeavors, a highly professional and dedicated development team was the key to handling the complex financing, design, construction, and management issues. Both buildings were planned, designed, and constructed using the design-build approach. Bringing the general contractors and their major subcontractors into the design process at the beginning enabled the development to be constructed on budget.

As property manager Aiden McAleenan and residents exchanged a friendly greeting in the hallway of 111 Jones he noted, "It's a great place and the people are great. Good management is one key to this ongoing success. At the front desk we have a scrapbook with a photo of every family, their names, and important information. This is a way to get to know everyone in the building, assist them efficiently in an emergency, and watch for overcrowding in the units." Security elements at both 111 Jones and 201 Turk include a 24-hour desk clerk, key-operated elevators visible from the front desk, and two-way intercoms in the garages.

According to Arthur Evans, president of the company that entered a joint-venture with Chinese Community Housing to build 201 Turk, "People are amazed by this development. The federal housing administration sent their architects over to learn from it. The police and the neighbors say that this development has done more to reduce crime and raise property values than anything tried in the last 10 years."

Golden Gate Avenue elevation

201 Turk Street, children's playground   John Sutton

111 Jones Street, with St Anthony's   John Sutton

111 Jones Street, exterior stair from courtyard John Sutton

111 Jones Street, view from the street John Sutton

111 JONES STREET

OWNER/DEVELOPER
Mercy Charities Housing Development Corp.
Catholic Charities of the Archdiocese of San Francisco

ARCHITECT
Hardison Komatsu Ivelich and Tucker

LANDSCAPE ARCHITECT
David Heldt

CONTRACTOR
Cahill Construction

PROPERTY MANAGEMENT
Mercy Services Corp.

FUNDERS
	TYPE
San Francisco Redev. Agency	Loan
CA Dept. of Hsg. and Community Dev.	Perm. loan
Low Income Housing Tax Credits	
bought by FNMA	Equity
Allied Irish Bank	Loan

DEVELOPMENT TYPE
New construction mixed-use, rental flats, walk-up
and elevator-served.

RESIDENT PROFILE
Very-low- and low-income households,
incomes $9,500-36,950.

DENSITY
251 units per acre

DEVELOPMENT PROFILE
Type	N°/Units	Size (sf)	Rents
Studios	8	390	$323
1 BR	64	520-640	$365-503
2 BR	16	785-1,105	$396-594
3 BR	20	1,090-1,195	$421-670
TOTAL	**108**		

Retail/Commercial: 1,500 sf
Courtyard: 10,440 sf
Parking: 44 spaces, underground garage
Total site area: 18,905 sf or .43 acres

CONSTRUCTION TYPE
Nine-story reinforced concrete
(post-tensioned slabs/one level parking).

COSTS
Land Cost: $2,000,000; Constr. Costs: $11,859,552
($93.14/sf - incl. garage); Other Costs: $4,617,783; **Total
Development Costs: $18,477,335;** (Completed May 1993)

Marvin Rand

CHAPTER EIGHT:
THE SOUTHWEST AND SOUTHERN CALIFORNIA

Nine developments in the southwest and southern California
region were selected for review as two- and four-page case studies:

Rancho Sespe Farmworker Housing, Piru, California
Amistad Farm Laborers Housing, Hereford, Texas
Woodlands, Boulder, Colorado
Daybreak Grove, Escondido, California
Willowbrook Green Apartments, Los Angeles, California
Villa Esperanza, Los Angeles, California
Yorkshire Terrace, Los Angeles, California
Ocean Park Co-op, Santa Monica, California
St John's Hospital Housing, Santa Monica, California

Rancho Sespe Farmworker Housing Ventura, California

Rancho Sespe is the result of a heroic effort to assist 90 farmworker families to secure replacement of the housing from which they were evicted after a 10-year struggle. In Ventura County, one of the leading citrus producing areas in the world, the average farmworker family of six earns less than $20,000 a year, and often lives in overcrowded and substandard conditions. In 1979, when the Rivcom Corporation purchased the 4,500-acre ranch where the camp was located the new owners fired the workers and sought demolition permits for the two dilapidated housing camps. Many of the 250 families left, but the Cabrillo Economic Development Corporation (CEDC) helped the remaining 90 families to organize a non-profit organization to build replacement housing. Developed by CEDC, the new Rancho Sespe community is owned by the farmworkers' non-profit corporation, and has 100 dwelling units, a community center, and childcare center on a new 20-acre site.

The Rancho Sespe site, a former orange grove, is part of a continuous 10-mile strip of orange groves along Highway 126 bounded by mountains on the north and the Santa Ana River on the south. Because of insecticide spraying in the surrounding groves, the site required a 200-foot sideyard setback. Due to the 100-year floodplain, a 70-foot wide setback on the eastern side and a 400-foot rearyard setback were required. The new camp was designed as a series of identifiable small neighborhoods. Each neighborhood grouping faces one another or a courtyard, and is differentiated by its palette of stucco colors and landscaping materials. A central pedestrian spine connects all the groupings and a large, central courtyard. Anchoring the spine is a community complex with a multi-purpose room, a 60-student childcare center, and a soccer field beyond. Aesthetically, the community building is designed as a farmyard edged by a colonnade of ranch-type buildings with metal roofs, and a community room, which acts spatially as the barn.

The design approach for the residential groupings was to strengthen the idea of the neighborhood through the identity of the buildings. An emphasis on the identity of the individual unit, when multiplied by 100 units, achieves repetition, not identity. Therefore, eight different building types were developed by varying the mixture, arrangement and number of the three unit types (two-, three-, and four-bedroom). Further savings in the construction process were achieved by the use of only two lengths of prefabricated roof trusses. Two stepped buildings link phase I and phase II along the central pedestrian spine.

In the dwelling units, a porch is created by the projection of the second floor bedroom over the entry, which is then accentuated by an off-center column. This provides a major stepping element along the front facade at eye level. All the units have private rear gardens with sliding glass doors. The massing, sunshades, and earth colors recall a traditional architecture that uses strong sunlight to enhance the movement of sunlight and shadow across the facades. South orientation maximizes sunlight penetration in cool winter months; overhangs shade windows in the summer.

Rancho Sespe reaffirms the right of farmworkers to own their own housing in agricultural areas. The tenacity of the tenants (this was the longest eviction case in the history of the California appellate courts, and the development was vigorously opposed by nearly all the surrounding neighbors), the perseverance of CEDC and several public agencies, and the quality of the design contributed to a truly livable place that has given its residents a real sense of empowerment and community.

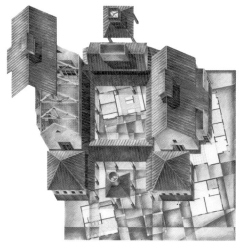

Exploded axonometric of community buildings

Eight unit building Ford Lowcock

Community buildings Ford Lowcock

Interior of community building Ford Lowcock

OWNER/DEVELOPER

Owner: Rancho Sespe Workers Improvement Assoc. Corp.
Developer: Cabrillo Econ. Develop. Corp.

ARCHITECT

John V. Mutlow, FAIA, Architects

LANDSCAPE ARCHITECTS

William Morgan (phase I)
Jordan and Gilbert (phase II)

CONTRACTOR

McGall Contractors (phase I)
Cabrillo Econ. Develop. Corp. (phase II)

PROPERTY MANAGEMENT

Hyder & Company

FUNDERS

	TYPE
County of Ventura/ CDBG-	Grant
Rosenberg Foundation	Grant
Farmers Home Admin. (FmHA)	Loan/grant
Ventura County National Bank	Loan
State of California HCD, FECP	Grant

DEVELOPMENT TYPE

New construction rental townhouses.

RESIDENT PROFILE

Very-low-income farm-worker families,
average income $17,731 for family of five.

DENSITY

5 units/acre

DEVELOPMENT PROFILE

Type	N°/Units	Size (sf)	Rents
2 BR	24	761–869	$345–405
3 BR	49	1,019–1,022	$395–455
4 BR	27	1,169–1,373	$445–505
TOTAL	100		

Parking: 293 carports and surface
Community/laundry: 6,400 sf (includes childcare facility);
3,812 sf (storage)
Courtyard/play: five-acre soccer/softball field, volleyball
court, basketball court, passive rec. area, and 2 tot-lots.
Total site area: 20 acres

CONSTRUCTION TYPE

One- and two-story woodframe, concrete slab,
roof trusses, stucco exterior, comp. shingle roof.

COSTS

Land Cost: $230,000; Constr. Costs: $6,639,711;
Other Costs: $1,252,909; **Total Development Cost:
$8,122,620 ($69.65/sf).** (Completed 1991 (phase I),
1993 (phase II))

Amistad Farm Laborers Housing

Subsidized housing had such a bad name in this small Texas panhandle town that there was heavy opposition to the development of Amistad in the town of Hereford. Fortunately the zoning for the apartments already existed so city approval was not necessary. Amistad is a community group that formed in 1985 when Motivation Education and Training, Inc. (MET) in Austin, Texas, began inquiries about interest in farm labor housing. The goal was to provide affordable housing for migrant farmworker families with incomes ranging from $3,000 to $16,000 a year, and to create community and private spaces sensitive to their needs.

After MET hired Tom Hatch as project architect, he began discussions about the design with Amistad representatives. Following numerous delays caused by the local Farmers' Home Administration office, the architect learned that the agency was reluctant to approve the development because, as one of the employees admitted, "the housing looked too nice!" Now that the housing has been built the surrounding community is quite pleased with it because it is very different from their past experience in other places. They think it is the "prettiest housing in town" and find it safe and clean.

Units are organized in groups of 10 around cul-de-sacs with parking off the main entrance street. This plan permitted generous open spaces between clusters. Buildings have different heights and a variety of forms to avoid the monotonous appearance of typical apartment blocks. Although the density is greater than that of the surrounding area, the buildings look smaller because of their varied form and staggered heights. Speaking about the design, architects Tom Hatch and Joel Martinez acknowledged that, "Good design for this type of housing takes extra effort—we had to be very creative in the use of similar floor plans throughout the development—but it is achievable and worth it." Since the design has units clustered around three cul-de-sac streets, the residents can observe outside activities. The tenants have formed a neighborhood watch and share the responsibilities of looking out for one another.

The housing has fostered community spirit and caused the city to pave adjacent streets. Local newspapers even feature success stories about the people at Amistad. The community supported the second phase of 20 units. The community garden, now in its third year, is a great success with many volunteers caring for it throughout the growing season. The managers and volunteers notify the tenants when the harvested vegetables are available and leave them in the laundry room for pickup.

Residents have also imposed a curfew on themselves that requires children and teenagers to be in their units by 10 pm and 11.30 on weekends. Mike and Angie Alonzo, a husband and wife team, manage Amistad and are always on call. They said that, "Amistad is beautiful, well designed, homey, and well managed. Now residents and town people alike take great pride in Amistad." Indeed, after word spread about the housing, people of varied income levels applied to live there and were surprised to find that it was reserved for farmworkers."

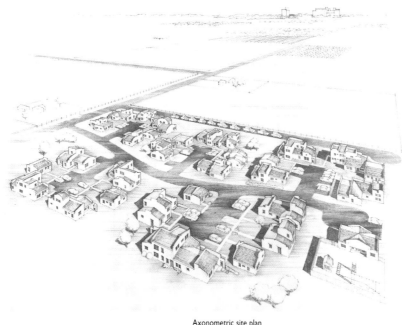

Axonometric site plan

Three- and four-bedroom apartments Joel Martinez

Children outside daycare center Joel Martinez

View looking east with grain elevators behind Joel Martinez

OWNER/DEVELOPER
Amistad Housing Development Corporation

ARCHITECT
Tom Hatch Architects

CONTRACTOR
Hallmark Builders

PROPERTY MANAGEMENT
Miguel and Angie Alonzo

FUNDERS	**TYPE**
Farmers Home Administration (FmHA)	Loan/grant

DEVELOPMENT TYPE
New construction rental townhouses.

RESIDENT PROFILE
Very-low-income families, incomes $3,000–16,000.

DENSITY
8 units/acre

DEVELOPMENT PROFILE

Type	Nº/Units	Size (sf)	Rents
2 BR	12	779	$355
3 BR	12	937	$375
4BR	6	1,196	$390
TOTAL	30		

Community/laundry: 2,083 sf (includes maint. shop)
Parking: 60 surface
Total site area: 423,612 sf (9.7 acres)

CONSTRUCTION TYPE
One- and two-story woodframe, with stucco exterior, comp. shingle roofs.

COSTS
Land Cost: $36,250; Constr. Costs: $1,200,000; Other Costs: $73,000; **Total Development Cost: $1,273,000 ($42,433/unit).** (Completed 1990)

In Boulder, where single parents head 20 per cent of all households, one-third of the single-parent households live in poverty with income levels below 50 per cent of the area median. The City and County Housing Authorities worked with Project Self-Sufficiency (PSS) to plan and construct Woodlands, which has 35 units of affordable housing with job training and childcare, to enable these families to achieve financial independence. PSS is a HUD-funded program in which participants attend a variety of "life skills" classes on topics such as parenting and budgeting, and receive organizational assistance as they begin a busy life as students and parents on their way to self-sufficiency. Three out of four graduates find work in stable jobs, breaking the cycle of poverty.

Located in a mixed-use neighborhood in central Boulder, the site was a vacant lot that was difficult to develop. Early in 1991, the architectural firm of Barker, Rinker, Seacat and Partners was selected to design Woodlands. The City of Boulder Housing Authority (CBHA) and the architects held a number of community meetings with potential residents, neighbors, and service providers who, according to project architect Phil Lawrence, shared valuable information that helped locate the major elements on the site. "The community design team (which included current participants in the PSS program) established a set of design concepts that were crucial to the success of the plan", said Cindy Brown, project manager for the CBHA. These included: indoor and outdoor private spaces, parking near front doors, a feeling of security and community, and a neighborhood rather than an institution. The final design has six buildings, consisting of 32 attached

two-story townhouses and three one-story wheelchair-accessible flats, a childcare center, and a community building. The apartments are articulated with gable roofs and front porches; wood brackets, picket fences, and lattices in the porch roofs make the facades more lively and inviting; large windows bring good daylighting to the interiors. The buildings surround a central green open space defined by a loop drive with parking spaces for the units. Each unit has a private rear patio off the kitchen, and a front porch facing the play area and parking. Lawrence noted, "The design creates community in that it is easy for residents to look out for each other. The kitchen sink is often located at the front windows so that children may be watched." Lawrence cautioned, "The center green is a safe place to play, but we recognize that the roadway also becomes a play space. We narrowed the required parking and drive widths beyond zoning standards and added speed bumps to slow people down."

The development process was not always smooth. According to Cindy Brown, complex guidelines governing the use of Section 8 certificates, funding for the childcare center, and negotiations to protect tax-credit investors against risk caused major time delays and uncertainty. In the end there were over 20 sources of financing! However, toward the end of construction Brown noted, "Every day I talk to families who are excited to have a new place with high quality childcare on-site. Those brief moments make all the long hours worth it."

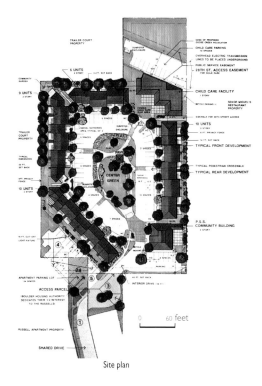

Site plan

Overall site Jerry Butts

OWNER/DEVELOPER
Boulder Woodlands, L.P.

ARCHITECT
Barker, Rinker, Seacat Partners

LANDSCAPE ARCHITECT
Matrix Gardens

CONTRACTOR
Casson Building Corporation

PROPERTY MANAGEMENT
Diversified Properties

FUNDERS	TYPE
Boulder City/County Hsg Authority	Devel. loan
Low-Income Hsg Tax Credits by Enterprise Social Investment Corp.	Equity
Colorado State Division of Hsg	Grant for land
Colorado National Bank	Constr. loan
Federal Home Loan Bank	Constr. grant
The Catherine McAuley Foundation of Mercy Housing	Constr./bridge loan
Columbia Savings/First National	Perm. loan
City of Boulder-CHAP	Grants
City of Boulder-CDBG	Grants
United Way	Grant/oper. funds
Knight Boettcher Foundation	Grant for childcare
Gates Foundation	Grant for childcare
IBM Corporation	Grant for childcare
Local banks	Grant for childcare
Head Start	Grant for childcare
St Johns (Boulder)	Grant for comm. ctr

DEVELOPMENT TYPE
New construction rental attached townhouses and flats.

RESIDENT PROFILE
Very-low-income families enrolled in Project Self-Sufficiency.

DENSITY
12.5 units/acre

DEVELOPMENT PROFILE

Type	N°/Units	Size(sf)	Rents
2 BR	23	672–896	$657
3 BR	11	928–1,058	$928
4 BR	1	1,260	$1,083
TOTAL	**35**		

Community/laundry: 2,700 sf
Childcare/center green: 3,300/5,000 sf
Parking: 70 surface
Total site area: 2.8 acres

CONSTRUCTION TYPE
Two-story woodframe, wood siding, comp. shingle roofs.

COSTS
Land Cost: $276,090; Constr. Costs: $2,513,863; Other Costs: $1,739,014; **Total Development Cost: $4,528,967 ($125,000/unit).** (Completed December 1993)

Front door/typical porch Jerry Butts

The need for affordable housing for people with low incomes is especially acute in California where land values and construction costs are abnormally high relative to most of the rest of the country. Among the neediest candidates for affordable housing are women with children; many applicants are new immigrants. Although Daybreak Grove is modest in size, comprising 13 units on less than an acre of land, it provides the families who live there—mainly headed by women—the security and stability they need to improve the quality of their lives.

Daybreak Grove is located in a desirable neighborhood of single-family houses, apartments, and condominiums with schools, parks, stores, social services, and bus lines nearby. The city of Escondido is a rapidly urbanizing agricultural community northeast of San Diego with a large Latino—immigrant population. Not surprisingly, the residents of the single-family area immediately behind the site circulated a petition against the proposed housing that obtained over 100 signatures.

Sponsoring the development was the North County Housing Foundation (NCHF), a non-profit organization with a board of directors entirely composed of residents of the community. At least one-third are either members of low-income house-holds themselves or residents of low-income neighborhoods, many the mothers of young children. A former mayor of Escondido with twenty-two grandchildren sold the site at a bargain rate to the NCHF.

Approval for the housing was obtained after the developers dealt with many issues, including addressing the neighbors' complaints by increasing the height of the rear wall from six to eight feet, and removing windows from the north building elevations that faced the single-family neighborhood. NCHF applied for and received two density bonus units and a reduction in parking. The latter was an important victory because under the existing parking ordinance, the ten

additional spaces required would have adversely affected the site plan and building design. According to Amy Rowland, Executive Director of NCHF, obstacles to the development that arose in the financing process were probably not unusual considering that it had six sources of financing, not including predevelopment and construction loans and grants.

Because this was the first multi-family housing development that the City of Escondido had participated in, City officials were eager to show that low-income housing did not have to look low-budget. This attitude encouraged the creation of a showcase design, one that set striking forms and colors in the traditional southern California setting of the bungalow court. Although few older bungalow courts remain in Escondido, they were familiar to board members, some of whom had recently rehabilitated one of them.

Bungalow courts were popular and practical housing developments produced in great numbers from the 1910s through the 1920s in the suburbs of both southern and northern California cities. Small parcels of land could be developed to a higher density with modest buildings and still retain open space and even such amenities as fountains and pergolas. The open space framed by buildings on three sides created both community and privacy. Since the older bungalow courts were designed in the style of the moment, the use of contemporary forms and materials for Daybreak Grove is appropriate. Architects Davids and Killory, who are based in San Diego, have studied the Spanish legacy of urban planning. They considered the courtyard plan a useful settlement prototype and observed that, "the flexible courtyard integrates easily with other housing types, including single family. As neighborhood opposition to multi-family projects usually diminishes in proportion to their size, courtyard housing is a particularly suitable type for a variety of urban and surburban neighborhoods, especially smaller lots in stable residential areas."

Isometric site section across courtyard

View east from the west entrance Davids/Killory

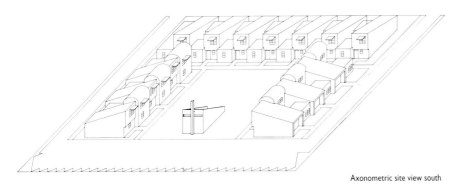

Axonometric site view south

OWNER/SPONSOR
The North County Housing Foundation

ARCHITECT
Design Architect: Davids Killory Architects
Architect of Record: Studio E. Architects

CONSULTANTS
Leslie Ryan, RLA

CONTRACTOR
Hidden Valley Construction

MANAGEMENT
The CBM Group

FUNDERS

FUNDERS	TYPE
California Equity Fund	Equity, Tax credits
California Department of Housing and Community Development	Loan
City of Escondido Community Development Commission	Loan
Local Initiatives Support Corp.	Predev. Loan
Bank of America	Constr. Loan
Citibank	Loan
Dr. William and Mrs. Lorraine Boyce	Land discount

RESIDENT PROFILE
Families with incomes between $9,000–$28,000/year

DEVELOPMENT TYPE
New construction rental housing.

DENSITY
18 units/acre

DEVELOPMENT PROFILE

Type	Nº/Units	Size (sf)	Rent
2 BR	7	730	$278–$454
3 BR	6	860	$304–$504
TOTAL	13	10,270	

Parking: 20 Carports
Court: 11,200 sf
Total site area: 36,590 sf (.84 acres)

CONSTRUCTION TYPE
Two-story stucco over woodframe

COSTS
Land Costs: $6.86/sf ($101k donated); Constr. Costs: $75/sf; Other Costs: $64/sf; **Total Development Cost: $1.7m; $131,000/unit.** (Completed July 1993)

The contiguous units have a lively roof profile that alternates barrel-vaulted and shed-roofed forms on the east and west sides and flat and shed-roofed forms on the south side. The buildings step backward and forward, creating a variety of patterns as well as privacy in recessed entryways. The colors, deep red and grey, also serve to break up the forms. The basic uniformity and compactness of the unit plans is complemented by a rich variety of private and public outdoor spaces: a front yard and porch, a back yard and porch, as well as a small internal patio, which provides both a private outdoor living space and natural light and cross ventilation for the rooms. Having the kitchen face the courtyard acknowledges its importance to family life and allows supervision of children without interrupting housework. The courtyard has a laundromat, and an outdoor theater set in grassy play areas. The landscaping features drought-resistant shade trees, edible species such as citrus and pomegranite, and includes plots for gardening.

In assessing the influence of Daybreak Grove, Amy Rowland observed that its existence and design qualities have made getting approvals on subsequent projects much easier. "Many other organizations have sent local decision-makers to visit to give them a positive impression of affordable housing." But she added that the positive impression made on city staff and elected officials by award-winning design does not always convert the opposition. "We recognize", Rowland said, "that in addition to good design, the main thing that will convince the neighbors is wise tenant selection and good, sound property management practices over many, many years."

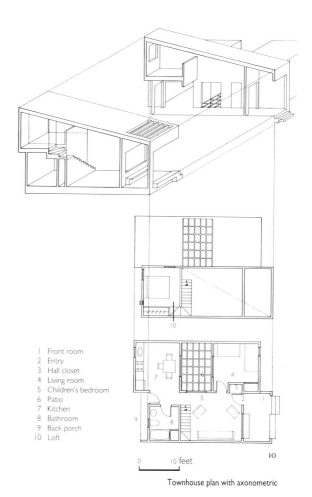

1 Front room
2 Entry
3 Hall closet
4 Living room
5 Children's bedroom
6 Patio
7 Kitchen
8 Bathroom
9 Back porch
10 Loft

0 ——— 10 feet

Townhouse plan with axonometric

Front porches along East Washington Avenue Davids/Killory

Back doors facing the courtyard Loisos/Ubbelohede

Southwest court view Davids/Killory

View from courtyard looking south Davids/Killory

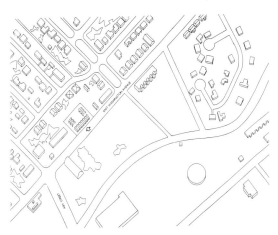

Neighborhood massing axonometric Grant Smith

Willowbrook Green Apartments Los Angeles, California

Willowbrook Green is an oasis in a tough neighborhood in south central Los Angeles. Two-story buildings surround a generous, well-landscaped courtyard containing a community building and a children's play area. Architect Ena Dubnoff designed the buildings with a scale in between that of the institutional and the residential buildings in the surrounding area. Drew University and Martin Luther King Medical Center have facilities located next door; an elementary school is across the street. A childcare and development center for 60 children, not yet built, was planned as part of the complex to occupy a site adjacent to the housing. The center will serve neighborhood children as well as those living at Willowbrook. At present, Drew University uses the community building's multi-purpose room for classes in parenting and related subjects. The location of the university and the hospital nearby has created employment and training opportunities for Willowbrook and neighborhood residents.

The two-story townhouses face each other across the court. As resident Venitta Cunningham, a mother with three children, observed, "The arrangement allows us to keep an eye on each other. It feels very safe." The neighborhood is a high-crime area, which made security a major design consideration. Originally, the units were to have entrances from both the street and the courtyard, but a review of security concerns led to a single secured entry to the courtyard. Once inside the courtyard there is no connection to the street or traffic. Dubnoff noted, "The final design created layers of security: gates at the parking entrance and main entrance, gates at the perimeter of the courtyard, gates at the private patio entrances, and, finally, at the front door." The front patios are raised a few steps above grade to give families added privacy. Low fences surround the patios giving residents privacy and the ability to see their children playing. In addition to the play area for younger children, there is a basketball hoop for the older kids and a barbecue for family picnics.

Because of the high requirement for parking—100 spaces for 48 units including 12 guest spaces—it was decided to locate all resident parking in one area to reserve as much open space as possible for the courtyard and to separate vehicular traffic. As a result, some of the units are relatively far from the parking area, although this walk is through the secure courtyard. The windows of townhouses in the rear building look over the well-lit parking lot for security, and carports protect the vehicles from the weather.

Willowbrook Green took an extraordinary amount of planning and negotiation. Carla Dartis, project manager for Drew Economic Development Corporation remarked, "The project was in the planning stages for five years. In 1984, the concept was used as a prototype for developing the legislation that led to Proposition 184—the State program that helped fund thousands of units of well-designed affordable rental housing in California." In addition to the housing, the program included childcare, intergenerational living, and on-site tutoring, which required multiple funding sources. After eight years, Willowbrook was completed. Dartis noted, "It was a labor of love, and the residents take a lot of pride in it." Resident manager Susan Glover Hamilton observed that the housing was much better than that in the rest of the neighborhood, "A lot of people cannot afford a home so you have to design rental housing as well as possible because this is often a long-term home for residents." Venitta Cunningham said her family was particularly fortunate in that among the many programs for children, the Saturday Science Academy engaged the interest of her oldest son so completely that he excelled to the point of being interviewed on World News and even met Hillary Clinton. The tutoring programs have benefited her children and, with the ability to live independently because of the low rents, Venitta is pursuing job training so that she can move off welfare. "Many of the good changes in my life would not have happened if I had not been a resident at Willowbrook."

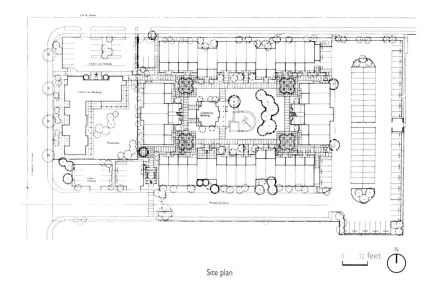

0   32 feet   N

Site plan

Section Looking West through Courtyard

0 16 feet

View across the courtyard toward the northeast Jim Simmons

Site location map

OWNER/DEVELOPER
Drew Economic Development Corporation

ARCHITECT
Ena Dubnoff

CONSULTANTS
Landscape Architect: Rios/Pearson
Development Consultant: Channa Grace

CONTRACTOR
R.D. Boykin

PROPERTY MANAGEMENT
Drew Economic Development Corporation

FUNDERS / **TYPE**

FUNDERS	TYPE
HUD Section 8	Rent subsidy
State of California Comm.	
Hsg. Fin. Agency	Perm. loan
County Community Dev. Comm.	Loan/land
Bank of America	Loan/grant
The Ford Foundation	Grant
Local Initiatives Support Corp. (LISC)	Grant

DEVELOPMENT TYPE
New construction rental attached townhouses.

RESIDENT PROFILE
Very-low- and low-income families,
40% single parents, 60% couples, 8 seniors,
1 disabled and 80 children.

DENSITY
19 units/acre

DEVELOPMENT PROFILE

Type	Nº/Units	Size (sf)	Rents
1 BR	16	672–780	$446
2 BR	24	960	$500
3 BR	8	1127	$550
TOTAL	48		

Community/laundry: yes (+ kitchen, offices);
w/d at each unit
Courtyard/play: childcare (future .5 acre)
Parking: 113 surface
Total site area: 2.5 acres

CONSTRUCTION TYPE
Two-story woodframe with stucco exterior, flat roofs.

COSTS
Land Cost: $0 (donated); Constr. Costs: $2,853,573;
Other Costs: $897,352; **Total Development Cost:**
$3,902,965 ($81,312/ unit). (Completed October 1990)

TYPICAL GROUND LEVEL

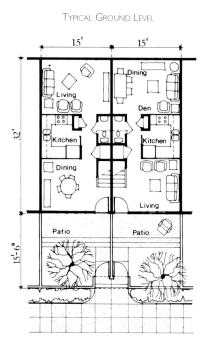

Unit Count

	no.	gross area
1 Bedroom Accessible	4	672 sf
1 Bedroom Townhouse	8	780 sf
1 Bedroom Flat	4	672 sf
2 Bedroom Townhouse	24	960 sf
3 Bedroom Townhouse	8	1,127 sf
TOTAL	**48**	

Unit entries from courtyard Jim Simmons

Units and courtyard Jim Simmons

Units and courtyard Jim Simmons

Courtyard toward community building Jim Simmons

Play structure and courtyard Jim Simmons

1 BEDROOM/3 BEDROOM
UPPER LEVEL

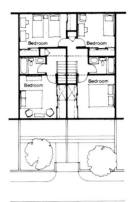

2 BEDROOM/2 BEDROOM
UPPER LEVEL

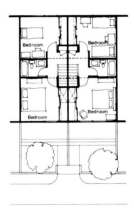

1 BEDROOM FLAT

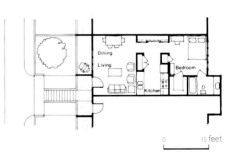

0   15 feet

Villa Esperanza Los Angeles, California

Villa Esperanza exemplifies the success of a low-income community's effort to take control of their neighborhood. In 1985, residents of a south central Los Angeles neighborhood led by Sister Diane Donoghue from nearby St Vincent's Church successfully opposed the local development of another garment factory. They formed the Esperanza Community Housing Corporation (ECHC) and, in partnership with the Los Angeles Community Design Center (LACDC), eventually purchased the original garment factory site to build 33 units of affordable housing, childcare services, and a neighborhood center.

At the beginning of the development process, the LACDC distributed questionnaires to help pinpoint specific needs in the community. Later, schematic designs were presented to a neighborhood committee. The provision of services, including English language classes, a literacy center, a computer lab, and parenting classes has significantly improved the quality of life in the community, according to Melanie Stephens, assistant director of ECHC. "But," she added, "it is very difficult to merge housing with another use, because the people and agencies that fund each of these uses do not necessarily agree with or understand each other."

The housing is organized around two courtyards built over a semi-underground parking structure. One courtyard serves as play area for the childcare center, and both receive full sun. Because Villa Esperanza is larger than other structures in the neighborhood, the architects kept its height as low as possible. Three-story sections were placed on the interior of the site and along Maple Street across from a light industrial building. Two-story portions were placed along streets adjacent to one- and two-story residential buildings. Separated entrance stoops break up the long elevations, as do gable-roofed bays, projecting balconies, and bold colors taken from murals on neighboring buildings.

Architect and deputy director of LACDC Bill Huang noted, "This development endeavors to provide much more than a decent affordable place to live. The units are designed with separate entries, townhouse configuration, and individual open space to allow each resident to feel a sense of ownership." A strong resident council and ECHC community organizers jointly direct educational and recreational activities at the neighborhood center, helping to build skills and relationships that will help this neighborhood survive and grow in the long term.

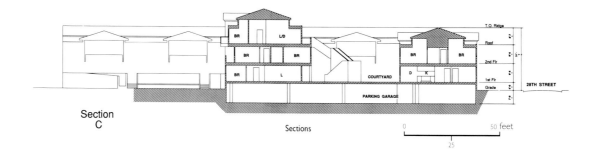

Section C

Sections

0   50 feet

25

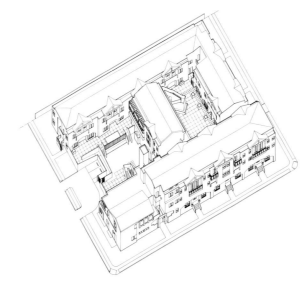

Site axonometric

Detail of north facade Marvin Rand

Interior view of unit Marvin Rand

Interior courtyard from southwest Marvin Rand

OWNER/DEVELOPER
Co-general Partner: Esperanza Community Housing Corp.
Co-general Partner: L.A. Community Design Center

ARCHITECT
L.A. Community Design Center

LANDSCAPE ARCHITECT
Lost West

CONTRACTOR
Edwin G. Brown Co.

PROPERTY MANAGEMENT
Solari Enterprises Inc.

FUNDERS	TYPE
Community Redev. Agency of L.A.	Loan
World Vision	Loan
National Urban and Rural Ministries Project	Grant
Local Initiatives Support Corporation (LISC)	Loan
Sisters of St Joseph of Orange	Grant
Wells Fargo Bank	Loan
Low Income Housing Tax Credits syndicated by the California Equity Fund	Equity
Citibank	Loan
State Dept. of Housing & Community Dev.	Loan

DEVELOPMENT TYPE
New construction rental townhouses and flats.

RESIDENT PROFILE
Very-low- and low-income families from local neighborhood.

DENSITY
29 units/acre plus community center

DEVELOPMENT PROFILE

Type	N°/Units	Size (sf)	Rents
3 BR	22	1,200	$350–475
4BR	11	1,500	$400–525
TOTAL	33		

Community/laundry: yes, + childcare and adult educ.
Courtyard/play: 3,000 sf two separate courtyards
Parking: 88 surface
Total site area: 50,094 sf (1.15 acres)

CONSTRUCTION TYPE
Three-story woodframe with stucco exterior,
concrete parking garage.

COSTS
Land Cost: $850,000; Constr. Costs: $4,000,000;
Other Costs: $2,700,000; **Total Development Cost:
$6,700,000 ($131.38/sf).** (Completed August 1994)

Yorkshire Terrace is an 18-unit infill development in Los Angeles's largely Hispanic, Pico-Union community. Located in a redevelopment area, it was developed by the Pico-Union Housing Corporation (PUHC), a branch of the Pico-Union Neighborhood Council (PUNC). Architect John V. Mutlow had directed the Pico-Union Neighborhood Council's planning and housing program from 1969 to 1973. He has designed 11 other affordable housing developments in the district—most of them larger than Yorkshire Terrace—that were sponsored by either PUHC or PUNC. This experience gave him a broad knowledge of the neighborhood and its residents.

Once part of an affluent neighborhood, Bonnie Brae Street retains a stand of two-story, wood-sided, early 20th century houses, most of which have been rehabilitated by the Los Angeles Community Redevelopment Agency (CRA). Many of the houses had been converted into four-unit apartment houses, but three of them, which stood on 50 by 150-foot lots, were demolished because they were judged to be economically unfeasible to rehabilitate. The demolition created the site for Yorkshire Terrace. Under the redevelopment plan 28 units could have been built (this number was half the maximum permitted by the zoning.) Only 18 units were built for a variety of reasons: a third of the site was designated for open parking, and two units were removed to provide an outdoor play area. In addition, Mutlow felt that housing for families should be limited to two stories, which fit in with the existing context.

The stacked two-bedroom flats are organized around a central linear court, a space which fosters social interaction, and which serves as the entry to all of the units. The architects eliminated the need for air-conditioning by designing the buildings so that the court allows the units to receive light and air on a second side yet provides shade from the hot afternoon sun. Individual entries are sheltered by second level bay windows, and sliding doors to the outdoor patios are both recessed and shaded by balconies above. A gazebo with a pyramidal roof indicates the location of the main entrance from the courtyard and is a favorite place for residents to sit in the shade. The play area next to the laundry proved to be too small. According to resident Zilda Stone, a student nurse with three children, "Most kids don't play there because of complaints about the noise and about balls flying around." However, an old stagecoach also next to the laundry is a popular place to play.

The building facades present a crisp composition of integrated Modern forms that resonate with the architectural history of the Los Angeles region. Mutlow designed the street elevation with a 30-inch bay that contains closets and recessed windows, buffering those openings from the street edge. The stepping in and out of the wall breaks up the linear facade with a series of elements in scale with the context, enriches the play of light and shadow, and gives expression to individual units. Mutlow worked out a subtle palette of shades of green to further enhance the forms. However, since 1988, when the

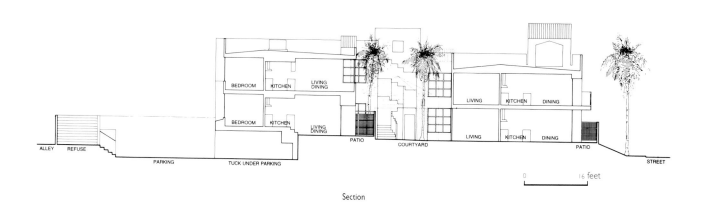

Section

0   16 feet

Entry Marvin Rand

Gazebo at court Marvin Rand

OWNER/DEVELOPER
Owner: Pico Union Housing Corp.
Developer: Housing Development Services, Inc.

ARCHITECT
John V. Mutlow FAA, Architects

LANDSCAPE ARCHITECT
Barrio Planners

CONTRACTOR
J.H. Hedrick & Co

PROPERTY MANAGEMENT
AWFMEX Inc.

FUNDERS	**TYPE**
Community Redev. Agency of City of L.A.	na

DEVELOPMENT TYPE
New construction rental stacked flats.

RESIDENT PROFILE
Low-income families.

DENSITY
35 units/acre

DEVELOPMENT PROFILE

Type	N°/Units	Size (sf)	Rents
2 BR	18	827–839	$74–601
TOTAL	18		(HUD pays difference FMR & 30% income)

Laundry: 150 sf
Courtyard/play: 3,008 sf; tot-lot 360 sf; stage 160 sf; gazebo 144 sf; patio 575 sf; roof terrace 155 sf
Parking: 23 surface/tuck-under
Total site area: 22,500 sf (.52 acres)

CONSTRUCTION TYPE
Two-story woodframe, stucco exterior, flat roofs.

COSTS
Land Cost: $250,000; Constr. Costs: $782,000; Other Costs: $235,000; **Total Development Cost: $1,267,000 ($70,388/unit).** (Completed 1987)

complex was finished, the colors have faded, and repainting patio walls has not been consistent, pointing up the necessity of scrupulous maintenance for the kind of stucco-over-wood-frame buildings that are standard construction in Los Angeles. In general, maintenance is excellent and the construction quality is good. According to Mutlow, "By working with the general contractor early on, you can lower the costs by learning how they build and where their major costs lie. The single-unit type with three plan alternates, and the single plumbing wall for two units provided both simplicity and repetition which helped the client to obtain very good prices from the contractor." Pico-Union also involved the community during construction to help reduce theft and vandalism.

Since security is a major concern because of neighborhood gang activity, there is a single intercom entry gate from the street. Parking is in the rear of the lot with one row of cars tucked under the back bedroom of the apartments and the other row open. Even though parking is secured by an automatic gate off an alley, Zilda Stone said, "People have jumped over the low walls in the front and stolen things from the cars." Manager Gregory Matthews acknowledges the walls are too low and says they are planning on making them higher. Stone said, "Management here is good. I like the place because it is open and breezy, and usually quiet."

As with most affordable housing, the financing for Yorkshire Terrace was complex and required significant assistance and reviews from the CRA. Michael Cracraft of the CRA noted, "We strongly encouraged Pico-Union. The building is definitely an improvement on the surrounding area and sets a high standard. Unfortunately, there is not much affordable housing being built here any more." Despite this, more development has followed the housing. Next door is a neighborhood occupational training center for the older children run by PUNC, which, according to Matthews, is very successful. Stone noted that she too values the training center, saying, "It gives the children a better alternative to being on the streets."

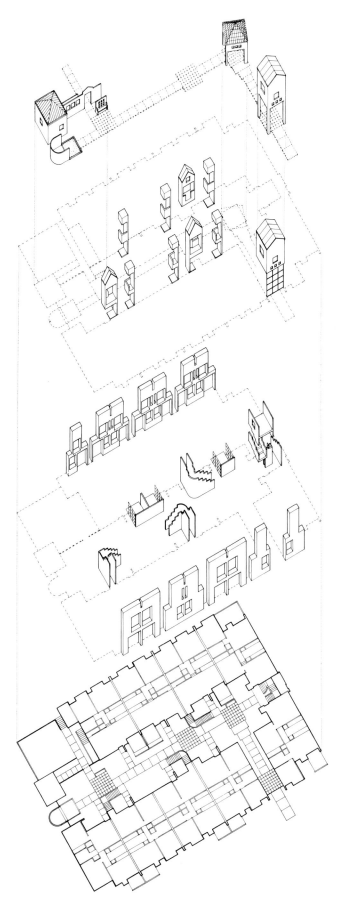

Exploded axonometric

Street facade Marvin Rand

Courtyard Marvin Rand

Ocean Park Co-op Santa Monica, California

The Ocean Park Housing Co-operative (OPC) has 43 dwelling units located on five sites in an older mixed-income section of the Ocean Park neighborhood. The development is part of a 55-unit program that replaced a portion of the housing lost to nearby redevelopment in the early 1960s. Santa Monica has a progressive housing policy that both seeks to preserve the character of existing neighborhoods and encourage private developers to build on vacant sites rather than tearing down existing homes. According to former mayor Denny Zane, "The community had sued a market-rate developer planning to build high-rise condominiums in the neighborhood. Part of the money resulting from that settlement was used to build OPC." The Community Corporation of Santa Monica (CCSM) was chosen by the city as the sponsor for the replacement housing.

The community had a significant role in shaping the designs of the complexes during the three open workshops. The first workshop focused on evaluating the sites in the context of the neighborhood; the second reviewed conceptual site design options, design criteria, and existing neighborhood building designs; and the third reviewed site-specific schematic designs. Architect Ralph Mechur noted, "It was invaluable to interact with neighborhood residents and develop a design that they felt would be beneficial to the community. Ignoring their concerns would have created a huge obstacle." Community input also led to the initial program of rental housing for families with low incomes, which shifted to a mixed-income, intergenerational co-op for households with incomes ranging from very low to moderate.

The buildings are designed as village-like complexes around common entry courts. Although their density is higher, the developments are similar in height and massing to the older buildings in the area. The small sites and the higher density required that the parking be semi-subterranean, accessible to the courtyards by stairs. The units share the entry court, and each has a private yard or patio off the living room. The architects derived the building design from the early 20th century California bungalows which are well represented in Santa Monica, and set them around the courtyards, which are intended to encourage neighborly interaction. Joan Ling, executive director of CCSM cautioned, "Intergenerational housing does work, as long as applicants are aware of the presence of children up front, and management deals with tenant conflicts quickly."

The community process created a positive climate of opinion for the housing and for the future residents, who were welcomed as community members. Many neighbors became convinced that higher density affordable housing designed to meet programmatic and contextual concerns could be more harmonious than for-profit development that builds the maximum unit size, building mass, and height. Today, people taken on tours of the area, who do not know that the Ocean Park Co-operative is subsidized housing for people with low incomes, often choose it rather than the market-rate condominiums across the street as the place they would prefer to live.

642 Marine Street: streetfront and entrance Alex Vertikoff

536 Ashland Avenue: corner landscaping with housing behind   Alex Vertikoff

518 Pier Avenue—Section through courtyard

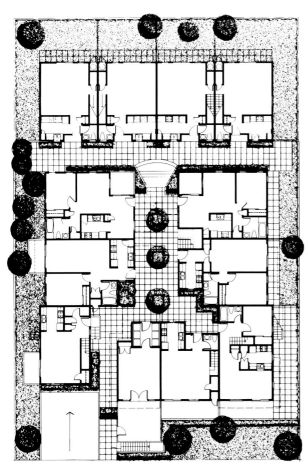

518 Pier Avenue—First floor plan/site plan

0   20 feet

OWNER/DEVELOPER
Community Corporation of Santa Monica

ARCHITECT
Appleton Mechur & Assoc., Inc.
(now: Ralph Mechur Architects and Appleton & Assoc., Inc.)

LANDSCAPE ARCHITECT
Burton and Spitz

CONTRACTOR
Alpha Construction Co. Inc.

PROPERTY MANAGEMENT
Community Corporation of Santa Monica

FUNDERS	TYPE
HUD Hsg Opportunity Dev. Action Grant	Grant
City of Santa Monica Redevelopment Agency	Loan
Wells Fargo Bank	Loan

DEVELOPMENT TYPE
New construction rental flats and townhouses.

RESIDENT PROFILE
Low- and moderate-income households, 50–120% of AMI.

DENSITY
41 units per acre

DEVELOPMENT PROFILE

Type	N°/Units	Size (sf)	Rents
1 BR	16	700	$383–631
2 BR	13	850	$444–1,049
3 BR	13	1,000	$545–1,167
4BR	1	1,150	$1,183
TOTAL	**43**		

Laundry: Laundry at each site
Courtyard/play: Courtyard at each site
Parking: 77 parking garage
Total site area: 5 sites, 45,200 sf (1.04 acres)

CONSTRUCTION TYPE
Two- and three-story woodframe over semi-subterranean parking, wood siding, comp. shingle roof.

COSTS
Land Cost: $1,278,900; Constr. Costs: $3,300,000; Other Costs: $714,069; **Total Development Costs: $5,29,96900 ($123,092/unit).** (Completed April 1989)

St John's Hospital Housing Santa Monica, California

In the early 1980s, St John's Hospital and Health Center (SJHHC), located on a tight site in densely populated Santa Monica, needed to expand its campus for medical uses. The hospital was established as an 89-bed facility in 1942 and over the following 45 years grew to 551 licensed beds, with an ambulatory care facility opened in the late 1970s. In the 1980s, the need to develop additional ambulatory care space, medical office space, and adjacent convenient parking became a priority. Land for such facilities was limited to a strip of residentially zoned property that contained rental units. These units had been acquired in the 1970s by the hospital, with the ultimate intention of demolishing them for expansion.

However, with the passage of the Rent Control Charter Amendment in April 1979, 31 of the 35 units were deemed to be under rent control and could not be demolished. The hospital had a problem. It sought relief through the courts but did not prevail. A new approach was then devised to meet the goals of the hospital, the tenants, the city, and the neighborhood.

The outcomes of the conflict resolution were: the hospital won access to the use of its land and property for its public purpose; the city gained a net increase in the number of affordable units; the rent control board protected the supply of affordable rent-controlled units; Community Corporation of Santa Monica (CCSM) was recognized as a developer which could supply new housing for the neighborhood; the former tenants won the right of either first refusal to reoccupy the new replacement units, or to take a cash contribution. All the affected tenants accepted the cash option, and moved out, allowing the new housing to be rented to tenants with low to moderate incomes; the neighborhood gained a site that was free of buildings that were becoming an attractive nuisance for crime and graffiti.

According to Tom Pyne, the representative for the hospital who helped to facilitate the solution, "There were no losers in this deal. We had a strong interest in resolving the issues in a fair manner. From 1985 to 1989 we worked out a resolution of what seemed like an impossible public dilemma—how to allow the hospital to expand and how to preserve affordable rental housing stock in the neighborhood. What was needed was flexibility by all."

The replacement housing was planned for four sites. One site consisted of a simple relocation of four units from one side of the street to the other. Architectural work was performed by Koning Eizenberg Architecture who designed the other three complexes of 28 units that were either built or re-located on sites between 23rd and 18th Streets, all within a few blocks of the hospital campus. Color and the play of light and shade give identity to individual units. At the Arizona Street site, the units are entered through a secure courtyard; at the 18th Street and Berkeley Street sites, sideyard entry portals lead to stacked flats that are canted to enhance the rhythm of the facades. According to Joan Ling, executive director of CCSM, "Because our development process is not driven by the market to maximize square footage, there is more latitude for the architects to be creative." The architecture blends in well with surrounding buildings. Architect Julie Eizenberg noted, "The beauty of infill housing is that it makes no visible change in the community. I believe this is the optimum way to absorb affordable housing into stable, middle-class neighborhoods."

Santa Monica is a diverse yet integrated community both economically and physically. This is in part due to proactive policies initiated by elected officials and planning staff. For example, Santa Monica was one of the first cities in California to adopt a type of inclusionary zoning. Former mayor, Denny Zane, observed that, "The City of Santa Monica is very active in creating affordable housing policies. We down-zoned the allowable density for market-rate units and adopted State laws that gave density bonuses for affordable housing. We simplified and reduced parking requirements, increased the allowable height, and decreased setbacks. The city has found that small infill developments—often mixed-income or mixed-use—developed by community organizations are the best type for Santa Monica."

Artist's sketch

Entry detail: north elevation Grant Mudford

Side entries: north elevation Grant Mudford

DEVELOPER
Community Corporation of Santa Monica

ARCHITECT
Koning Eizenburg Architecture, Inc.

CONTRACTOR
A.J. Turrentine Co.
Norm Salter Construction

PROPERTY MANAGEMENT
Community Corporation of Santa Monica

FUNDERS	TYPE
Bank of America	na
City of Santa Monica	na
St Johns Medical Center	na
CHFA	na

DEVELOPMENT TYPE
Scattered-site relocation and remodel of rental apartments, new construction of rental flats.

RESIDENT PROFILE
Low-income families, singles, seniors.

DENSITY
45 units/acre

DEVELOPMENT PROFILE
Type	N°/Units	Size (sf)	Rents
1 BR	1	550–650	$540
2 BR	4	751–1,052	$420–630
3 BR	19	892–1,047	$540–920
TOTAL	28		

Community/laundry: yes
Courtyard/play: yes
Parking: 29 surface

CONSTRUCTION TYPE
Two- and three-story woodframe, some over concrete underground parking, stucco exterior.

COSTS
Total Development Cost: $1,577,575 ($35–$44/sf).
(Completed 1988)

CHAPTER NINE:
THE CENTRAL STATES

Five developments in the central states region were selected for review as two- and four-page case studies:

Lyton Park Place, St Paul, Minnesota
Field Street, Detroit, Michigan
West Town II, Chicago, Illinois
The Reservoir, Madison, Wisconsin
West Town Cluster Housing, Chicago, Illinois

Lyton Park Place St Paul, Minnesota

Justin Properties, the developer of Lyton Park Place, worked co-operatively with the non-profit organization Habitat for Humanity and other organizations to build 21 single-family homes for people with low to moderate incomes on a block just north of the state capitol. David Van Landschoot, president of Justin, and his wife, Terri, assumed responsibility for financing the development and built 13 of the houses. Habitat built the other eight using volunteers and future homeowners, who each gave 350 hours of work as their "sweat-equity" share in the construction process. Because some 80,000 hours were donated for the Habitat homes they sold for about half the price of Justin's union-built homes and were affordable for people with much lower incomes.

The nearly five million dollars of funding for Lyton Park Place came from a combination of federal, state and city sources. The funds were spent to acquire the site, to allow the City of St Paul to own and transfer the land at no cost to the Justin and Habitat team, to pay residents' relocation expenses, and to prepare the site. The 42 deteriorated, pre-World War I structures standing on the site were demolished and the soil was repaired. New sidewalks, alleys, and other street improvements such as lights, and site utilities were installed. Since Habitat's policy is not to take government money for their housings, monetary gifts from individuals, churches, and corporations financed the Habitat homes.

Recently, the state programs that helped to fund this development were terminated, causing communities to wonder how to develop affordable housing and build neighborhoods for the increasing numbers of families in need.

The firm of LHB Engineers and Architects designed Lyton Park Place using traditional Midwestern prototypes for the houses. The two-, three-, and four-bedroom homes, which have eight different floor plans, fit well with their turn-of-the-century neighbors. The traditional massing, front porches, and horizontal siding give the homes a comfortable feeling. Parking is in garages off a rear alley, keeping the front streetscape agreeable for pedestrians and visitors. Resident Mike Lewis expressed his happiness upon moving in, "We never thought we could afford a home of this quality. There are lots of little extras that make it special, and there is a park across the street that the kids use."

Justin's president, David Van Landschoot said, "I have learned that it is very important to do master planning and to do a development of a size that can affect the neighborhood." Even though community opposition in the beginning delayed the start of construction by about six months without really changing the design, the entire neighborhood has been renewed as a result of the Lyton Park Place.

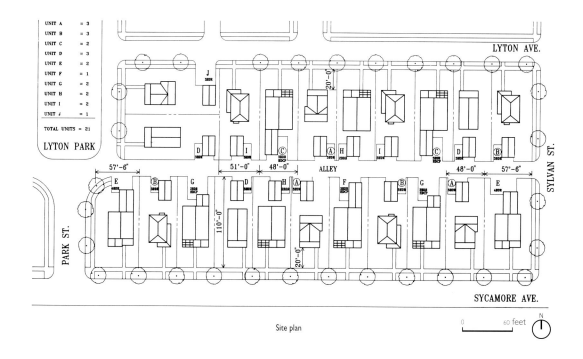

Site plan

0   60 feet

3 BR House–Main floor/lot plan   0   20 feet

Unit E off Sycamore and Sylvan Franz Hall

Units D and J on Lyton and Park Franz Hall

OWNER/DEVELOPER
Justin Properties, Inc.

ARCHITECT
LHB Architects and Engineers

CONTRACTOR
Justin Properties, Inc.

FUNDERS	**TYPE**
City of St Paul Planning and Econ Devel./	
Housing Redevelopment Authority	Grant
Local Initiative Support Corporation	Loan
Western Bank and Insurance	Loan
State of Minnesota	Land

DEVELOPMENT TYPE
New construction for-sale single-family homes.

RESIDENT PROFILE
Low- to moderate-income families,
incomes $15,000–45,000.

DENSITY
7 units/acre

DEVELOPMENT PROFILE

Type	N°/Units	Size (sf)	Sale Prices
2 BR	2	1,250	$55,000
2 BR Accessible	2	1,300	$60,000
3 BR	12	1,300	$35,000–67,500
3 BR Accessible	3	1,500	$35,000–67,500
4 BR	2	1,600	$70,000–75,000
TOTAL	**21**		

Total site area: 3 acres

CONSTRUCTION TYPE
One- and two-story woodframe with aluminum siding,
comp. shingle roof.

COSTS
Land Cost: $0; Constr. Costs: $2,100,000; Other Costs:
$300,000; **Total Development Cost: $2,400,000**
($114,285/unit). (Completed October 1991)

Field Street Detroit, Michigan

The 21 units of the Field Street infill housing are located in the Island View Village area of Detroit about three miles east of downtown. The development was sponsored by the Church of the Messiah Housing Corporation (CMHC), a non-profit organization established by the church in 1978 on Detroit's lower east side. CMHC also administers the City of Detroit's Neighborhood Opportunity Fund and HOME grants for home repair and rehabilitation, and conducts other activities related to housing needs and inner city revitalization.

The homes were built on sites that had been cleared of previous structures and required excavation and removal of fill material. Architect Abraham Kadushin saw this condition as both a problem in terms of added cost and an opportunity because, he said, "It provided an impetus for designing full basements for the buildings, a significant residential amenity for residents because they provide extra living space for future needs." Kadushin described the design, "The site plan utilizes the pattern of residential buildings parallel to the street so that front entrances face the public street, and rear entrances face the semi-public alley. Parking off the alleys is on paved areas behind the residences. The building designs are interpretations and adaptations of traditional duplex and row house dwellings in the neighborhood. Front porches, horizontal siding with special shapes and corner trim, window types and patterns, gabled roofs and other exterior features express this compatibility with existing buildings. Since the development is small, public space was difficult to support, but common back yard areas provide semi-public open space for the families, and a small tot-lot with mature trees and vegetation has been completed."

Dwelling units are arranged in four building types: duplexes, fourplexes, quadraplexes, and a modified fourplex that contains two townhouses and a stacked flat with the lower level a wheelchair-accessible unit. The homes have separate front and rear entrances reached directly from both the street and back yard. The characteristic midwestern woodframe construction of working-class Detroit neighborhoods was used, augmented by pre-fabricated wood trusses for roofs and floors, which lowered costs. The site plan allows easy monitoring of open spaces and entries. Even the alleys, previously locations of criminal activities, have been improved and are actively used by residents going to and from parking. Units are equipped with full security systems and have ample windows to allow visual connection between inside and outside areas.

Abraham Kadushin summed up his firm's experience with the Field Street housing by saying, "The positive catalyzing effect of new infill housing development in a severely distressed urban neighborhood cannot be underestimated. While rehabilitation of existing deteriorated structures is extremely important, the symbolic and tangible rebirth represented by new construction is a powerful revitalizing force, attracting substantial attention and additional resources. This is especially significant when the developer is a non-profit, community-based organization undertaking responsibility for the planning, design, development, and management of the project, as was the case in Island View Village."

The 'Grand'

Walkway   Lafayette Greenbelt

Grand Boulevard East Elevation

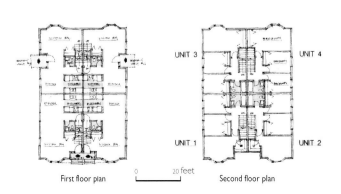

First floor plan   0   20 feet   Second floor plan

View of fronts of new townhouses along Field Street Kadushin Associates Architects Planners

View of quadruplex looking north along East Grand Boulevard Kadushin Associates Architects Planners

View of front elevations looking south along Field Street Kadushin Associates Architects Planners

OWNER/DEVELOPER
Church of the Messiah Housing Corp. (CMHC)

ARCHITECT
Kadushin Associates Architects Planners

LANDSCAPE ARCHITECT
MH Consulting

CONTRACTOR
Fairview Construction

PROPERTY MANAGEMENT
Church of Messiah Housing Corp.

FUNDERS	TYPE
Michigan State Hsg Dev. Authority	Mortgage
Nat'l Equity Fund	Equity
Lilly Endowment	Grant
First Federal of Michigan	
Federal Home Loan Bank AH Prog.	2nd mortgage
Hudson-Weber Foundation	Grant
Field Street Limited Partners	Grant

DEVELOPMENT TYPE
New construction rental attached townhouses.

RESIDENT PROFILE
Very-low- and low-income families with incomes 25–50% of AMI.

DENSITY
12 units/acre

DEVELOPMENT PROFILE

Type	N°/Units	Size (sf)	Rents
2 BR	10	900 + bsmt.	$367
3 BR	11	1,050 + bsmt.	$425
TOTAL	21		

Laundry: in each unit
Courtyard/play: playlot under development
Parking: 36 surface
Total site area: 97,740 sf (2.24 acres)

CONSTRUCTION TYPE
Two-story woodframe with vinyl siding, comp. shingle roofs.

COSTS
Land Cost: $34,209; Constr. Costs: $1,262,329; Other Costs: $445,671; **Total Development Cost: $1,708,000 ($81,333/unit).** (Completed September 1993)

West Town II Chicago, Illinois

Bounded on one side by the Chicago River, West Town is only 3 miles northwest of the Loop. Its 180,000 residents form one of the city's great ethnic melting pots. Two-thirds of West Town's population is Latino; most of the other residents are Polish, Ukrainian, Italian, and African-American. Once a strong and solidly Polish neighborhood, population shifts and economic decline have raised unemployment in the area to twice the national average. Elderly people and large families have few housing options; more than half the housing units were built before 1910, and most residential development occurred before 1939. Vacancy rates were running above 10 per cent in substandard housing.

The Bickerdike Redevelopment Corporation (BRC), a community organization, joined West Town Housing Partners, private developers, to build the housing with architects Weese Langley Weese and Peter Landon. Robert Brehm, director of BRC stated, "We are emphasizing housing for large families— 75 per cent of the units will be three- or four-bedroom townhouses. We are acquiring only existing vacant land, and the housing clusters are targeted for blocks with high levels of demolition." Bickerdike purchased the mainly 25-by-100-foot lots from the city, which had acquired the land through demolition liens over a two-year period. The development consists of 113 three- and four-bedroom, single-family, attached-townhouses on 30 scattered, vacant sites. Floor plans were varied to take advantage of different site conditions such as standard infill lots, corner lots, and combined lots

with buildings facing a common on the interior of the lot. A Section 8 grant from the US Department of Housing and Urban Development (HUD) was crucial to the construction of the housing. Unlike most city construction projects, West Town II employed a large number of neighborhood residents through a jobs-for-residents program that was based on the principle that city work paid for with government money should go to city residents when possible.

The design process, from planning through finishing details, incorporated community input. City and HUD guidelines also required heavy administrative scrutiny of the process. Dennis Langley, principal at Weese Langley Weese, described the townhouses as, "efficient but well appointed with large windows in living areas, individual laundries, good storage, and quality materials." Low ornamental fencing was used on small private front yards with higher fencing on rear and side yards. The architects focused on the use of enduring materials and on various strategies for creating maximum variety and texture for the facades. The buildings' first floors were raised a few steps above grade and strong roof forms were used to fit in with the older housing stock in the neighborhood. Parking is off side streets or back alleys; on some sites the housing shares entry courts from the parking to the homes. Resident Sheryl Jackson praised the apartments because, "They are large, with lots of cabinet space, lots of storage, and light everywhere!"

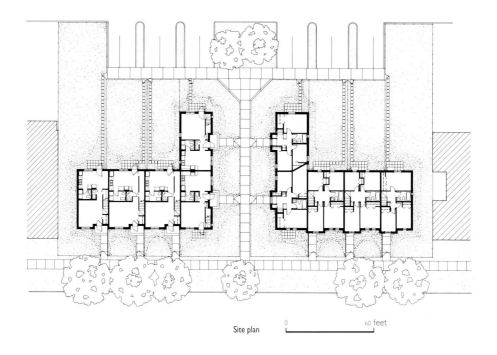

Site plan   0   60 feet

Interior view of projecting bay—3 BR unit Wayne Cable

Typical rear entry facade of corner unit Wayne Cable

OWNER/DEVELOPER
Bickerdike Redevelopment Corporation

ARCHITECT
Weese Langley Weese Architects, Ltd
with Peter Landon Architects

LANDSCAPE ARCHITECT
Mormino Landscaping

CONTRACTOR
Linn-Mathes

PROPERTY MANAGEMENT
Bickerdike Redevelopment Corporation

FUNDERS	TYPE
HUD Section 8	Grant/rent subsidy
Low Income Housing Tax Credit	Equity
Local bank	FHA-insured loan

DEVELOPMENT TYPE
New construction and rehab. scattered-site rental townhouses.

RESIDENT PROFILE
Very-low income families, Section 8 eligible.

DENSITY
17 units/acre (ave.)

DEVELOPMENT PROFILE

Type	N°/Units	Size (sf)	Rents
3 BR	65	900	(HUD pays diff. between
4BR	48	1,100	FMR and 30% HH income)
TOTAL	**113**		

Community/laundry: in each unit
Courtyard/play: private rear yards, some front shared courts
Parking: 113 surface
Total site area: 30 scattered sites; 281,775 sf (6.4 acres)

CONSTRUCTION TYPE
Two-story woodframe, some with basements, brick walls, comp. shingle roofs.

COSTS
Land Cost: $895,000; Constr. Costs: $12,137,544; Other Costs: $2,663,118; **Total Development Costs: $15,695,662 ($71,680 /unit).** (Completed 1989)

West Town II

In an interview, Andy Soto, property manager for West Town, expressed strong support for tenant organization, "The tenant organizations that come out of Bickerdike are very active in the neighborhood in promoting new affordable housing. There is a tenant newsletter run and organized by tenants, which serves as a venue for both tenants and management to have a voice. Before starting any development we hold public meetings. We don't want people to spend their lives in Section 8 housing so we are starting a program that trains people to do property management—we want to create jobs and housing."

One incentive that the tenant organization has used with considerable success to get people involved in the community is to require anyone who wants an on-site parking sticker to attend two of their monthly meetings a year. Soto explained, "Once they go to the meetings, they see how their lives are affected and they keep going." Since moving in, Sheryl Jackson has been able to find steady work. "Living at West Town allows me to focus not so much on how I'm going to pay the rent, but on what I can be."

Exterior sketch

Street facade of combined site units Wayne Cable

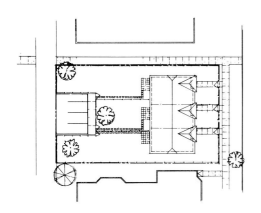
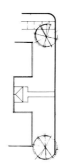
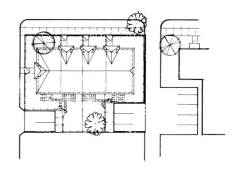

Typical site plans

Inside "street" of combined units site Wayne Cable

Street facade of typical infill units Wayne Cable

Entry facade of typical unit infill scheme Wayne Cable

The Reservoir is a resident-managed, limited equity co-operative designed for families, and singles. It consists of 28 units arranged in two-story flats and attached townhouses, with a number of units specifically designed to accommodate people with disabilities. The density of 20 units per acre matches that of the surrounding neighborhood as do the street setbacks, roof shapes, building widths, bay windows, and building materials. Wood construction was used throughout except for the historic brick livery stable on the site, which was retained and remodeled to contain two apartments, a laundry, and meeting space for the complex. Buildings were grouped to provide the largest possible back yards, community gardens, and two playgrounds. Two parking lots are located within short walking distances of the units so that cars do not dominate the site. In respect to security, all parts of the site are visible from within the units, and the residents supervise the commons as communal space.

The City of Madison owned the site and offered it to developers who would meet the city's development and design criteria, which became strong determinants of the site planning and design. The non-profit owner–architect team, Madison Mutual Housing Association (MMHA) and Design Coalition, Inc., were required to compete with for-profit developers. The site was six blocks from the state capitol and the downtown business district between an underutilized industrial area with a rail corridor and a neighborhood occupied by a working-class and student population. Subsequently the use of the marshy site as a landfill for building materials made it necessary to excavate the site and haul in new soil. The new housing not only made a positive use of long vacant land but also sparked rehabilitation efforts on adjacent blocks. In the last five years for-profit developers have added about 150 more units both in rehabilitated warehouses and new construction.

At the outset, community support was divided—the antagonists outnumbered the advocates. The development faced strong opposition because neighborhood residents were concerned about the effect on the neighborhood of the families with low incomes who would move in. This situation changed during the design process to which the owner invited opponents of The Reservoir, residents of the Mutual Housing Association's other co-ops, representatives from local non-profits serving older adults and persons with disabilities, and neighborhood residents. The two major changes that neighborhood concern brought about were the reduction of units from 40 to 28 and more parking. Susan Hobart, former executive director of the Madison Mutual Housing Association, believes that the additional months of planning committee meetings were key to the eventual acceptance of The Reservoir, and improved the overall building and site design.

Lou Host-Jablonski, one of Design Coalition's architects, commented that, "In my experience much more thought, care, and energy was lavished on The Reservoir than is typical of conventional, market-rate housing. The latter is typically easier because it attempts little that is new. Infill affordable housing projects like this one present a more complicated political context, financial complications such as many sources of funds, overlapping and sometimes conflicting requirements, tight deadlines, and greater scrutiny by the community and governing officials. The Reservoir could not have been accomplished without a strong, committed and clear-minded client."

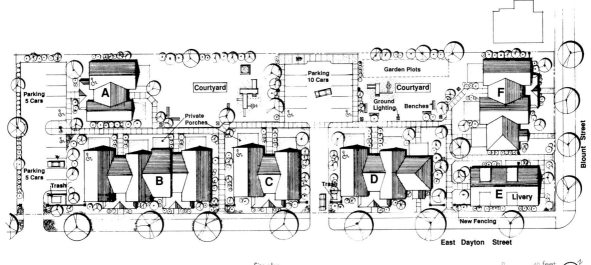

Site plan

0   40 feet

View west down Dayton Street of front facade Lou Host-Jablonski

Row houses north of Livery Lou Host-Jablonski

Building B–first floor   Building B–second floor

0   32 feet

OWNER/DEVELOPER
Madison Mutual Housing Assoc.

ARCHITECT
Design Coalition
& Glueck Architects

LANDSCAPE ARCHITECT
Vandewalle and Associates

CONTRACTOR
Connery Bldg. Corp.

PROPERTY MANAGEMENT
Meridian Group, Inc.

FUNDERS	TYPE
City of Madison, Comm'ty Devel. Authority	Loan
Madison Mutual Housing Association	Equity
Wisconsin Housing and Econ. Development	Loan
City of Madison, CDBG - UDAG	Loan
Tax Increment Funds	

DEVELOPMENT TYPE
New construction rental flats and townhouses, 4 barrier-free units; and historic preservation of former "livery".

RESIDENT PROFILE
Mixed-income, mixed-age, mixed able and disabled persons; 25% low-income, 50% moderate-income, 25% market-rate.

DENSITY
18 units/acre

DEVELOPMENT PROFILE

Type	N°/Units	Size (sf)	Rents
1 BR Flat	5	525	$300–525
2 BR Flat	19	800	$381–620
3 BR Flat	2	1,000	$400–675
3 BR TH	2	1,100	$775
TOTAL	28		

Community/laundry: 1 for each 4-unit building; MHA offices community/kitch./off rehabed livery
Courtyard/play: one for older kids, one for younger kids; raised garden beds for wheelchair bound
Parking: 20 surface
Total site area: 67,082 sf (1.54 acres)

CONSTRUCTION TYPE
Two-story woodframe, horiz. siding, comp. shingle roof.

COSTS
Land Cost: $240,000; Constr. Costs: $1,987,368; Other Costs: $207,282; **Total Development Cost: $2,434,650 ($86,952/unit).** (Completed 1988)

West Town Cluster Housing Chicago, Illinois

Starting in 1966 with a lawsuit, Chicago housing activists fought for over 20 years to reverse the federal and local housing policies directed toward putting people with low incomes in high-rise developments. Only in recent years has the effort to scatter low-rise, low-income housing throughout the city been successful in building over 1,600 units of scattered-site housing in integrated neighborhoods on Chicago's north and near west sides. In contrast with the past, the new housing has met little resistance from neighbors because it fits into the neighborhood context. Yet the strength of the former opposition was such that court orders to build low-income housing throughout the city were appealed and even city mayors favorable to the idea were unable to implement the program (which had finally been established in 1974) because of political pressure. The principal advocacy group, Business and Professional People for the Public Interest, headed by lawyer Alexander Polikoff, repeatedly sought to have a private receiver hired to oversee the scattered-site program so that approval of all plans by both the US Department of Housing and Urban Development and the Chicago Housing Authority would no longer be required. In 1987, the CHA agreed to appoint the non-profit Habitat Corporation, a private developer and real estate management firm, as the receiver.

Habitat's first challenge was the 85 buildings, most in very deteriorated condition, that were already in the program; 42 of these were rehabilitated and the rest torn down or sold. Habitat administrators said that initially their biggest problem was dealing with the HUD regulations, especially the "modest designs and cost containment" regulation which was dropped in January of 1994. The neighborhoods welcomed Habitat's efforts to rehabilitate the abandoned buildings. Construction of new units caused some apprehension, but a rigorous screening process for the selection of tenants helped to assure neighbors that responsible development and effective property management were combined to bring accountability to the program.

The nine townhouse sites planned and designed by the architectural firm of Nagle, Hartray & Associates were scattered within a one-mile radius of the seniors' building. The exterior design of the buildings was based on 19th century workers cottages similar to those found throughout Chicago's working-class neighborhoods. Materials such as precast concrete lintels, matching sills, and copings colored to mimic limestone provided the exteriors with detail that satisfied HUD's cost containment guidelines for integrating structural and ornamental elements. The designers' main goal was to create efficient floor plans for three- and four-bedroom townhouses for families and studio and one-bedroom apartments for the elderly. The new units are clustered to permit the location of management and recreation in the seniors' building.

This housing program is a classic example of how dedicated advocates and professionals can succeed in changing the failed concept of warehousing the poor in tower blocks into a model of integrating families and seniors with low incomes successfully into neighborhoods.

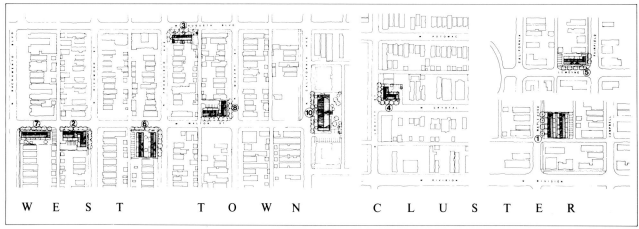

Site cluster

0   200 feet   N

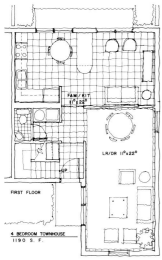

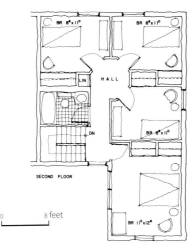

4 BEDROOM TOWNHOUSE
1190 S.F.

FIRST FLOOR

FAM/KIT
11⁰x22⁰

LR/DR 11⁰x22⁰

UP

SECOND FLOOR

BR 8⁴x11⁰

BR 8⁴x11⁰

LIN

HALL

DN

BR 8⁴x11⁰

BR 11⁰x12⁸

0   8 feet

4 BR townhouse–First floor   4 BR townhouse–Second floor

900–04 North Mozart facades David Clifton

1215 North Maplewood facades David Clifton

OWNER/DEVELOPER
The Habitat Co., Receiver for Chicago
Housing Authority Scattered Site Program

ARCHITECT
Nagle Hartray and Assoc. Co.

CONTRACTOR
Babco Construction Co.

PROPERTY MANAGEMENT
Luthern Social Services of Illinois

FUNDERS   **TYPE**
HUD Section 8   Grant/rent subsidy

DEVELOPMENT TYPE
New construction, scattered-site rental
townhouses and senior apartment building.

RESIDENT PROFILE
Very-low-income seniors, disabled individuals, and families.

DENSITY
Families 20 units/acre; seniors 102 units/acre

DEVELOPMENT PROFILE

Type	N°/Units	Size (sf)	Rents
1 BR	50	550	(HUD pays diff. between
2 BR	1	750	FMR and 30% HH income)
3 BR	50	1,000	
TOTAL	101		

Community/laundry: yes
Courtyard/play: private yards, large garden for seniors
Parking: 75 surface; 1:1 for families; 1:4 for seniors
Total site area: senior 26,000 sf; family 2.5 acres

CONSTRUCTION TYPE
Senior building: four-story block and brick; flat roofs.
Family townhouses: two-story woodframe with partial brick
veneer and drivit.

COSTS
Land Cost: $555,500; Constr. Costs: $6,272,700; Other
Costs: $1,292,800; **Total Development Cost: $8,121,000
(Senior: $69,600/unit; Family: $91,000/unit).**
(Completed 1995)

Steve Rosenthal

CHAPTER TEN:
THE NORTHEAST

Fifteen developments in the northeast region were selected
for review as two- and four-page case studies:

Battle Road Farm, Lincoln, Massachusetts
Crawford Square, Pittsburgh, Pennsylvania
West HELP, Greenburgh, New York
Hyde Square Co-op, Dorchester, Massachusetts
Waterside Green, Stamford, Connecticut
Parkside Gables, Stamford, Connecticut
Catherine Street, Albany, New York
Mutual Housing Association, New York
Melrose Court, Bronx, New York
CEPHAS Housing, Yonkers, New York
Roxbury Corners, Roxbury, Massachusetts
Charlestown Navy Yard Rowhouses, Boston, Massachusetts
Ninth Square Redevelopment, New Haven, Connecticut
Langham Court, Boston, Massachusetts
Tent City, Boston, Massachusetts

Lincoln, Massachusetts

Suprisingly, households in affluent suburbs often need housing assistance. Battle Road Farm exemplifies this situation. It became apparent to town officials that many young families who grew up there could not afford to buy their own home, and that municipal employees—teachers, policemen, and others—had to live elsewhere and commute to work. The town's response was to purchase a large tract of land in the north part of town and designate 24 acres for mixed-income housing. Through an extensive planning process, a consensus favoring affordable housing was established before the developer was selected—a welcome and unusual situation.

When completed, Battle Road Farm will have 120 condominium units in 34 buildings. At this writing 96 units have been built. The irregular site plan responded to a wetlands area; two cul-de-sac roads partly enfold the wetlands area and an open meadow. Architect William Rawn achieved a village-like character by grouping buildings on opposite sides of 24-foot-wide roads. Only one road enters the site from an arterial, and the absence of sidewalks furthers the impression of a rural community. There are no garages, but two parking spaces per unit are available in small paved lots adjacent to the homes. Six housing types fit into three types of building. Most are fourplexes articulated to recall the New England farmhouse, a formal building on the street with a gable roof and generous porch linked by two smaller connecting units and ending with a barn-like building at the back. The other building type is a two-family structure evocative of turn-of-the-century carriage houses.

Only first-time home buyers were eligible to purchase a unit, and a lottery was held to select buyers. Half of these homes were reserved for past or present residents or their relatives, municipal staff members, and employees of local non-profit organizations in Lincoln. Local public officials approved the masterplan by a vote of ten to one. However, during delays caused by the design and development of the sewer treatment plant (an innovative tertiary treatment system integrated with the wetlands), the recession hit the northeast in full force. The real estate market contracted severely and the original construction lender was taken over by the FDIC, making marketing more challenging than expected. Although the original agreement called for 60 per cent of the homes to be affordable, that has been adjusted to 40–50 per cent to allow the development to remain financially viable.

Developer Bob Keuhn reports that Battle Road Farm has been a worthwhile venture, although it may not make any money. In retrospect he would have been more cost-conscious about the design, negotiated more favorable acquisition terms with the town, and phased the development more gradually. The saving grace during the problem period was the local political support which made a big difference in the flexibility of the development process. Keuhn noted, "This developer prefers to work only where no adversarial relationship exists within the governing jurisdiction."

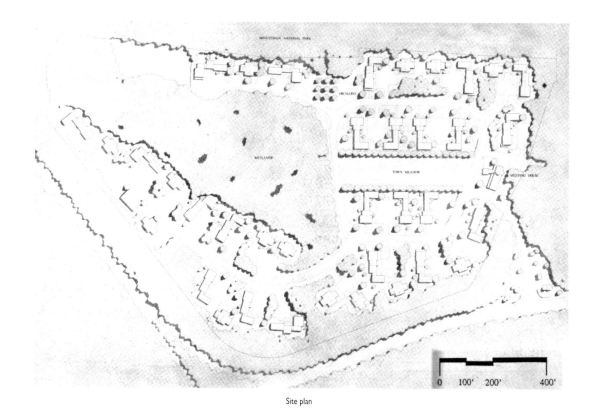

Site plan

SECOND FLOOR

FIRST FLOOR

0   32 feet

Unit plans of duplex

Exterior: front porch with chair William Rawn

DEVELOPER
Keen Development Corporation

ARCHITECTS
William Rawn Associates, Inc., (phase I)
The Architectural Team (phase II & III)

LANDSCAPE ARCHITECTS
Michael van Valkenburgh Assoc., Inc. (phase I & site)
William Fleming Assoc. (phase II & III)

CONTRACTOR
Wolf Construction Corp.
CWC Builders

PROPERTY MANAGEMENT
First Realty Management

FUNDERS

FUNDERS	TYPE
Eliot Bank	Loan
Massachusetts Hsg Finance Agency	Loan
First Trade Union Saving Bank	Loan
Massachusetts Hsg Partnership	Interest subsidies/grant

DEVELOPMENT TYPE
New construction for-sale attached townhouses.

RESIDENT PROFILE
60% low- and moderate-income households,
40% market-rate.

DENSITY
10 units/acre

DEVELOPMENT PROFILE

Type	N°/Units	Size (sf)	Sale Prices
2 BR	80	1,100–1,500	$86,000–184,000
3 BR	40	1,400–1,800	$130,000–234,500
TOTAL	120		

Community: town common, community meeting house.
Courtyard/play: private yards/patios
Parking: 240 surface
Total site area: 24 acres

CONSTRUCTION TYPE
Two-story woodframe, some with basements, horiz. siding,
comp. shingle roofs.

COSTS
Land Cost: $1,400,000; Constr. Costs: $13,000,000;
Other Costs: $3,300,000; **Total Development Cost:
$16,300,000 ($107/sf).** (96 completed by 1995,
phase III under constr.)

Exterior: front porch angled Lucy Chen

Exterior: farm house from a distance Lucy Chen

Crawford Square Pittsburgh, Pennsylvania

Once a vital urban area known for its jazz clubs and ethnic diversity, Pittsburgh's Hill district had deteriorated by the 1950s and, in the 1960s, suffered great damage during riots following the assassination of Martin Luther King Jr. The Urban Redevelopment Authority (URA) had already begun the acquisition and clearance of sites in the area, which became an urban wasteland like many others created by stalled redevelopment projects across the country. When the community organized to prevent further expansion of downtown development, Crawford Street was established as a boundary.

Today, revitalization of the district has begun thanks to the completion of Crawford Square, a mixed-income development on 17.5 acres in the lower Hill district. Crawford Square is the result of the combined efforts of the city of Pittsburgh and McCormack Baron & Associates, a St Louis developer experienced in converting blighted inner-city neighborhoods into communities that are attractive to a broad range of residents. As the development coordinator, McCormack Baron formed a joint venture with the Hill Community Development Corporation, the Hill Project Area Committee, and the URA. Speaking of the site, which the URA acquired in 1990, Richard Baron noted, "It has spectacular views of the downtown area and is a five-minute walk from the business district and cultural activities."

The first development phase, completed in 1993, consists of 203 rental apartments and townhouses, which are 50 per cent market-rate and 50 per cent subsidized. Resident Sheryl King, who used to live in nearby public housing, now lives in a two-story, three-bedroom townhouse with her two sons. She remarked, "It is very safe here. When I leave to go to work at 5.00 am it is well lit. Having two levels makes my place feel more like a house than the apartment." Since few homes have been built in the city in recent years, there was a market for potential homebuyers. To reach this market, 9 townhouses and 18 detached homes, designed by Tai + Lee Architects were offered for sale in phase II. When completed, Crawford Square will have 1,000 residents, 550 homes with complete recreation facilities, and a rebuilt shopping district.

The masterplan for Crawford Square was designed to fit in with the neighborhood and the city as a whole. Three traditional parks have been planned to create a new address for the community and to link the neighborhood to the nearby business district. Ray Gindroz of UDA Architects commented, "The buildings are designed as houses whether they are single-family houses, townhouses, or apartment houses. Their scale, materials, and architectural forms are related to typical Pittsburgh neighborhoods of a scale similar to the Hill district. Crawford Square, therefore, proudly serves as the gateway to a neighborhood immediately adjacent to downtown."

The architects held working sessions with the project area committee at every stage of planning and design during which such key issues emerged as the participants' desire to make the scale and character of Crawford Square as much like a traditional neighborhood and as different from a "project" as possible. Brick was considered the most desirable material for the facades despite its cost. UDA developed design guidelines to establish the vocabulary of the site plan and architectural elements. Narrower street widths, front porches, bay windows, and dormers, create interesting and useable spaces for residents and project an image of quality and stability to the neighborhood. Vince Bennett, project manager for McCormack Baron noted, "The development's design quality, and income and racial diversity far exceeded the community's best expectations."

Aerial perspective of Protectory Place

Aerial close-up, Protectory Place Tim Buchman

Centre Avenue rental flats Tim Buchman

Centre Avenue rental flats Tim Buchman

OWNER/DEVELOPER
McCormack Baron & Assoc.

ARCHITECT
UDA Architects and Planners, Inc. (phase I)
Tai + Lee Architects (phase II)

LANDSCAPE ARCHITECT
LaQuatra Bonci

CONTRACTOR
Snavely-Waller-Whiting-Turner; Louis Waller Contr.
Whiting-Turner Contracting Co.; Kee Construction

PROPERTY MANAGEMENT
McCormack Baron & Assoc.

FUNDERS	TYPE
Urban Redevelopment Authority of Pittsburgh	Loans and grants
Pennsylvania Housing Finance Agency (HOME)	Loans/bond proceeds
Local lender consortium: PNC Bank, Mellon Bank, Dollar Rent-a-car, Landmark Integra	Loans and grants
Department of Community Affairs	Loans
Local Foundations: R.K. Mellon Foundation Howard Heinz Foundation, Vira I. Heinz Found. Pittsburgh Foundation	Grants
Low-Income Housing Tax Credits	Equity
General Partner/Developer	Equity

DEVELOPMENT TYPE
New construction rental attached townhouses; for-sale
detached and attached single-family homes.

RESIDENT PROFILE
Low-income and market-rate singles, couples, and families.

DENSITY
16.2 units/acre

DEVELOPMENT PROFILE

Type	N°/Units	Size (sf)	Rents/Sale Prices
1 BR	101	674–703	$279–495
2 BR	155	862–1154	$337–650
3 BR	18	1,205–1,230	$391–795
3&4BR (for-sale)	57	1,940–2,780	$89,000–139,700
TOTAL	331	(phase I & II both rental and for-sale)	

Community/play: 2,500 sf; pool/deck 4,500 sf; tot-lot 750 sf
Parking: 304 surface
Total site area: 10.4 acres

CONSTRUCTION TYPE
Two- and three-story woodframe, brick veneer and
vinyl siding, comp. shingle roofs.

COSTS
Total Development Cost: $35,671,202 ($41/sf for for-sale
units, $45/sf for rental units).
(Stage I is complete and stage II is 90% complete as of
June 1995)

Commenting on some of the difficulties of the process, Ray Gindroz said, "The architecture could have been simpler and, therefore, more cost effective if variety had been achieved with more building types, as determined by a number of different developers." However, it is ultimately more important to have a co-ordinated marketing plan that takes into account the demands of potential residents. In fact, according to Gindroz, "The community and the market have pushed the for-sale program more towards detached houses, which has caused the rental program to be scaled back." The construction process was not simple, and was made especially complex by the 15 per cent slope and bad soil conditions. A variety of local minority firms worked with several general contractors to build the housing. Despite some difficulties with the construction process in the beginning, city design review along with developer commitment ensured that Crawford Square was built to high standards. The complexity of the funding also required great co-operation between the public and private partners. As Bennett pointed out, "Each participant was necessary to the deal and provided an element of credibility which convinced the others to be involved."

Crawford Square stands as a symbol of hope and pride for a community that has endured its share of struggles. Sheryl King reflected, "It not only fits in, but it has improved the look of the neighborhood. Everyone looks out for each other here, and I can sleep at night because I don't have to worry so much for my children's safety." Property manager David Hefflin noted, "More cities should look into housing like this. It has a sense of community. People seem to have a sense of responsibility and take pride in the fact that they qualified to live here. I grew up in this neighborhood, and for residents of the Hill area this is a dream come true."

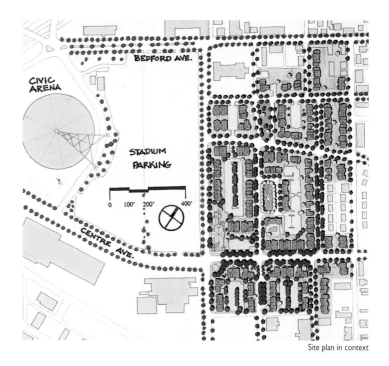

Site plan in context

Protectory Place, rental townhouses Tim Buchman

Perspective from the porch

Dining Room
12'.0¹/⁸" × 8'.3"

HW

A/H

Kitchen
7'.8" × 8'.7³/⁴"

DW REF

Living Room
15'.1" × 12'.0¹/⁴"

up

First floor

Centre Avenue rental flats Tim Buchman

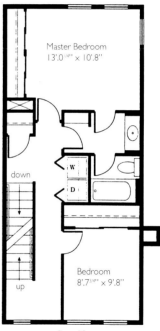

Master Bedroom
13'.0¹/⁴" × 10'.8"

down

W

D

Bedroom
8'.7³/⁴" × 9'.8"

up

Second floor

The city of Pittsburgh as a backdrop to Crawford Square Paul Rocheleau

down

Bedroom
12'.0¹/⁴" × 16'

Third floor

This housing for homeless families in a semi-rural area of upstate New York is a sensible, gracious solution to a critical and controversial problem. Initiated as a partnership by president and founder of HELP, Andrew Cuomo, Andrew O'Rourke, county executive for Westchester County, and Anthony Veteran, Greenburgh town supervisor, the intent was to find a decent place for homeless families from Westchester County to live, while avoiding the overconcentration of such programs in urban areas. Six acres on the campus of Westchester County Community College were identified as a quiet yet accessible site for the development. Initial community opposition to the size of the project led to a number of costly and difficult lawsuits. However, negotiations eventually allowed the development to proceed on the condition that after 10 years the housing would revert to city-owned affordable housing for seniors or students.

Not everyone opposed the program. "Families become homeless for many reasons," neighbor and West HELP Community Advisory boardmember Candyce Corcoran noted, "These people are where they are because of hardship. For example a young woman whose partner has walked out on her, or a family whose house has burned down. These people all want to get a job and don't want to be on welfare. With social services backing they have a great start."

The 108 units are designed in eight residential buildings and a community center organized around a rolling open meadow. A welcoming appearance speaks strongly of a communal lifestyle quite unfamiliar to single parents with preschool children. Residents anticipate living here for six to nine months on their way to employment and more permanent housing. According to architect Roland Baer of Cooper Robertson and Partners, "The premise for the site plan stemmed from both social concerns and security issues."

For the safety of residents the site is enclosed with unobtrusive fences between buildings and a single entry point at the community center.

The simple one-bedroom units are designed with moveable panels between them to convert to a studio and two-bedroom unit if a larger family needs more space. Baer noted, "The construction people were on board from the schematic phase, so costs and scheduling were monitored from the beginning. This was critical due to the fixed budget and tight deadlines, all of which we were able to meet."

The community center, clearly defined by the rotunda at the entry, has facilities for daycare, healthcare, substance abuse counseling, and education. Resident manager Dennis Powers commented, "The multi-purpose room is spacious, practical for all types of events, and architecturally pleasing. Our expanding programs require us to partition it for multiple uses, but the acoustics of the cathedral ceilings make this difficult." The residents are encouraged to take full advantage of the programs to assist them to get back on their feet. Resident Wanda Alston said she values the counseling programs and the environment provided for the children, "I feel safe here, and the neighbors are very respectable."

West HELP has settled into this community of middle-class housing and a country club without the negative side effects people feared. Paul Finer, town supervisor noted, "People are relieved that it hasn't contributed to crime, that it's well maintained and well controlled." Baer summed up the architects' feelings, "The lesson learned is that one can design affordable housing to conventional standards and not have to spend additional money making it vandal proof. People respond to the quality of the housing by respecting and taking care of it."

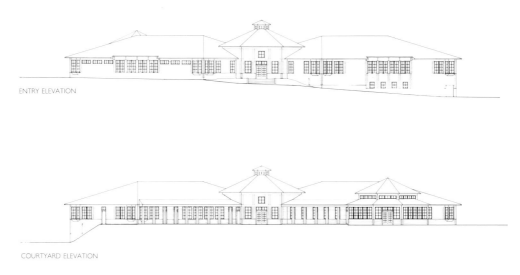

ENTRY ELEVATION

COURTYARD ELEVATION

Community center

Detail of exterior housing finishes and stair Jock Pottle

OWNER/DEVELOPER
HELP

ARCHITECT
Cooper Robertson & Partners

CONSULTANTS
Landscape Architect: Mark Morris Assoc.,
Development Consultant: Tishman-Speyer,

CONTRACTOR
Alder/Valentine Assoc., Ltd.

PROPERTY MANAGEMENT
DiNardis Assoc., Inc.

FUNDERS	TYPE
N.Y. State Housing Finance Agency	na
Westchester County Dept. of Social Services	na

DEVELOPMENT TYPE
New construction, transitional housing, rental attached flats.

RESIDENT PROFILE
Formerly homeless families.

DENSITY
18 units/acre

DEVELOPMENT PROFILE

Type	N°/Units	Size (sf)	Rents
1 BR	108	440	na
TOTAL	**108**		

Comm'ty/laundry: 18,000, comm'ty center, medical, daycare, social services, and recreation facilities
Protected play areas: 8,000 sf
Parking: 63 surface
Total site area: 6 acres

CONSTRUCTION TYPE
Two-story woodframe, wood shingle siding, comp. shingle roofs.

COSTS
Land Cost: $1/year; Constr. Costs: $4,275,000; Other Costs: $1,425,000; **Total Development Cost: $5,700,000 ($75/sf.).** (Completed January 1991)

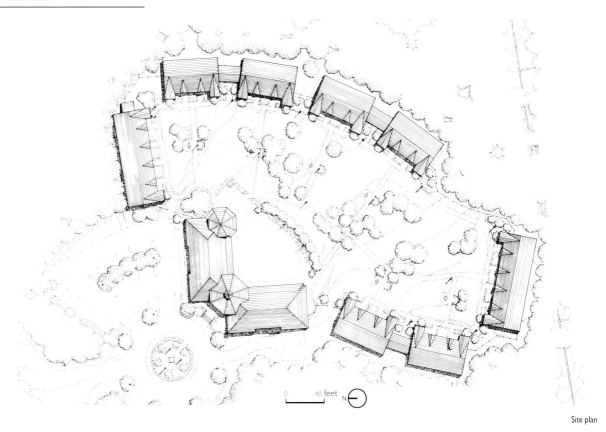

Site plan

Courtyard view of housing and community center   Jock Pottle

Close-up of two housing buildings   Jock Pottle

Community center through protected play area Jock Pottle

Entrance Jock Pottle

Courtyard view of housing through protected play area Jock Pottle

Hyde Square Co-op Jamaica Plain, Massachusetts

Hyde Square developed around the turn of the century as a working-class neighborhood of woodframe buildings for one to three families. Until recently, a patchwork of undersized and underutilized lots in the Hyde Square neighborhood often served as dumping grounds and eyesores. Now, 41 families own co-operative homes in 17 new buildings that restore the streetscape at a comfortable density. With extensive input from the community, architects Domenech Hicks and Krokmalnic developed three building types based on the architectural style and layout of several two- and three-family buildings around the city. The three-family building type is a variant of the original "three-decker" with two side-by-side townhouses over a flat; the two-family buildings have individual entries off a common front porch. All units have back decks looking over a private yard area next to well-lit off-street parking.

This housing began with efforts to organize the community by staff from the Jamaica Plain Neighborhood Development Corporation (JPNC). Organizer Betsaida Gutierrez and former project manager Ricanne Hadrian went from door to door in the neighborhood to build political support and to identify building sites. Lizbeth Heyer, project manager, spoke of the extensive community involvement in shaping and contributing to the design process. Potential residents attended several two-hour, multi-lingual sessions to educate themselves

about the development process and participate in the design. Reviewing worksheets with alternative home designs, people prioritized their housing needs and made design tradeoffs in order to develop final designs that would best serve the future occupants. Basements, half baths, and combined or separate kitchen and dining areas were some of the issues discussed with regards to security, cost, and cultural attitudes. Presentation material resulting from these workshops were often left on display at the JPNDC office.

Architect Fernando Domenech believes that the result of this approach is that, "the development is a successful example of balancing attractive design well suited to the neighborhood and residents with the fiscal responsibility required by a tight budget." Resident and community organizer Karen Chacon lives in a three-bedroom townhouse with her husband and two daughters, Kimberly and Karen. She commented, "I feel very lucky to be at Hyde Square Co-op. One of the best things is the sense of community, and that we have a voice in what happens. The rent is affordable so we have enough for the kids' tuition and clothes. Eventually we hope to buy our own home." Although the JPNDC hopes that Hyde Square Co-op will serve as an inspiration for nearby property owners to continue the revitalization of the neighborhood, this new stock of affordable family housing will also serve to maintain socio-economic diversity in the long term.

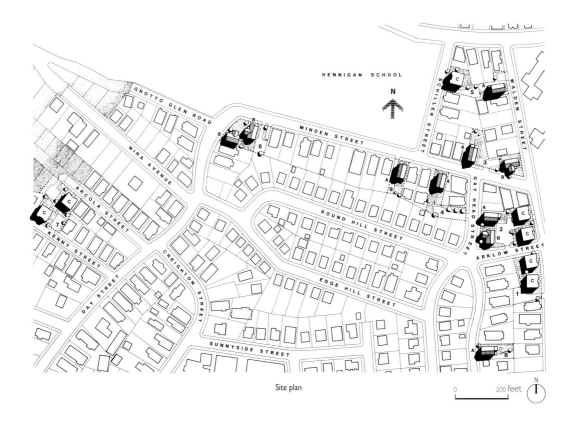

Site plan

0   200 feet

View from 37 Walden Street looking west Peter Vanderwarker

View at corner of Arklow and Gay Head Streets looking east toward Walden Street Peter Vanderwarker

Corner of Walden and Minden Streets looking west Peter Vanderwarker

OWNER/DEVELOPER
Owner: Hyde Square Limited Partnership
Developer: Neighborhood Dev. Corp. of Jamaica Plain

ARCHITECT
Domenech Hicks Krockmalnic

CONSULTANTS
Landscape Architect: The Halvorson Co.
Development Consultant: The Community Builders

CONTRACTOR
CWG Builders

PROPERTY MANAGEMENT
Maloney Properties, Inc.

FUNDERS	TYPE
Metropolitan Boston Hsg Partnership	
City of Boston, Public Facilities Dept.	Grant
Massachusetts Housing Investment Corp.	Grant
Executive Office of Communities and Dev.	Grant
Massachusetts Gov't Land Bank	Loan
Federal Home Loan Bank	Grant
HUD Section 8	Rent subsidy

DEVELOPMENT TYPE
New construction scattered site, co-op duplexes, triplexes.

RESIDENT PROFILE
Very-low and low-income families, incomes below 50–80% of AMI.

DENSITY
22 units/acre

DEVELOPMENT PROFILE
Type	N°/Units	Size (sf)	Rents
2 BR	13	1,017	$350–679
3 BR	24	1,180–1,322	$400–856
4 BR	4	1,651	$450–951
TOTAL	41		

Laundry: in each unit
Courtyard/play: private yards
Parking: 41 surface
Total site area: 80,075 sf (1.84 acres)

CONSTRUCTION TYPE
Two- and three-story woodframe, basements, wood siding, comp. shingle roofs.

COSTS
Land Cost: $0 (donated); Constr. Costs: $4m; Other Costs: $1.5m; **Total Development Cost: $5.5m ($134,146/unit).** (Completed September 1993)

Waterside Green is a development for homeowners with moderate incomes, that replaced an abandoned elementary school. It exemplifies the benefits of reclaiming underutilized inner-city land. The housing is an asset to the surrounding community as well as to the residents, a mix of small families, singles and couples chosen by lottery, with preference given to local people. Long-term affordability is guaranteed by silent second mortgages and resale restrictions. According to John Madeo, president of Fairfields 2000 Corporation (F2C), "The fundamental program was to create quality affordable homeownership with the character of single-family housing, but at a higher density."

F2C joined with New Neighborhoods, Inc., a local non-profit sponsor, to form the Stamford Watergreen Development Corporation (SWDC) a public/private partnership for the purpose of developing the housing. Although a community task force brought neighbors together to learn about and discuss the new homes, progress was slow because of opposition to removal of the school. "But", Madeo said, "the neighbors supported the project through the approvals process and comments have been overwhelmingly positive now that it is built."

The 75 units were divided into four building clusters grouped around semi-private courtyards. Each cluster differs because of the shape of the lot, giving the housing an unregimented appearance. By designing the one-bedroom units as third-floor walk-ups over three-bedroom townhouses, architect Zane Yost succeeded in giving the buildings the character of large houses, helping them fit in well with the Victorian character of the late 19th century neighborhood. Townhouses have front porches and yards with picket fences that give families secure, private outdoor space, which is rare in higher density housing.

Space for the inner courtyards was gained by putting vehicle parking in between the four clusters. A playground in the center of the block is connected to the housing by paved walks. Although the mixed-use neighborhood had an existing local ordinance permitting higher density for affordable housing, parking requirements reduced the amount of open space. In order to gain more open space, SWDC applied for and received minor variances to reduce parking from two to one-and-a-half cars per unit, to reduce parking spaces to 8 feet 6 inches, and to reduce setbacks from 15 feet to 7 feet.

John Madeo believes that despite some agencies' low design standards, developers must fight for the best quality and amenities that funders and markets will allow. Neighborhood acceptance, quick sales, and the winning of several prestigious industry awards have proved that struggle to have been worthwhile at Waterside Green.

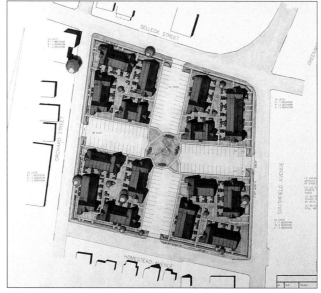

Site plan

View of Hickory townhouse patios David Todd

Close-up of Hickory townhouse patio David Todd

OWNER/DEVELOPER
Owner: Stamford Waterside Development Corp.
Developer: Fairfield 2000/New Neighborhood

ARCHITECT
Zane Yost and Assoc., Inc.

CONSULTANTS
Landscape Architect: Environmental Design Assoc.
Development Consultant: M & L Construction

CONTRACTOR
The Frank Mercedes Jr. Construction Group

MANAGEMENT
Plaza Realty and Management Corp.

FUNDERS	TYPE
State of Connecticut Dept. of Housing (CDH)	Grant for land
Connecticut Housing Finance Authority	Loans
Pitney Bowes, and other corps.	Constr. loan

DEVELOPMENT TYPE
New construction for-sale attached townhouses and flats.

RESIDENT PROFILE
Low- and moderate-income first-time homebuyer families.

DENSITY
27 units/acre

DEVELOPMENT PROFILE

Type	N°/Units	Size (sf)	Sale Prices
1 BR	21	651	$62,500
2 BR	32	1024	$86,000–89,000
3 BR	22	1236	$106,500–109,500
TOTAL	**75**		

Laundry: in each unit.
Courtyard/play: 4 playgrounds, private yards, central green
Parking: 112 surface

CONSTRUCTION TYPE
Two- and three-story woodframe, vinyl siding, comp. shingle roofs.

COSTS
Land Cost: $0; Constr. Costs: $4,734,605; Other Costs: $1,625,058; **Total Development Cost: $6,359,663 ($82/sf).** (Completed in 1994)

The 70 families who have lived in Stamford's Parkside Gables since 1991 are fortunate to have high quality housing in a region that is among the nation's least affordable housing markets (the median price of a single-family home was over $250,000). Residents of Parkside Gables, which is owned by the Mutual Housing Association (MHA) of Southwestern Connecticut, are not equity owners of the property. However, like co-operative or condominium owners, they exercise essential control of decisions and have a lifetime right of housing with the privilege of passing this right to other household or immediate family members who meet the selection criteria. Residents also have the advantages of professional property management and the services of a staff to assist them within the complex or in the community. One result of their influence is the West Side United Neighbors, an organization that, among other activities, has made improvements in the park and community center such as initiating a youth employment program. MHA also spearheaded the funding and approval of the renovation of a nearby 48-unit property foreclosed by HUD. Through a variety of community efforts Parkside Gables residents have truly reversed the negative image of this once crime-ridden area.

Peter Wood, Executive Director of MHA noted, "We organized potential residents to participate actively in the public approvals and design processes. The site design committee included 15 to 20 potential residents along with representatives from public, private, and non-profit sectors. The committee members provided the architects with a direction for the site plan and suggestions for specific architectural elements that potential residents considered important. Literally hundreds of Mutual Housing members and potential residents attended more than a dozen public hearings and spoke eloquently of the need for this development."

The committee favored opening the complex to the surrounding community rather than creating a fortress. A loop road runs through the site with entrances from West Main Street. Pedestrian walkways complement the road and serve as access points to a number of the apartments. All outdoor space within the complex is assigned to individual units to avoid no-man's lands that typically lack maintenance and surveillance. Since both the fronts and the backs of the buildings generate human activity, an informal neighborhood watch system exists, which is reinforced by neighborhood watch patrols. Residents note that the criminal element doesn't come around when they see that someone is concerned. One ongoing problem Wood described is that, "an adjacent liquor store, which NHS was unable to acquire, continues to detract from the quality of life of neighbors as public drinking and loitering is tolerated by the owner and police."

The 2.3-acre site is adjacent to several 1960s-to-1970s public housing towers. Architect Brad Perkins stated their goal for Parkside Gables: "to change the image of assisted housing from impersonal, high-rise apartment complexes to small-scale, traditional homes that would harmonize with the architecture of one of Stamford's 19th century neighborhoods." Adherence to these goals resulted in nine two- and three-story wood-frame buildings which house a mix of one-, two-, and three-bedroom units, each with its own entrance and small yard. The design gives the residents a sense of individual ownership by avoiding common corridors, stairs, and entrances and by providing inside and outside spaces that could be personalized. Creating this character at about 30 units per acre required that many of the cars be parked in garages under the housing. The garages, and some surface parking spaces are entered from rear courts also shared by pedestrians.

In order to individualize the homes, three different front doors were interspersed throughout the complex, and painted several different colors. Elements borrowed from Victorian residences in the neighborhood included general proportions

West Main Street elevation

Two-story units in center of site Fred George

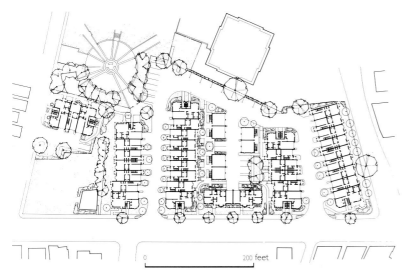

0   200 feet

Site plan

OWNER/DEVELOPER
Owner: Mutual Housing Assoc. of Southwest Connecticut
Developer: Stamford Neighborhood Housing Services

ARCHITECT
Perkins Eastman Architects PC

CONSULTANTS
Landscape Architect: Steve Wing
Development Consultant: Barbara Andrews

CONTRACTOR
The Frank Mercedes Jr. Constr. Group, Inc.

PROPERTY MANAGEMENT
Mont Enterprises/MHA of SW Connecticut

FUNDERS   **TYPE**
City of Stamford   Capital grant
Connecticut Dept. of Housing   Capital grant

DEVELOPMENT TYPE
New construction rental flats and townhouses.

RESIDENT PROFILE
Low- and moderate-income families, seniors, incomes
$7,000–54,000.

DENSITY
29 units/acre

DEVELOPMENT PROFILE

Type	N°/Units	Size (sf)	Rents
1 BD	19	670–800	$324
2 BD	33	890–1,240	$482
3 BR	17	1,400–1,500	$515
TOTAL	**69**		

Laundry: in each unit.
Courtyard/play: adjacent to public park
Parking: 76 surface and garage
Total site area: 102,366 sf (2.35 acres)

CONSTRUCTION TYPE
Two- and three-story wood frame, horiz. siding,
comp. shingle roofs.

COSTS
Land Cost: $4.7m; Constr. Costs: $4.98m; Other Costs:
$1,400,000; **Total Development Cost: $11.1m
($160,869/unit).** (Completed December 1991)

and the use of gabled forms, as well as colors, street lighting fixtures and low, ornamental fences. New products included thermal windows to save energy and a composite wood siding that looks like wood when painted but is more durable and economical. These design decisions involved all those with a stake in the end product, but particularly the residents whose identification with the buildings was needed to foster pride and reduce maintenance. The sense of value derived from their physical surroundings fulfilled a major goal of encouraging leadership abilities and helped to make the residents more productive members of the society at large.

Parkside Gables was constructed at a time when buildings costs were very competitive. Although the land costs were high, Peter Wood noted, "The job was well managed by the architects, the contractor, and the state agency monitor; it was delivered essentially on-time and on-budget with few significant problems." The use of direct grants from the state and the city allowed the housing to be affordable to residents with low to moderate incomes, and was a very efficient use of public funds in relation to operating subsidies. Although the City was very supportive of the development process, Robin Stein, Planning and Zoning Director recalls, "I don't remember a project that had to go through so many board approvals." In the end, all the effort was worthwhile. Stein noted, "Parkside Gables set a high standard —in the future we will view affordable housing very favorably."

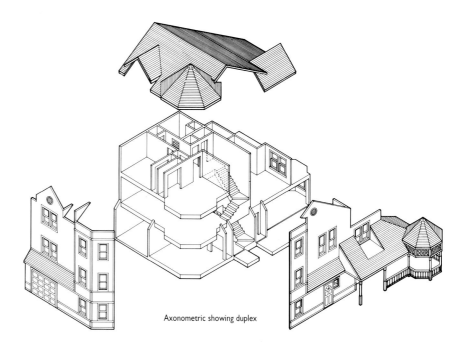

Axonometric showing duplex

Two-story units in center of site Fred George

Mews at western edge of site Fred George

SECTION HOUSE TYPE 'A

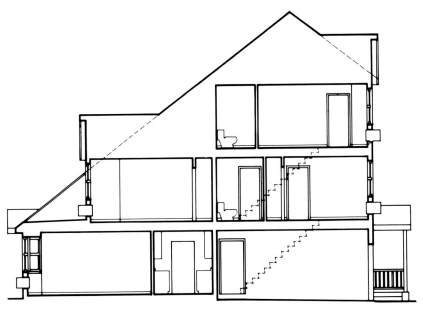

SECTION HOUSE TYPE B

Gazebo and community room/office corner Fred George

View from southwest corner showing 1970s public housing in rear Fred George

Catherine Street Albany, New York

The Catherine Street development is located in the South End/Grosbeckville Historic District of Albany, which is composed of modest two- and three-story brick or woodframe row houses built primarily between 1830 and 1870 for the city's working class. The Capitol Hill Improvement Corporation, a local, non-profit community design center with experience in design and housing counseling, conducted a detailed survey of prospective buyers' housing preferences: amenities, style, and unit size; and financial capacity: income, savings, and debt. The final program used this survey data as well as extensive discussions with neighborhood residents.

Of the 250 people surveyed, the majority indicated a preference for a three-bedroom home for one or two families with traditional styling, gas heat, a private yard, masonry construction, fenced yards, front porches, bay windows, and decks. Most prospective buyers' needs were met by a row house with a two-story duplex or maisonette owner's unit over a garden level two-bedroom flat. This dwelling type fits in well with the surrounding historic housing. The location of the housing in an historic district required detailed review by the Albany historic sites commission and by the state historic preservation officer. This review limited acceptable siding materials to painted wood or brick masonry and required the solution to respond to the rhythm, proportions, and details of existing buildings.

Community participation was very important in shaping this development. But the confrontational style and mistrust in public dialogues made the community process challenging. Local residents' skepticism about government-initiated new construction in the area was reflected in their motto, "South End against the world". Neighborhood oversight extended to daily inspection of the construction site. Major savings in the cost of construction were achieved by the developer, who served as construction manager and hired small, local sub-contractors. Although this strategy met community objectives of employing local residents and members of minority groups, the use of numerous subcontractors and limited professional services also complicated supervision and the interaction between trades, and has resulted in several construction defects.

Despite the success of the Catherine Street housing and subsequent new construction in the neighborhood, many conditions in the community have declined. In the view of architect Kathleen Dorgan, "This development points out again how important it is to have strong continuing redevelopment in the neighborhood. There needs to be an integrated local policy for addressing the continuing needs of the community."

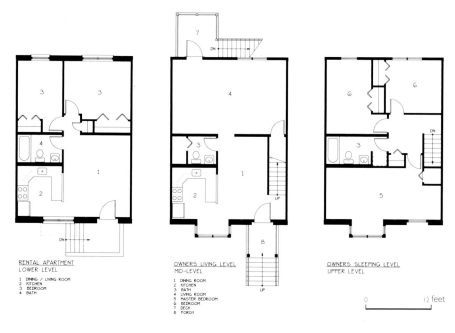

RENTAL APARTMENT
LOWER LEVEL

1 DINING / LIVING ROOM
2 KITCHEN
3 BEDROOM
4 BATH

OWNERS LIVING LEVEL
MID-LEVEL

1 DINING ROOM
2 KITCHEN
3 BATH
4 LIVING ROOM
5 MASTER BEDROOM
6 BEDROOM
7 DECK
8 PORCH

OWNERS SLEEPING LEVEL
UPPER LEVEL

0   12 feet

Typical floor plan Dan Langer

South side entrance with owner's decorations Robert Kerr

SPONSOR/DEVELOPER
Sponsor: City of Albany, Dept. of Econ. Development
Developer: Vulcan Affordable Hsg Corp.
Community Consultants: Capitol Hill Improvement Corp.
  United Tenants of Albany

ARCHITECT
Langer, Dion Associates Architects P.C., in assoc.
  with David Sadowski, P.C.
Dorgan Architecture and Planning

CONTRACTOR
Vulcan Affordable Hsg Corp.

FUNDERS	TYPE
N.Y. State Affordable Hsg Corp.	Loan
Norstar Bank of Upstate NY	Loan
Key Bank of New York	Loan
Pioneer Savings Bank	Loan
City of Albany & County	Land

DEVELOPMENT TYPE
New construction, two-family for-sale townhouses
with rental flats.

RESIDENT PROFILE
Owners: Low- to moderate-income families,
incomes $12,700–37,000.
Tenants: Very-low-income.

DENSITY
37 units/acre

DEVELOPMENT PROFILE
Type	N°/Units	Size (sf)	Sale Prices
2 BR	65	600	$95,000–97,000
3 BR	65	1,200	$95,000–97,000
TOTAL	130		

Laundry: in each unit
Courtyard/play: private yards
Parking: 93 on-street
Total site area: 15,246 sf (3.5 acres)

CONSTRUCTION TYPE
Basement and first floor concrete block, second floor
woodframing, with brick facing or horiz. siding, flat roofs.

COSTS
Land Cost: $0; **Total Development Cost: $6,240,000
($48,000/unit).** (Completed 1990)

North side of Catherine Street row Robert Kerr

Mutual Housing Association Brooklyn, New York

In 1985, local residents acting with the Association of Community Organizations for Reform Now (ACORN) occupied 25 vacant, city-owned buildings in the East New York section of Brooklyn causing a political uproar. Two years later, the Pratt Institute Center for Community and Environmental Development (PICCED) and the Consumer Farmer Foundation (now the Meyer Parodneck Foundation) negotiated a deal. The squatters agreed not to take over any more buildings and to become "homesteaders" and members of a new entity, the Mutual Housing Association of New York (MHANY). This gave them a legal status that allowed the City to grant them title to their apartments and to allocate $2.7 million of a revolving loan fund to finance rehabilitation work and to pay for technical assistance.

This was the first test in New York City of mutual housing, a much-discussed low-income housing development in which a city would give a neighborhood collective of homesteaders money and technical assistance to rehabilitate buildings for their own use in return for restrictions on their resale rights. When a family decides to move, MHANY has the first option to buy the unit for resale to a member on the waiting list and can restrict the sale price, thereby maintaining long-term affordability. MHANY membership is open to any New York City resident whose family income is less than 80 per cent of the area median income and who is not a city property owner.

In the 10 years since the original protest squat, the program has evolved. In the beginning the rehabilitation tasks were divided between the homesteaders and the contractors. However, the slow pace of these early projects and the growing list of new applicants forced a shift to the use of contractors for everything but painting of the interiors. Today, although architects from the Pratt Architectural and Planning Collaborative develop plans and supervise the construction, MHANY members still must do at least 40 hours work either painting or cleaning out rear yards to qualify for an apartment. Homeowners also select the colors and patterns for the bath tile, countertops, and kitchen flooring.

The buildings in the MHANY program range in size from single-family houses to nine-unit buildings and are now located in three other Brooklyn neighborhoods. The program validates the use of the older building stock, which permits a density that could not be re-created in new construction. Some of these large units have enough space for small business activities such as tailoring, bicycle repair, or catering.

In cities like New York, which have a great number of vacant buildings and an even greater number of people waiting for public housing, this is a very attractive type of program. It is a grass-roots effort to repair the physical and social fabric of a damaged neighborhood using existing housing stock, sweat-equity, and a local workforce. E. Perry Winston, senior architect of the Pratt Collaborative and project manager for MHANY from 1990 to 1995, called the program, "One of the best I have worked on from the point of view of long-term affordability, size of units, quality of materials, opportunity of resident participation, involvement of small local contractors, pace of production, and cumulative impact on the physical environment."

301 Bradford Street 'before' Perry Winston

301 Bradford Street 'after' Perry Winston

271 Milford Street, two d.u. with duplex on top floors Perry Winston

459 and 462 Wyona Street (left and right of the red building) Perry Winston

OWNER/DEVELOPER
Mutual Housing Assoc. of N.Y.

ARCHITECT
Pratt Planning and Architectural Collaborative

CONTRACTORS
Clermont G.C.; Cracovia G.C.; H & V Allen Constr.;
Penn Constr.; The Loranco Corp.; Strategic Constr.;
Strathaim Construction.

FUNDERS	TYPE
The Meyer Parodneck Foundation	Servicing agent
ACORN	Admin. budget
NYC Dept. of Hsg, Preserv.	
& Dev. (HPD)	Loan/land
N.Y. Landmarks Conservancy	Loan
HUD	HOME grant
Chemical Bank	Recoverable loans
East New York Savings Bank	Recoverable loans
Bank of N.Y.	Recoverable loans

DEVELOPMENT TYPE
Rehabilitation, scattered-site, co-operative,
attached townhouses.

RESIDENT PROFILE
Low-income families with max. income $28,500
for family of 4.

DENSITY
Average 54 units/acre

DEVELOPMENT PROFILE

Type	N°/Units	Size (sf)	Rents
Studio	9	350–400	$325
1 BR	31	510–650	$375
2 BR	105	640–750	$425
3 BR	108	760–900	$475
4BR	54	930–1,100	$525
5 BR	10	1,100–1,600	$575
6 BR	1	1,800	$575
TOTAL	318		

Parking: 0 on street
Laundry: in cellar
Courtyard: two playlots, private rear yards
Retail: one storefront

CONSTRUCTION TYPE
Two-, three-, and four-story brick exterior walls, wood and
steel framing.

COSTS
Land Cost: $1/lot; Constr. Costs: $24,021,227
(ave. $74,600/unit); Other Costs: $5,765,094
(ave. $17,504/unit); **Total Development Cost:**
$29,786,321 (ave. $92,504/unit). Ongoing program.

Melrose Court Bronx, New York

Most people associate the South Bronx with crime, bombed-out buildings, and despair. This image is being transformed by the hard work and vision of architect Marvin H. Meltzer and Procida Organization (among many others) into one of resettlement, reinvestment, and hope. Melrose Court is the first mixed-income homeownership housing to be developed in the area of Melrose Commons. The Melrose Commons plan includes the revitalization of 200 square blocks with approximately 2,000 units of housing.

Community input during the master-planning process generated guidelines that helped shape Melrose Court, three blocks of three- to four-story buildings surrounding secure courtyards at a density of 60 units per acre. Parking spaces located on demapped streets between the housing blocks are controlled by an owner-operated, locking metal bar secured to the pavement. The courtyards, which have become a focal point of activity for the residents, are friendly places to congregate with their stoops, colorful canopies, and attractive light fixtures.

Most apartments have individual entries from the courts; others are entered from the street. No entry is more than one-and-a-half flights up. The appearance from the courtyards is of individual townhouses. All apartments are two- and three-bedroom townhouses over flats with the bedrooms facing the street and the living rooms overlooking the courtyard for security.

According to Marvin Meltzer the flat street facades are in deliberate contrast to the vibrant scale and texture of the courtyards. Some of the older character of the Bronx has been lost in recent years due to extensive demolition and it is very difficult, given today's budgets, to create a new character to match what has been lost. This is especially true when building for first-time homebuyers, since fewer funding sources are available to help subsidize homeownership as compared to rental housing. Creating interior courtyards provides a level of security and privacy not typical of the area. Resident Sarah Morales, a 37-year-old, working mother of two boys, who moved here from poorly managed public housing and feels much safer at Melrose Court, said, "The people here are all working people who have a stake in the community."

The fact that banks such as Chemical Bank and European American Bank have reconsidered their lending criteria to support reinvestment in this community is an inspiring example of new thinking in a traditionally conservative sector. The long-term contribution that the entire Melrose Court development team has made to revive a community suffering from three decades of disinvestment has both physical and social rewards. The new families at Melrose Court have added almost 1,000 new people to a neighborhood known as a place to leave. The reduction in crime and blight is attracting still more community development.

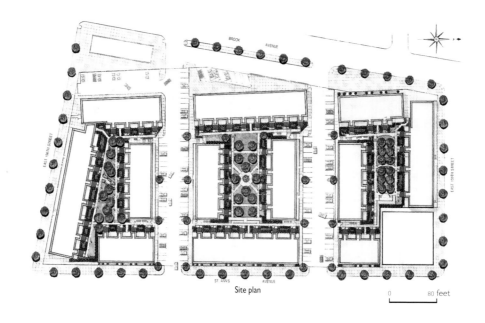

Site plan

0   80 feet

Entry to units Michael Moran

Facade, 158th to 159th Street Paul Warchol

OWNER/DEVELOPER
Procida Construction Corp.

ARCHITECT
Marvin H. Meltzer Architects, P.C.

CONSULTANTS
Landscape Architect: Mark Morrison Assoc.,

CONTRACTOR
The Procida Organization

PROPERTY MANAGEMENT
Classic Realty Corp.

FUNDERS	TYPE
Chemical Community Development Corp.	Loan
N.Y. City Housing Partnership	Subsidy
Office of Bronx Boro. President	Subsidy
N.Y. City Hsg Preservation and Devel.	Subsidy
Affordable Housing Corp., State of N.Y.	Subsidy

DEVELOPMENT TYPE
New construction, for-sale stacked flats and townhouses.

RESIDENT PROFILE
Low- and moderate-income families, incomes $22,000–53,000.

DENSITY
60 units/acre

DEVELOPMENT PROFILE

Type	N°/Units	Size (sf)	Sale prices
2 BR	99	833	$51,227
3 BR	166	1,067	$72,256
TOTAL	265		

Laundry: in each unit
Courtyard/play: 3 courtyards, all secured.
Parking: 137 surface
Total site area: 4.3 acres

CONSTRUCTION TYPE
Three- and four-story masonry bearing walls and concrete plank floors.

COSTS:
Land Costs $131,500; Constr. Costs: $24,920,000; Other Costs: $2,983,400; **Total Development Cost: $28,034,900 ($105,800/unit).** (Completed Nov. 1993 (phase I), Nov. 1994 (phase II))

As more and more people have become homeless, communities like Yonkers have looked for ways to build quality affordable housing for them. Beginning in 1991, St Peter's Roman Catholic Church worked with CEPHAS Housing and The Housing Action Council to secure funds from New York State and Yonkers, and find a way to maximize use of the site. The former site of an old school building had been vacant for over 15 years when architect Duo Dickinson, working with the non-profit Board, designed an innovative building on its steep site to house formerly homeless families. Two-story townhouses over accessible flats are designed with gabled roofs and horizontal siding to fit in with turn-of-the-century homes along Stanley Avenue on the upper side. On the downhill Riverside Avenue edge, the building rises 6 stories to blend with St Peter's and adjacent apartment building. Despite its height, no families have to walk up or down more than two flights of stairs to their home. Most of the homes have two or three bedrooms for families with children, which is the fastest growing group of homeless people today.

This housing dealt creatively with several significant regulatory issues. A parking variance allowing no new parking spaces was granted because of the topography, the homeless population's low rate of automobile ownership, and the ability to share the church parking lot. Parking for units on the upper side is on the street; families with cars in the lower units park in the church lot. The building is in a Fire District, which required a two-hour-rated cladding of concrete siding and trim screwed to a heavy steel frame, both of which added significant costs to the budget. This situation did allow zero or minimal setbacks, helping to make the development more feasible. Dickinson notes, "The key to the success of this housing is the privacy of entry, the compatibility with existing massing patterns, and the "bottom-up" planning." In 1994 Cephas Housing won the Westchester AIA Community Design Award in recognition of its success.

Perspective from Stanley Avenue

Site section looking south

0   20 feet

View from Stanley Avenue showing individual entries off stairwell Mick Hales

Westerly view from Riverdale Avenue Mick Hales

OWNER/DEVELOPER
Owner: CEPHAS
Developer: Housing Action Council

ARCHITECT
Duo Dickinson

CONTRACTOR
Bedell Associates

PROPERTY MANAGEMENT
West Hab

FUNDERS
	TYPE
City of Yonkers	Grant
N.Y. State Homeless Hsg Assist. Program	Grant

DEVELOPMENT TYPE
New construction rental stacked flats.

RESIDENT PROFILE
Section 8 eligible/formerly homeless families, usually single parent with children.

DENSITY
65 units/acre

DEVELOPMENT PROFILE
Type	N°/Units	Size (sf)	Rents
2 BR	4	800	$500
3 BR	10	950	$700
4 BR	1	1100	$800
TOTAL	**15**		

Courtyard/play: back and front yard paved areas
Parking: 15 surface, off-site
Total site area: 10,000 sf (.23 acres)

CONSTRUCTION TYPE
Six-story, heavy-gauge steel construction with cast concrete siding.

COSTS
Land Cost: $70,000; Constr. Costs: $1,700,000; Other Costs: $150,000 ; **Total Development Cost: $1,850,000; ($123,333/unit).** (Completed 1993)

Roxbury Corners stands on two parcels of land in the Lower Roxbury section of Boston's South End historic district. The westerly parcel has a new structure of four-and-a-half stories; two rehabilitated buildings and a new four-story addition stand on the other parcel. Surrounding buildings are multi-family, low-income housing projects in high- or low-rise blocks that date from the last 25 years and 19th century brick row houses with front stoops and mansard roofs. At 65 dwelling-units per acre, Roxbury Corners is less dense that many of the nearby buildings.

Roxbury Corners was part of the South End Housing Initiative, the goal of which was to develop good, multi-family, affordable housing with some form of homeownership within the context of an overheated real estate market that excluded many people with low incomes. Community groups participated extensively in a series of community meetings and voiced their concerns about architectural design, security, parking, and site planning. The United South End/Lower Roxbury Development Corporation (UDC) was created in 1979 to participate in a wide range of business and real estate development activities that create employment and housing opportunities for people with low and moderate incomes and people of color. Prior to the construction of Roxbury Corners, this section of Lower Roxbury was abandoned. Now, almost 6,000 square feet of commercial space is leased to businesses that provide goods and services previously unavailable in this part of the neighborhood.

According to Syvalia "Val" Hyman III, President and CEO of UDC, Roxbury Corners has had a significant positive impact both physically and socially on the neighborhood. Mr Hyman recommended that affordable housing should always be designed from the beginning, "with the highest quality products and amenities. It is virtually impossible to significantly upgrade already specified products and amenities in a development, even when funding is available."

The development had to undergo review by the Landmarks Commission in respect to setbacks, height, materials, and architectural detailing—all of which had a major effect on the design. Because so many agencies, as well as the non-profit developer and the development consultants, had the right to review the design, the process was quite lengthy. According to architect Fernando J. Domenech, "It was a great challenge to design buildings that met the desires and expectations of many groups with very different agendas. Also, affordable housing developers do not have a real project until their financing is in place, and then they must move quickly to obtain occupancy in time to meet their tax credit deadline. Given the complexity of this development, preparation of construction documents under those constraints was very difficult."

Daniel DeSantis, a neighbor, stated in a recent interview, "Over the past few years, I have had the opportunity to mix with the residents of Roxbury Corners over crime issues in the neighborhood. Boston's South End is an ethnically and economically diverse community so the people at Roxbury Corners are not significantly different. Someone's income should not be a concern to neighbors. I think it is very important for affordable housing to blend in with the surrounding structures so that residents feel they live in a place as good as everyone else's. Roxbury Corners achieves this very successfully."

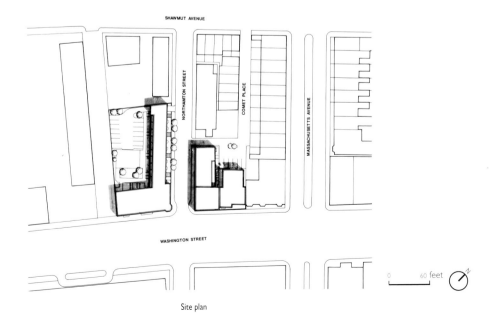

Site plan

View of common courtyard at parcel 29-A (south side of Northampton) Ralph Hutchins

Stoops and townhouse entrances along Northampton Street Ralph Hutchins

SPONSOR
United South End/Lower Roxbury Dev. Corp. [UDC]

ARCHITECT
Domenech Hicks Krockmalnic

CONSULTANTS
Landscape Architect: Halvorson Company
Development Consultant: The Community Builders

CONTRACTOR
Peabody Construction

PROPERTY MANAGEMENT
The Community Builders

FUNDERS

	TYPE
Boston Redevelopment Authority	Loans/grants
City of Boston Neighborhood Hsg Trust	Linkage loan
Massachusetts Housing Finance Agency	First mortgage
Hsg Innovations Fund Prog. (HIF)	Loan
EOCD/ Retail Dev. Action Loan	Loan
Low Income Housing Tax Credits bought by NYNEX, Boston Bank of Commerce, State St. Bank and Trust Co.	Equity

DEVELOPMENT TYPE
New constr. and rehab. limited-equity for-sale flats and townhouses.

RESIDENT PROFILE
Families: 63% low-, 17% mod.-income, and 20% market-rate.

DENSITY
65 units/acre

DEVELOPMENT PROFILE

Type	N°/Units	Size (sf)	Rents
Studio	2	368–410	$390
1 BR	5	562–650	$600
2 BR	25	860–1,070	$747–850
3 BR	19	1,126–1,425	$845–1,096
4BR	3	1,490–1,615	$1,096
TOTAL	54		

Community: 850 includes office
Parking: 19 surface
Retail: 5,000 sf
Total site area: 36,224 sf (.83 acres)

CONSTRUCTION TYPE
Two buildings; four-story steel frame with brick and precast block and plank.

COSTS
Land Cost: $350,000; Constr. Costs: $7,020,832; Other Costs: $2,020,773; **Total Development Cost: $11,602,227 ($190,200/unit).** (Completed May 1991)

Charlestown Navy Yard Rowhouses Boston, Massachusetts **67 units/acre**

In responding to the historical 19th century buildings of a former navy yard, the Charlestown Navy Yard Rowhouses complement the attractive and expensive residential properties of the surrounding community, making possible the residents' continuing pride in their neighborhood. Moreover, since the Rowhouses is not easily identifiable as housing for families with lower incomes, their residents are not stigmatized as second-class citizens. Just a block away, similar market-rate townhouses have sold for over $500,000.

William Rawn, architect of the Rowhouses, has described the goals of the housing as follows: "The fundamental goal was to provide housing units that, in terms of function, addressed the family housing needs of first time home buyers. The fundamental goal of our client, the Bricklayers Non-Profit Development Corporation, was to fulfill the community's need for affordable housing and, in doing so, to illustrate the civic role of unions and to demonstrate the affordability of construction provided by unions. A third goal, realized in the course of design and construction, was to make this development a model for union-sponsored affordable housing."

Developer Tom McIntyre is proud of the fact that since it was partly financed by the Union's pension fund, the housing used less public funds than other affordable housing. The special brick detailing along the main facade is the mark of

skilled tradespeople from the Union. The building's L-shaped plan makes easy surveillance of the interior court and backyard possible. The stacked townhouse units running through the building from front to back have private yards at ground level and open decks on the upper floor. This allows their occupants to oversee both the street and the interior court. Forty-seven of the 50 units have views of the harbor.

In respect to urban design, one of the achievements of this development is to create continuity both with the simplicity and solidity of the older industrial buildings on First Avenue and the long linear forms of the Charleston Navy Yard buildings that run perpendicular to the waterfront. The tall, gabled front of Building One establishes an appropriate scale for a building located on First Avenue. The six-unit tower building on the waterfront end of the Rowhouses is slightly canted to make it perpendicular to the boardwalk, a major public amenity of the waterfront area. If location is paramount for affordable housing, the Rowhouses have a virtual guarantee of success. In about 20 minutes, residents can reach the central business district via an inexpensive water shuttle or by walking across a bridge from the Navy Yard.

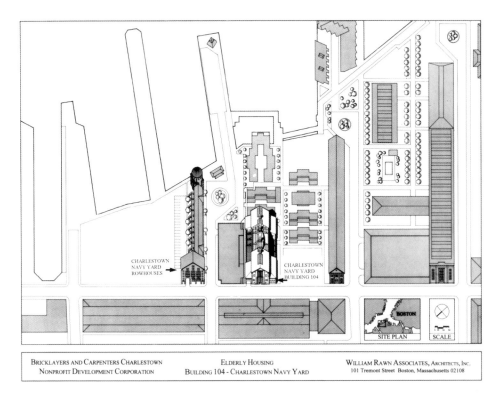

BRICKLAYERS AND CARPENTERS CHARLESTOWN
NONPROFIT DEVELOPMENT CORPORATION

ELDERLY HOUSING
BUILDING 104 - CHARLESTOWN NAVY YARD

WILLIAM RAWN ASSOCIATES, ARCHITECTS, INC.
101 Tremont Street Boston, Massachusetts 02108

Site plan axonometric

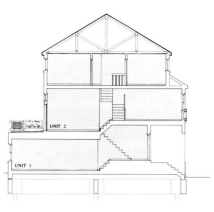

Building length, through window Steve Rosenthal

Typical Rowhouse section/elevation

UNIT 2

UNIT 1

OWNER / DEVELOPER
Bricklayers and Laborers Non-profit Housing Corp.

ARCHITECT
William Rawn Associates

LANDSCAPE ARCHITECT
Michael Van Valkenburgh

CONTRACTOR
Mirabassi Associates

FUNDERS	TYPE
Bricklayers and Laborers Pension Fund	Development support
City of Boston Linkage Program Funds	Subsidy
Private Bank	Loan

DEVELOPMENT TYPE
New construction for-sale stacked townhouses.

RESIDENT PROFILE
Low- and moderate-income families, incomes
$22,000–34,000, at or below 80% of AMI.

DENSITY
67 units/acre

DEVELOPMENT PROFILE

Type	N°/Units	Size (sf)	Sale Prices
1 BR	29	750	$67,500–87,500
2 BR	13	1150–1300	$77,500–100,000
3 BR	6	1350	$87,500–102,500
4 BR	2	1560	$95,000–102,500
TOTAL	50		

Parking: 50 surface
Outdoor space: private yards, one deck/pair of units.
Courtyard/play: boardwalk, tot-lot
Total site area: 32,670 sf (.75 acre)

CONSTRUCTION TYPE
Three- and four-story brick, metal and comp. shingle roofs.

COSTS
Land Cost: $1.00 for 99 years; Constr. Costs: $5,444,175;
Other Costs: $789,466; **Total Development Cost: $6,233,641.**
(Completed October 1988)

Interior: kitchen area Steve Rosenthal

Tower from the water Steve Rosenthal

CHARLESTOWN NAVY YARD ROWHOUSES 195

Ninth Square Redevelopment New Haven, Connecticut

The name "Ninth Square" was given to one of the original nine squares of New Haven's town plot, which was laid out in 1638. It was the last of the city's original squares to be redeveloped, and, as a result, many of its historic buildings were vacant or underutilized. In the early 1980s, the City of New Haven began the process of nominating the area to the National Register of Historic Places. The city's goal was to facilitate private investment in the Ninth Square's historically significant architecture. At the same time, a group of outside investors, planners and preservationists approached the city with an ambitious plan for redevelopment.

Inspired by the energy of the outside group, city staff and citizens came together to plan a revitalized safe, attractive, well-managed, urban district where a diversity of people live, work, shop and play. Creation of a district improvement association known as the Ninth Square Association (NSA) comprising property owners and tenants grew out of these early planning efforts. However, by 1985 it became clear that the original development group would not succeed. The NSA, the City, and other downtown interests sought a replacement developer and, in 1986, chose McCormack Baron and Associates, Inc. (MBA) of St Louis, Missouri, a firm that specializes in urban affordable housing. Together with its partner, the Related Companies, MBA steered Ninth Square through the downturn in New England's economy and on to completion in the spring of 1995.

The first 24 apartments on Orange Street opened in early 1994; they were followed by 311 more apartments which opened later in 1994 and early 1995. In the first phase over 500 residents will live within walking distance of all that downtown has to offer, including Yale University. Newly paved streets, new trees, sidewalks, and historic lighting standards create a safe and attractive place. Local merchants hope that the shopping and night life will attract students, workers and visitors. Low-income housing tax credits helped finance the development and provided the guarantee that more than half of the apartments would be affordable to such households. If the neighborhood continues to revitalize, the financing restrictions will keep those units affordable for households with modest means.

Richard Baron, President of MBA noted, "We received considerable and necessary support from the local community for Ninth Square over the years, although many doubted we would succeed when the economy went into a tailspin. We simply refused to give up and kept on pushing." Resident and Ninth Square Association board member Bill Sherr enthused, "This neighborhood has fantastic potential. I hope this is the start of a lot more building and development in the area."

Master Planners Herbert S. Newman and Partners saw restoration of the historic architecture as key. Upper floors of existing structures have been converted to apartments and ground floor spaces readied for retail. Voids along the street were filled with new mixed-use buildings and two parking garages—all detailed to match the character of the historic structures. Rear lots have been cleared to create landscaped courtyards within the blocks. Stonehill House, the taller of the new apartment buildings, is an L-shaped structure with 7- and 9-story wings and an 11-story tower at the intersection of two of the main streets. In Ninth Square it is a neighborhood landmark and a symbol of the hard work and vision that is making downtown New Haven an affordable and exciting neighborhood.

Aerial view looking northwest

Interior Terence Falk

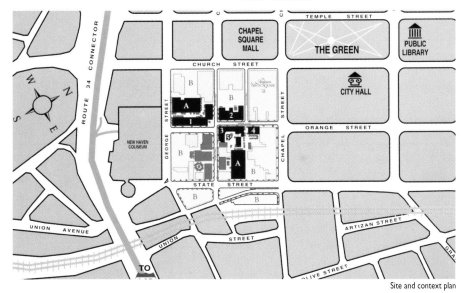

Site and context plan

Stonehill house, looking down Orange Street Terence Falk

OWNER/DEVELOPER
Ninth Square Project Limited Partnership; a joint venture of McCormack Baron & Associates, Inc., & The Related Companies, L.P.

ARCHITECT
Herbert S. Newman and Partners,
 P.C (Master planning and new construction)
Trivers Assoc. (Owners' representative)
Smith Edwards Architects (Historic rehabilitation)
Seelye, Stevenson, Value & Knecht (Public improvements)
Lev Zetlin Associates, Inc. (Garages)

LANDSCAPE ARCHITECT
Rolland/Towers

CONTRACTOR
The Fusco Corp. (new construction)
W.E. O'Neil Construction

MANAGEMENT
McCormack Baron & Associates, Inc.

FUNDERS	TYPE
Yale University	Loan
Connecticut Housing Finance Authority	Loan
City of New Haven	Loans/grants
State Depts. of Housing and Econ. Develop.	Loans/grants
HUD - Urban Development Action Grant	Loan
SunAmerica, Inc.	Equity

DEVELOPMENT TYPE
New construction, historic rehab., mixed-use, rental flats over retail/commercial, and garage.

RESIDENT PROFILE
Low- and moderate-income households (56% of units); market-rate.

DENSITY
84 units/acre

DEVELOPMENT	PROFILE		
Type	N°/Units	Size (sf)	Rents
Studio	25	434–560	$525–575
1 BR	149	632–724	$635–745
2 BR	161	856–1,054	$860–1,010
TOTAL	**335**		

Com'nty/laundry: W/D in each unit; rehabed historic stable
                    meeting room, kitchen & exercise facility.
Courtyard/play: three interior courtyards
Parking: 628 in garages; 300 surface spaces
Retail: 50,000 sf
Total site area: 4.2 acres, excluding surface parking area

CONSTRUCTION TYPE
Rehab: masonry and wood structures.
New: concrete, steel, masonry.

COSTS
Land Cost: $10.2m; Constr. Costs: $43.7m; Other Costs: $32.7m; **Total Development Cost: $86.6m.** (Construction complete June 1995; 85% leased)

Langham Court Boston, Massachusetts

The history of Langham Court began in 1986 when the Boston Redevelopment Authority called for proposals to develop vacant property that had contributed to the decline of the neighborhood for a long time. The location of the site in an historic neighborhood meant that the architecture of the housing had to respond to a context mainly composed of tall, brick townhouses with bay windows and fine detail. The program called for 84 units of mixed-income housing in a configuration and design compatible with the neighborhood's historic character; parking was to be below grade.

The developer chosen for the housing was the non-profit Four Corners Development Corporation, a group of South End housing advocates which had incorporated itself specifically to develop Langham Court as a limited equity co-operative, and to demonstrate that excellence in design and affordable housing were not mutually exclusive. The firm selected to design the development, Goody, Clancy & Associates, had a history of work in mixed-income housing going back to the late 1960s. John Clancy, the project designer, noted that the inclusion of market-rate units, "makes the standards higher for the affordable housing." The owner's and the architect's commitment to designing the best living environment possible for all residents extended to uniform detailing so that market-rate units would not differ from the subsidized units, which are distributed randomly within the complex. The mix of one-third heavily subsidized, one-third partly subsidized, and one-third market-rate reflects the neighborhood demography, which has adjacent zones of affluence and poverty.

Langham Court has three street frontages: one, Shawmut Avenue, is a major east–west thoroughfare; it is wide, with heavy traffic and taller buildings often at the street intersections. The other two, more narrow streets, Worcester and West Springfield, are lined mainly with four-story townhouses. These buildings have raised stoops leading to primary entrances and facades that feature bay, bow, and oriel windows, and mansard and pitched slate roofs with a variety of dormers. Although the new buildings could not copy these now luxurious features, the architects successfully interpreted them within their limited budget using economical building materials, methods, and systems. The Shawmut Avenue frontage is a five-story block with the corners accentuated at street intersections while the frontages on Worcester and West Springfield Streets are designed as four-story townhouses. The design generally reflects the massing and character of the surrounding neighborhood in the use of: dormers, oriels, and bay windows; arched and vaulted entryways; a combination of mansard and flat roofs, string courses and textured brickwork; and a palette of materials that includes multi-colored brick, granite, precast concrete, enameled aluminum, and glazed ceramic tile.

The 84 dwelling units are distributed in the four-story townhouses and the five-story apartment building with elevators. The units range in size from studios to three-bedroom townhouses. The larger townhouse units have front entries from the street. The rear entries lead to small private outdoor areas and the common courtyard beyond. These units are reserved for families with children. Studios, one-bedroom units, and some two-bedroom apartments are located in the five-story Shawmut Avenue portion of the development, which is served by elevators. All apartments in the elevator building and all ground-floor duplex townhouse units are accessible to people confined to wheelchairs, or with other disabilities. Public open space and its location was a lively community issue. Some of the neighbors favored a park on the street rather than an interior courtyard. However, the architects persuasively pointed out that the park would be difficult to maintain and thereby would not serve to improve the neighborhood.

Overview of city with Langham Court Goody Clancy & Associates

Entry arch at West Springfield Street Steve Rosenthal

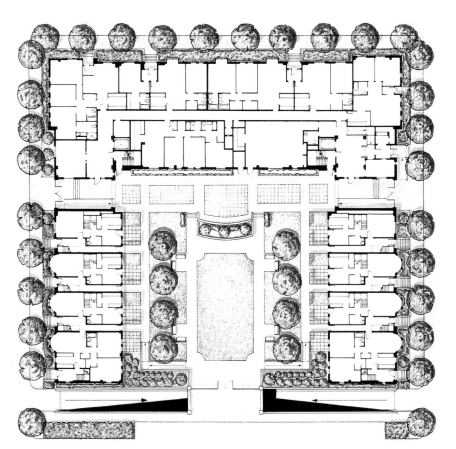

Site plan/unit plans

0   25 feet

SPONSOR
Four Corners Development Corporation

ARCHITECT
Goody Clancy and Associates

CONSULTANTS
Development Consultant: Community Builders
Landscape Architecture: The Halvorson Company

CONTRACTOR
Dimeo Construction Company

MANAGEMENT
Four Corners Development Corporation

FUNDERS	TYPE
Massachusetts Housing Finance Agency	Loan
City of Boston Linkage	Grant
Commonwealth of Massachusetts	Loan
Langham Court Co-operative Corp.	Loan

RESIDENT PROFILE
Mixed-income, families and singles with incomes ranging
from very low to median (market-rate)

DEVELOPMENT TYPE
New construction mixed-income rental elevator-served
midrise and stacked townhouses over parking

DENSITY
81.5 units/acre

DEVELOPMENT PROFILE

Type	Nº/Units	Size (sf)	Rent
Studios	15	300	$422–$503
1 BR	29	630	$492–$803
2 BR	27	840	$595–$1,029
3 BR	13	1,150	$752–$887
TOTAL	84	87,589	

Court: 8,800 sf
Community: 1,253 sf
Parking: 54 spaces, 23,060 sf
Total site area: 45,000 sf (1.03 acres)

CONSTRUCTION TYPE
Four-five stories brick veneer over steel frame on
concrete podium

COSTS
Constr. Costs: $11,098,555 ($99/sf); Other Costs:
$5,869,196; **Total Development Cost: $16,967,751
($201,997/unit).** (Completed September 1991)

The resulting south-facing, central courtyard provides a sunlit, landscaped retreat for all residents, including the senior residents of adjacent Washington Manor. Two-story vaulted entranceways from both Worcester and West Springfield Streets admit the immediate neighbors into the building's community. The courtyard provides both semi-private rear terraces for first floor units and larger public landscaped terraces, seating areas, and lawns.

The architects report "tremendous co-operation" from community organizations that cared deeply about the process. The Boston Redevelopment Authority was also supportive of the development, which was part of the City's South End Neighborhood Housing Initiative. Because Langham Court is located in the South End Landmarks District, the Boston Landmarks Commission was importantly involved in design review.

From the perspective of the resident property manager, Mary Manuel, Langham Court has succeeded in contributing positively to the neighborhood. "Architecturally, the building feels as if it was always here," she said. She also commented that, "The co-op is a good concept; people are encouraged to actively participate in events and to get to know their neighbors and meet each other in places such as the lobby and the courtyard. People have a stake in their property and an incentive to maintain the property." In 1993 the architects and the owner jointly received the coveted Honor Award from the American Institute of Architects.

Corner view with tower at Shawmutt Avenue and Worcester Street Steve Rosenthal

Aerial view of courtyard Steve Rosenthal

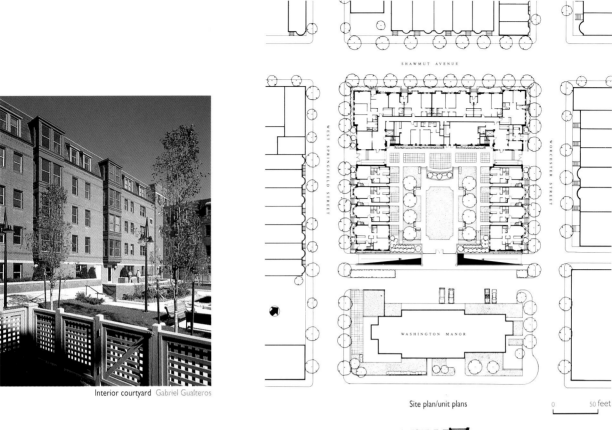

Interior courtyard Gabriel Gualteros

Site plan/unit plans

SHAWMUT AVENUE

WEST SPRINGFIELD STREET

WORCESTER STREET

WASHINGTON MANOR

0   50 feet

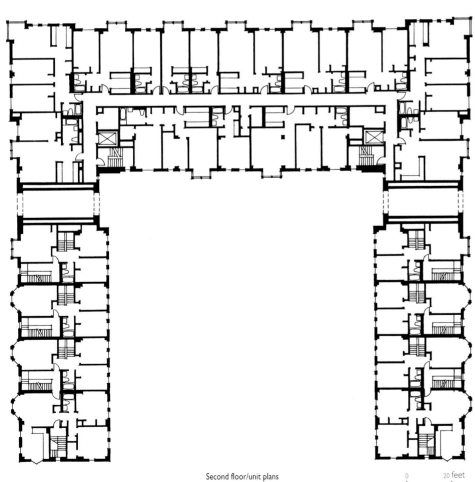

Second floor/unit plans

0   20 feet

Tent City Boston, Massachusetts

Formerly occupied by townhouses that were torn down for urban redevelopment in the 1960s, Tent City's 3-acre site remained vacant for about 20 years. Protesters resisting commercial development on the site organized a nonprofit housing development corporation, which eventually developed housing. The name "Tent City" recalls the tents that the housing advocates pitched on the vacant land. Located in Boston's South End Historic District, Tent City is next to Copley Place, a huge redevelopment project, and serves as a transition area between the high-density housing of Copley Place and the South End, which has three-and-a-half- to four-story townhouses. The density of Tent City is similar to that of the South End on two-thirds of the site and increases to 12 stories in the area next to Copley Place. Overall the density is 81.5 units per acre with 212 parking spaces per acre below grade. The parking was developed by the Copley Place developers and serves both projects.

The units are a mix of 25 per cent low-income, 50 per cent moderate-income, and 25 per cent market-rate housing. According to architect John Clancy, the absence of any distinction between the market-rate units and other types has been successful partly because the location is very desirable. Clancy emphasized that location is very important to the success of housing for low-income people and added that the provision of amenities for the wider community facilitated the integration of Tent City into the older social

fabric. The three- and four-bedroom units are in four-story townhouses, or two stacked two-story units. All have individual entries and stoops on the street, rear exits onto private patios, and access to the shared courts beyond. The one- and two-bedroom units are in midrise buildings with elevators and have laundries and lounges as well as access to the shared amenities. On Copley Place the facade is relieved by a sweeping curve, the result of the shape of the subway tunnel below. The historic district's guidelines influence the design, but, according to John Clancy, the level of detail required was less than if the site was in the heart of the SEHD.

Ken Kruckemeyer of the Tent City Development Corporation, a neighbor of the site, first got involved in the effort to build housing in 1974 when the Boston Redevelopment Agency planned to build a high-rise tower with an above-grade parking structure and only 10 per cent subsidized housing. In a recent interview he commented, "It is hard to make a block-sized new development seamless with an existing Victorian neighborhood. There remains some stereotyping by people on both sides. The important success is that a very high quality, mixed-income development has been created in the midst of an existing but gentrifying neighborhood. A strong stand to preserve the mix of income and races has been made, and it helps create a level of trust and tolerance among all."

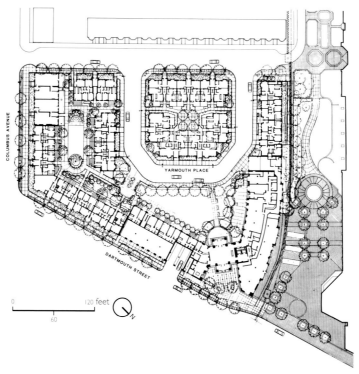

Site plan Goody, Clancy and Associates

Townhouse entry Steve Rosenthal

Rear court Steve Rosenthal

Columbus Avenue townhouses Steve Rosenthal

DEVELOPER
Tent City Corporation

ARCHITECT
Goody Clancy & Assoc., Inc. Architects

CONSULTANTS
Landscape Architect: The Halvorson Co.
Development Consultant: The Community Builders

CONTRACTOR
Turner Construction

PROPERTY MANAGEMENT
The Community Builders

FUNDERS	**TYPE**
Boston Redevelopment Authority	Grant
Mass. Hsg Finance Agency	Loan
Commonwealth of Mass., Executive Office of Communities and Development	Equity
Low Income Housing Tax Credits	Equity

DEVELOPMENT TYPE
New construction three- and four-story rental attached townhouses, 6–12 story stacked flats with elevator.

RESIDENT PROFILE
Families, seniors, singles: 25% low-, 50% moderate-income and 25% market-rate.

DENSITY
89 units/acre

DEVELOPMENT PROFILE

Type	N°/Units	Size (sf)	Rents
Studio	1	580	na
1 BR	93	600–650	$217–850
2 BR	92	825–850	$215–1,200
3 BR	66	1,130–1,200	$360–1,600
4 BR	17	1,450–1,525	$405–1,850
TOTAL	269		

Community/laundry: daycare for 50 kids; shared laundry
Courtyard/play: yes
Parking: 212 underground garage
Retail: 4 shops
Total site area: 3 acres

CONSTRUCTION TYPE
Brick veneer on steel frame, over 2-story underground parking or concrete piles.

COSTS
Land Cost: $0; Constr. Costs: $29,409,000; Other Costs: $6,573,000; **Total Development Cost: $35,982,000 ($110/sf).** (Completed 1988 (phase I), 1991 (phase II))

Brian Clements

CHAPTER ELEVEN:
THE SOUTH

Four developments in the southern region were selected for review as two- and four-page case studies:

Orchard Village and Oak Hill, Chattanooga, Tennessee
Charleston Infill Housing, Charleston, South Carolina
Randolph Neighborhood, Richmond, Virginia
Timberlawn Crescent, Bethesda, Maryland

Orchard Village and Oak Hill Chattanooga, Tennessee

Orchard Village and Oak Hill were the Chattanooga Neighborhood Enterprise's first attempts to develop infill housing for the revitalizing of a south Chattanooga district. Both developments were built on vacant parcels that had been problem spots. The smaller development, Oak Hill, has 10 single family houses built in 1992. Orchard Village, completed in 1991, occupies an 8.6-acre tract. All of the homes in both developments have sold.

The process of planning Orchard Village included input from the local urban design center and multiple branches of city government. Stroud Watson of the design center provided guidance in establishing a development plan emphasizing streets scaled for pedestrian comfort. The project architect, Brian Clements, developed building designs appropriate for narrow but deep lots with a front porch as the primary design element. Continuity in the design is provided by the steep but uniform roof pitches and the detailing of the porch and trim elements. Carports are included in each design, but they are placed far behind the front of the house to diminish their presence.

During the design process the housing encountered opposition from members of the minority community who felt that affordable housing would be developed with a minimalist approach and would turn the area into a ghetto. "Hearing of this attitude gave us an opportunity to understand the design priorities of the community," Clements said, "and increased our concern for building and landscaping features, and for establishing a homeowners association. The homeowners association cares for common landscaped areas and participates in a neighborhood watch program sponsored by the police department."

The Oak Hill homes use the same principles as Orchard Village, but at a smaller scale. "We modeled the houses after Tennessee bungalows," Clements said, "and after studying porch forms common to Chattanooga, we developed four different porch configurations for a single plan." Clements believes the design success of Oak Hill and Orchard Village stems from the use of simple building types designed to enhance the streetscape. The revitalization of the neighborhoods is expected to continue in response to demand for new housing supported by neighborhood participation.

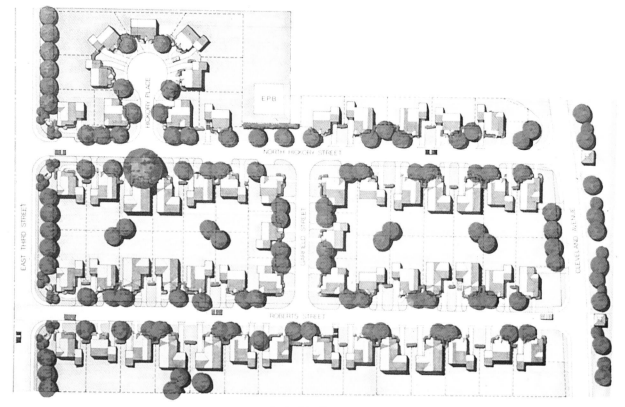

Site plan Brian Clements

The "Vintage": front elevation

The "Vintage": front elevation Brian Clements

The "Villager": front elevation Brian Clements

OWNER/DEVELOPER
Chattanooga Neighborhood Enterprise

ARCHITECT
Brian Clements, Architect
Stroud Watson, Architect

LANDSCAPE ARCHITECT
Hodgson & Douglas

CONTRACTOR
Various local firms

MANAGEMENT
Chattanooga Neighborhood Enterprise

FUNDERS	TYPE
Tennessee Housing Development Agency	Loans
Local lenders	Loans
Chattanooga Neighborhood Enterprise	Loans

DEVELOPMENT TYPE
New construction single-family for-sale homes.

RESIDENT PROFILE
Very-low- to moderate-income families and seniors, incomes $10,000–35,460.

DENSITY
6.8 units/acre

DEVELOPMENT PROFILE

Type	N°/Units	Size (sf)	Sale Prices
2 BR	I	920	$46,000
3 BR	47	966–1,350	$55,300
4BR	I	1,350	$60,000
TOTAL	49		

Open space/play: private yards, pavilions, 2,000 sf open area
Parking: 98 garage and surface
Total site area: 7.3 acres

CONSTRUCTION TYPE
One- and two-story woodframe, masonite siding, comp. shingle roofs.

COSTS
Land Cost: $7,810; Constr. Costs: $2,265,958; Other Costs: $431,102; **Total Development Cost: $2,704,870 ($55,200/unit).** (Completed 1991)

Viewing the rows of neat, well-mannered houses built in 1984 for families with low incomes in and near Charleston's premier historic district, it is difficult to imagine the opposition that the architects of Bradfield, Richards & Associates had to overcome to achieve their design. Not only were Charleston residents—justifiably proud of their architectural heritage and determined to protect it—opposed to housing that they assumed would be incompatible with the city's historic architecture, but the Department of Housing and Urban Development, the agency with the right of final approval, had to be convinced that the proposed radical departures from HUD standards would have positive results.

From the beginning the architects were determined to design buildings for Charleston, not for the South Carolina HUD guidelines, which they thought likely to increase costs without producing the desired architectural character. They chose as a prototype the 18th century "single house", a familiar type in the historic district. Long and narrow, this house fits nicely on the narrow Charleston lots, and, being one-room wide, provides cross-ventilation for the hot and humid climate. The duplexes have side porches, another climate-influenced feature of the side house. The architects added a false entry on the street side of the porch for privacy; the remaining street frontage is fenced for security and to strengthen the street edge. Instead of the brick veneer specified by HUD, the architects chose wood siding painted in light colors. By consulting some local builders who had restored modest houses in the area, they found ways to emulate historic details with inexpensive materials: railings were milled from standard two-by-fours, balusters were stock two-by-twos, columns were four-by-fours with chamfered edges.

Despite the careful attention paid to the buildings' appearance, the initial HUD design reviews contained pages of negative comments about nonconforming elements. However, in a series of conferences with HUD staff the architects and representatives of the Housing Authority won their case for the design by demonstrating that their solution, though different, was practical, efficient, and affordable. Because of a depressed construction industry, the low bid for the project was 4 per cent below the budget making the overall cost per square foot only $27.06.

The Housing Authority Board of Commissioners' executive director, Donald J. Cameron, and Charleston Mayor Joseph Riley were committed to locating the new housing in the historic district. Their decision was partly based on the fact that recipients of the housing were families with low and moderate incomes, some of whom were being displaced by gentrification within the district. Following the allocation of funds in 1978, more than 100 sites were reviewed before eight were selected for the 67 units of housing. The number of units per site ranged from 2 to 15 with an average density of about 12 units per acre. The dimensions of the sites, typically 25–30 feet wide and 125 feet deep, imposed their own restrictions on the design. Location in the historic district also carried with it the imposition of standards set by city, state and federal agencies.

Architect Richard H. Bradfield, FAIA reported, "This public housing did not reduce property values on adjacent sites, nor did it deter private investors. Most important, it did not inhibit the efforts of the communities to continue the rehabilitation and restoration of (other) historic sections." On Amherst Street where nearly 50 per cent of the lots had been vacant, development returned to the neighborhood for the first time in more than 20 years. The residents of the new housing are proud of their homes and interested in planting flowers and additional shrubbery to supplement the landscaping in the small yards. One resident registered her only complaint: "It should be mine," she said, "I take care of it."

In giving this housing an Honor Award in 1986, members of the national AIA awards jury commented that the architects' "skillful adaptation" allowed "the dignity of the architecture to nurture the dignity of the people who reside within it making this an example of what low-cost housing should be, but rarely is—shelter not just for the body, but for the human spirit."

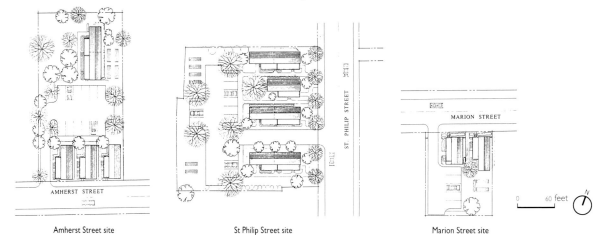

Amherst Street site   St Philip Street site   Marion Street site

Streetfront showing rebuilt neighborhood Richard Bradfield

Side view of duplex showing porch entry Richard Bradfield

Exterior side porch Richard Bradfield

OWNER/DEVELOPER
Housing Authority of the City of Charleston

ARCHITECT
Bradfield Richards and Associates Architects

CONTRACTOR
Mitchell Construction Co.

PROPERTY MANAGEMENT
Housing Authority of the City of Charleston

FUNDERS   **TYPE**
HUD, Public Housing Authority   Capital grant

DEVELOPMENT TYPE
New construction rental flats and townhouses,
spread over 8 sites.

RESIDENT PROFILE
Very-low- and low-income families, incomes below $20,000.

DENSITY
11 units/acre

DEVELOPMENT PROFILE

Type	N°/Units	Size (sf)	Rents
1 BR	18	659–693	30% of income
2 BR	11	907–915	
3 BR	29	1,279–1,138	
4 BR	9	1,350	
TOTAL	67		

Parking: 102 surface
Total site area: 6 acres

CONSTRUCTION TYPE
Two-story woodframe, wood siding, comp. shingle roofs.

COSTS
Land Cost: $907,486; Constr. Costs: $1,681,543 ($27/sf);
Other Costs: $770,887; **Total Development Cost:
$3,360,000 ($50,150/unit).** (Completed July 1983)

Randolph Neighborhood

Richmond's Randolph neighborhood experienced many of the problems of urban poverty and disinvestment typical of US cities in the 1960s. In the early 1970s large areas of it were razed and designated for redevelopment. For years local citizen activists worked with the Richmond Redevelopment and Housing Authority (RRHA) to plan how to rebuild the neighborhood. From the beginning, said resident Betsy Jones, "I participated, along with a whole lot of other people, in urging the city to renew this area. We were involved in all phases of the planning from street plans to parking plans to density. Now we have a healthy, vibrant community that is still developing—I'm proud of what we accomplished. However, we lost a lot of older residents through the original renewal efforts and that was very painful."

In order to accommodate community concerns that the neighborhood would not become gentrified, the first Randolph Redevelopment and Conservation Plan called for a significant amount of well-designed housing for households with low incomes. However, once HUD reviewed the plan they decided that it would concentrate too many people with minimal resources in one area. The RRHA was forced to re-evaluate the plan. Although the RRHA had begun to successfully rehabilitate older houses at the edge of the neighborhood, there was debate about the type of new housing to be built. In 1981 some new public housing and Section 8 subsidized rental units were built with HUD funds, and in the mid-1980s momentum began to grow for private housing.

In response to HUD, the RRHA developed a second plan with the goal of creating a mixed-income community. "Build a neighborhood, not a project," was its motto. UDA Architects was brought in and, working with the community, they began to develop a plan based on traditional design concepts. According to architect Ray Gindroz, "The many community meetings on front porches emphasized their importance and the pride that residents took in the brick facades of the houses. We designed a range of housing types that would fit seamlessly with the adjacent blocks of 1920s red brick houses with white-painted porches, mimicking the block size and the design of alleys of the adjacent neighborhood." A pattern book of houses was designed with townhouses and duplexes, each with a front and back yard and parking off a rear alley. The zoning was changed to conform to traditional patterns; this was a benefit of the designation of the district as a redevelopment area.

The community process was challenging because, according to Bob Everton of the RRHA, "At first the community was not in favor of the new plan. They reminded the RRHA that they did not want to change the socio-economic characteristics of the neighborhood, and they felt that the "urban-style" of the units would be better received by persons other than the African-American community. Only after many community meetings and public hearings was the urban-style concept approved."

Marketing the denser homes was hard at first, partly because it was difficult to see the neighborhood as a complete development. Gindroz remarked, "The plan called for public improvements to be done in advance of the housing. Unfortunately, the new streetscapes were put in after the model homes were built, which set the sales pace back." The neighborhood also had to compete with new suburban tracts at the edge of town, so the attached units were not as attractive to prospective buyers. Eventually, the team modified the design so that the townhouses were three feet apart and raised slightly above grade to give buyers a sense of their own home. The RRHA worked closely with local developers and contractors to ensure that the homes would sell and that the program would continue. Council member Henry Richardson, who sponsored and supported the program from the beginning, remarked, "Randolph shows how successful we can be if government agencies actually respond to citizen participation."

Townhouses on Idlewood Avenue

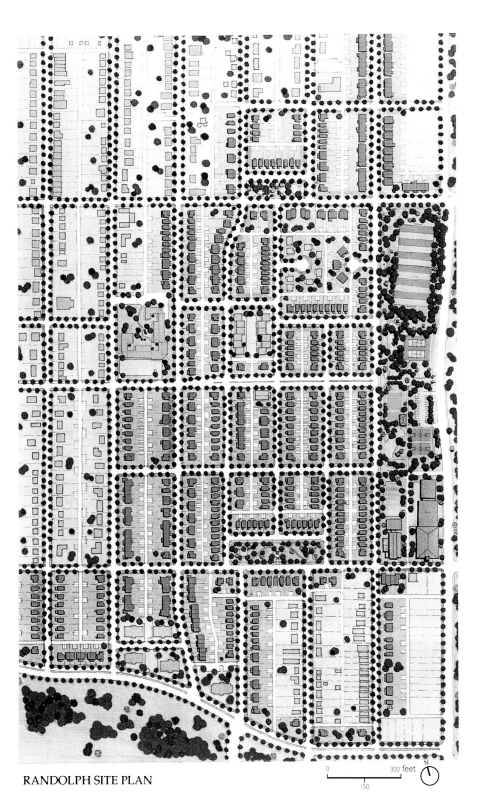

RANDOLPH SITE PLAN

DEVELOPER
Richmond Redevelopment and Housing Authority
(RRHA)

ARCHITECT
UDA Architects

CONTRACTOR
Richmond Homes
Various other local firms

PROPERTY MANAGEMENT
RRHA

FUNDERS	TYPE
HUD Section 8, and Mod. Rehab	Grant/rent subsidy
HUD Section 202	Grant
HUD - Public Housing	Grant
CDBG/CIP -	
Urban Homeownership Opp'ty	Loan
Virginia Housing Dev. Authority	Loan
Virginia Housing PF	Loan
Various banks	Loans

DEVELOPMENT TYPE
New construction and rehabilitation, rental and for-sale
flats and townhouses.

RESIDENT PROFILE
Very-low-, low-, and moderate-income seniors and families.

DENSITY
20 units per acre (ave.)

DEVELOPMENT PROFILE

Type	N°/Units	Size (sf)	Sale Prices/Rents
Senior			
1 BR	125	550	30% of income
Section 8/Public Housing			
1–5 BR	143	550–1,300	30% of income
Single Family (new and rehabilitation)			
2–4 BR	742	1,000–1,936	$27,500–108,000
TOTAL	**1,010**		

Courtyard/play: 3 public parks with multiple
                 rec. areas, tot-lots
Parking: garages, surface, carports
Total site area: 100 acres

CONSTRUCTION TYPE
One- and two-story single-family detached
Two- and three-story apartment buildings

COSTS
New SF: $23.8m; Rehab. SF: $6.9m; Senior Hsg: $4.6m;
Low-income family hsg: $6.4m; **Total Costs: $41.8m
($41,455/unit).** (In final phase.)

Randolph Neighborhood Continued

The Randolph development was envisioned as an extension of the existing neighborhood. The city of Richmond built three public parks as part of the development. One of them has a swimming pool, a large playing field, jogging track, tennis and basketball courts, and play areas for small children. The other two parks are smaller, but are carefully tended by residents. As Gindroz pointed out, "The best way to build this type of neighborhood is to design a group of houses around a park. When competing with suburban forms that have more land per unit, it is important that the advantage of urban life —a sense of community—can actually be experienced."

The area is exceptionally safe for one that includes a significant amount of public housing and other subsidized rental programs. However, the subsidized housing is balanced by a large number of owner-occupied, single-family houses. Along with an urban form that allows for individual identity while encouraging a sense of community, this balance has produced an environment in which residents actively maintain their security through surveillance of the street and front porch socializing. Beverly Burton bought one side of a duplex in 1983 where she raised her two children while she worked as an attorney. She commented, "This neighborhood is an attempt to get people from different backgrounds to all live together. There are people here who work in maintenance at the local hospital. It is very convenient to schools, transportation and community resources. It's like a little neighborhood right in the heart of the city!"

Townhouses on Idlewood Avenue Tom Bernard

Townhouses viewed from community park Tom Bernard

Early Saturday morning on Wallace Street Tom Bernard

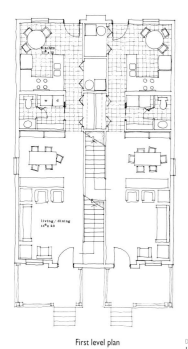

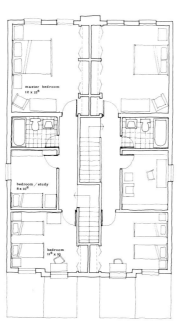

Townhouses with gazebo Tom Bernard

First level plan   0   16 feet   Second level plan

Timberlawn Crescent
Montgomery County, Maryland

Montgomery County, one of the wealthiest in the nation, has long been a desirable place to live. In the last decade housing had become so expensive that people with low and moderate incomes could not afford to rent or buy homes in the area. Fortunately, the county has policies that encourage the development of affordable housing by giving density bonuses and other concessions to developers. At Timberlawn Crescent, a mixed-income rental community, the original goal of 30 per cent subsidized and 70 per cent market-rate units changed to almost 60 per cent subsidized by the time the housing was completed. According to county councilman Neil Potter, "A major goal has been to integrate affordable housing units into the community at large rather than create pockets of low-income housing in the county." Architect Larry C. Kester commented, "The support and contributions of the county planning staff and the commitment of the owner to goals that would improve the lifestyle of the future residents was significant. Their goal was to build a high quality design that would last for many years." The development has become a model for other public agencies and developers throughout the region.

The developer planned to build Timberlawn Crescent to make the market-rate units indistinguishable from those that were subsidized. However, Kester reported, "Although numerous meetings were held to solicit neighborhood input during the planning process and suggestions were included, residents of the surrounding community vigorously opposed the development before the planning commission. They did not believe that we were telling them the truth about our design." But when they saw the actual buildings the neighbors' opposition vanished. Neighbor John Spano commented, "It turned out much better than we expected. They allow us to use their community center for board meetings, which is a benefit."

The moderate density is generally equivalent to surrounding communities, with the buildings designed as two-story townhouses over flats. Each unit has a ground level patio or balcony, which helps interaction between neighbors. To save energy, heat pumps were used for heating and cooling, and triple pane windows reduce heat loss and unwanted noise from the nearby freeway. In phase II, the apartments incorporated a "bonus room" which residents can use as an extra bedroom, study, or home office. Parking is distributed in open lots a short walk from each apartment. The architect was able to weave the buildings into the site to save as many of the existing tulip trees as possible. Although the loss of some trees was unavoidable, enough were saved to create screening between buildings and filtered views.

Timberlawn is a successful mixed-income community. Residents of market-rate apartments have not reacted negatively to the presence of people with low incomes in the complex. Resident Helen Biyer moved there in 1992 after looking at a lot of different apartments to rent. She picked Timberlawn because of the affordability, convenience, and security. She plans to move on to market-rate accommodations elsewhere, but noted "Timberlawn is in itself a neighborhood. I will hate to give up this great place."

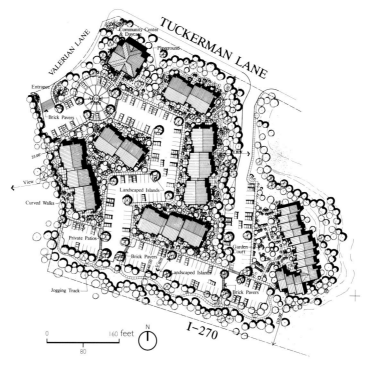

Site plan

0   16 feet

Building elevation

Three-story townhouse over flat Larry Kester

Community center and childcare Larry Kester

OWNER/DEVELOPER
Housing Opportunities Commission of Montgomery County

ARCHITECT
Architects Collective

LANDSCAPE ARCHITECT
Lewis, Scully and Gionet

CONTRACTOR
Tudor Construction
Hame Commercial

PROPERTY MANAGEMENT
Dryfuss Management

FUNDERS	TYPE
Montgomery County Housing Initiative Fund	Loan
State of Maryland Housing Production Prog.	Loan

DEVELOPMENT TYPE
New construction rental flats and townhouses.

RESIDENT PROFILE
Very-low-income, low-income, moderate-income, market-rate singles and families.

DENSITY
22 units/acre

DEVELOPMENT PROFILE

Type	N°/Units	Size (sf)	Rents
1 BR	12	750	$142–950
2 BR	2	1,050	$180–1,200
2 BR TH	76	1,120	$180–1200
3 BR	17	1,100	$175–1,175
TOTAL	107		

Community/daycare: 1,800 sf
Courtyard/play: tot-lot, barbecue area, fitness trail
Parking: 215 surface
Total site area: 237,000 sf (5.4 acres)

CONSTRUCTION TYPE
Three- and four-story woodframe, horiz. siding, comp. shingle roofs.

COSTS
Land Cost: $0 (donated); Constr. Costs: $6.3m; Other Costs: $1.3m; **Total Development Cost: $7.6m ($71,000/unit).** (Completed 1989 (phase I), 1991 (phase II))

Eric Mitchell

CHAPTER TWELVE:
ADDITIONAL CASE STUDIES OF MERIT

Thirty additional developments in the
five regions were selected for review as
one-page case studies:

The Central States:

    Quincy Homes, Chicago, Illinois

    Harriet Square, Minneapolis, Minnesota

    International Homes, Chicago, Illinois

    Westminster Place, St Louis, Missouri

The Northwest and Northern California:

    Lake Park Townhomes, Klahanie, Washington

    Holladay Avenue Homes, San Francisco, California

    Open Doors, Los Gatos, California

    Lucretia Gardens and Julian Street, San Jose, California

    Horizons, Campbell, California

    Paula Avenue Apartments, San Jose, California

The Southwest and Southern California:

    Blacklands Transitional Housing, Austin, Texas

    La'ilani at Kealakehe, Hawaii

    La Ramona Morales Apartments, Benson, Arizona

    Viviendas Asistenciales, Tucson, Arizona

    West Hopkins Townhouses, Aspen, Colorado

The Northeast:

    Fineview Crest, Pittsburgh, Pennsylvania

    Capen Green, Stamford, Connecticut

    Columbia/Hampshire St Housing, Cambridge, Massachusetts

    University City Family Housing, Philadelphia, Pennsylvania

    Dorado Village, Philadelphia, Pennsylvania

    Sojourner Truth Homes, Brooklyn, New York

    Regent Terrace Apartments, Philadelphia, Pennsylvania

    Oak Terrace, Boston, Massachusetts

    Spring Creek Gardens, Brooklyn, New York

    Lee Goodwin Residence, Bronx, New York

    Crotona Park West, Bronx, New York

    Sarah Powell Huntington House, New York, New York

The South/Southeast:

    Middle Towne Arch, Norfolk, Virginia

    Dermott Villas, Dermott, Arkansas

    Mer Rouge Villas, Mer Rouge, Louisiana

Quincy Homes Chicago, Illinois

DEVELOPER
The Shaw Company

ARCHITECT
Schroeder Murchie Laya Associates Inc.

CONTRACTOR
The Shaw Co.

FUNDERS | **TYPE**
City of Chicago "New Homes Program" | Grant
Bank of America Illinois | Loans

DEVELOPMENT TYPE
New construction, for-sale single-family homes.

RESIDENT PROFILE
Moderate-income families.

DENSITY
9 units/acre

DEVELOPMENT PROFILE

Type	N°/Units	Size (sf)	Sale Prices
3 BR	40	1,224–1,690	$84,000–94,000
TOTAL	**40**		

Parking: 80; 54 surface, 26 garage
Total site area: 194,952 sf (4.47 acres)

CONSTRUCTION TYPE
Two-story woodframe, brick veneer and vinyl siding, comp. shingle roof.

COSTS
Total Development Cost: $116,000/unit.
(Completed January 1992)

Quincy Homes is a development of the "New Homes for Chicago" program sponsored by the City of Chicago's Department of Housing. Initially, this was a five-year program introduced in 1990 with the goal of encouraging affordable homeownership and revitalization in communities that private development had overlooked. Quincy Homes, located in the South Austin district of Chicago, was the first New Homes development. The 40 single-family houses include three bedrooms, two baths, a family room, large yards and an attached one-car garage. All homes sold in a short time; the average buyer was 39 years old and earned $40,000 a year. The new buildings are smaller than the dominant neighborhood housing, which is typically three-story brick stacked-flats. According to architects Schroeder Murchie Laya, the design challenge was, "to make a 900- to 1,200-square-foot unit look appropriate on the street." To increase their apparent size the architects placed them on raised berms and put garages below the living quarters, which, in turn, created raised entrance porches. Attic stories were also added, and brick was used on the first level to link the materials with the adjacent structures. The sale of new homes is intended to attract long-term residents with higher incomes to stabilize the neighborhood without gentrifying the community.

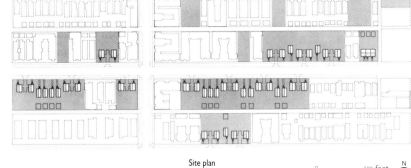

Site plan

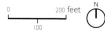

0   100   200 feet   N

Quincy Street with new homes William Kildow

Front entry of new home William Kildow

Completed in 1986, Harriet Square townhouses interprets the forms and elements of the traditional Minnesota home in a row-house type, increasing the density by several times. Organized as a street-front building with parking off the court behind the homes, the 27 two- and three-bedroom townhouse-units that comprise Harriet Square have split-level plans. The lower level has a garage and half-basement; the ground level has living, dining, and kitchen, and the top level has bedrooms and a full bath. Paul Madson, project architect of BRW Elness Architects, designed the housing to fit seamlessly into the neighborhood by observing characteristics of the older residences such as placing the buildings on a raised berm and giving them a uniform setback. The traditional practice of entries preceded by screened porches raised a half-level give the units more privacy. The gabled roofs, bay windows, and use of white vinyl, lap-siding and wood latticework below the porches also echo the styling of nearby houses. By bringing the roofline of the two-and-a-half-story units down to the first floor the appearance of bulk is reduced.

All units were sold to first-time homebuyers (with re-sale restrictions) before construction was finished. When Harriet Square received a MSAIA Honor Award in 1986, the judge's comment was, "With restraint and an economy of means, the designers have produced modest, yet elegant architecture."

DEVELOPER
Brighton Development Corp.

ARCHITECT
BRW Elness (formerly Arvid Elness Architects, Inc.)

LANDSCAPE ARCHITECT
Damar Farker Assoc.

CONTRACTOR
Watson-Forsberg Construction

MANAGEMENT
Homeowners Association

FUNDERS   **TYPE**
First Capital Resources Corporation   Loan

DEVELOPMENT TYPE
New construction for-sale attached townhouses.

RESIDENT PROFILE
Moderate-income first-time homebuyers.

DENSITY
10 units/acre

DEVELOPMENT PROFILE

Type	Nº/Units	Size (sf)	Sale Prices
2 BR	16	1,280	$77,500
3 BR	8	1,440	$84,500
TOTAL	24		

Parking: 48 surface
Total site area: 2.5 acres

CONSTRUCTION TYPE
Two-story split level, woodframe, horiz. siding, comp. shingle roofs.

COSTS
Land Cost: $225,000; Constr. Costs: $1,204,000; Other Costs: $721,000; **Total Development Cost: $1,925,000 ($80,208/unit).** (Completed 1985)

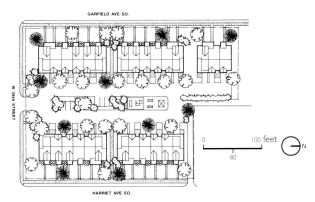

Site plan

Front entry as seen from Harriet Avenue Arvid Elness

International Homes Chicago, Illinois

DEVELOPER
Voice of the People In Uptown, Inc.

ARCHITECT
Weese Langley Weese Architects Ltd.

CONTRACTOR
Thrush Construction, Inc.

FUNDERS	**TYPE**
La Salle/Cragin Bank	Grant
Federal Home Loan Bank	Grant
Illinois Dept. of Energy and N.R.	Grant
City of Chicago, Dept. of Hsg.	Grant
Uptown Nat'l Bank of Chicago	Loan
LISC	Predev. grant

DEVELOPMENT TYPE
New construction, scattered-site, for-sale attached townhouses.

RESIDENT PROFILE
Low- and moderate-income first-time homebuyers.

DENSITY
14 units/acre

DEVELOPMENT PROFILE

Type	N°/Units	Size (sf)	Sale Prices
3 BR	28	1,200	$72,000–80,000
TOTAL	**28**		

Parking: 28 surface

CONSTRUCTION TYPE
Two-story woodframe, concrete basements, vinyl and wood siding, wood truss roofs and floors.

COSTS
Land Cost: $103,832; Constr. Costs: $2,240,000; Other Costs: $334,168; **Total Development Cost: $2,678,000 ($95,642/unit ave.).** (Completed 1993–94)

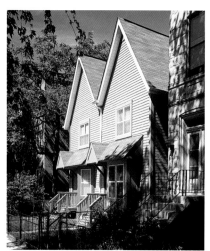

Street facade (front entry) Wayne Cable

Planned and implemented in co-operation with neighborhood organizations, the International Homes offered the opportunity for home ownership at affordable prices to diverse groups of people. Located on vacant lots mostly owned by the city, the development has 28 attached row houses with 1,200 square feet plus a full basement and a private outdoor space. Weese Langley Weese designed the buildings to blend with the traditional architecture and streetscape of Chicago's Uptown neighborhood. The homes are grouped together with high roofs to fit the scale of the high density neighborhood; gables and porches emphasize the individuality of the homes.

Voice of the People in Uptown, Inc., a non-profit housing development corporation that has been active in the Uptown community for 25 years, conducted workshops to familiarize prospective buyers with the application and purchase process. The buyers reflected the racial and ethnic diversity of Uptown and included African, African-American, Asian, Hispanic, Middle Eastern, Native American, and Caucasian households. Buyers were able to purchase the houses with a minimal downpayment and must sell the houses to qualified families with low-incomes. The community gained both stability and vitality with the replacement of dangerous vacant lots with quality homes, without gentrifying the neighborhood.

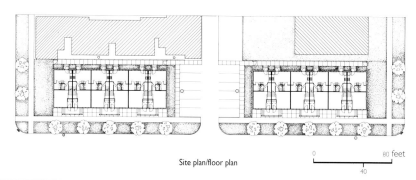

Site plan/floor plan

0   40   80 feet

Typical street facade Wayne Cable

Westminster Place St Louis, Missouri

During the 1970s the once affluent Westminster area of St Louis became crime-ridden and declined to the point of near abandonment. Westminster Place is a new multi-phased 392-unit mixed-income residential community that consists of one-, two-, and three-bedroom units configured in two-story townhouses and three-story garden apartment buildings. McCormack Baron worked closely with the architects at Trivers Associates to develop the building and unit design. The master plan involved blocking the primary street to create a private, tree-lined drive with landscaped apartment buildings and well-lit parking behind the buildings. As the area blossomed into a neighborhood that residents once again felt safe to walk in, the slowing of traffic, use of entry markers, and street lighting continued to be a success. In addition to pioneering the

rebuilding of inner-city neighborhoods, McCormack Baron provides professional property management to ensure stability in the community and the long-term viability of their investment.

The large scale of Westminster Place had created a substantial new community to support commercial, institutional, and cultural activities adjacent to the site. Residents live in a truly mixed social/economic environment in which everyone enjoys the same amenities. Project Manager Tom Cella said, "The blend of affordable with market-rate housing is crucial to the success of our developments. The positive impact of urban areas being reborn provides a catalyst for the needed commercial infrastructure to invest once again in the area."

OWNER / DEVELOPER
McCormack Baron & Assoc. Inc.

ARCHITECT
Trivers Associates

CONTRACTOR
E.M. Harris Building Co.

MANAGEMENT
McCormack Baron & Assoc. Inc.

FUNDERS	TYPE
SunAmerica Housing Funds	Equity partner
AFL-CIO Housing Investment Trust	Loan
Land Clearance for Redev. Auth. of Kansas City	Bond issue
Community Development Agency	Soft loan
Missouri Housing Development Commission	Loan
Boatmen's Bank	Loan
The Related Companies	Equity syndicator
Northside Preservation Commission	Soft Loan
Mark Twain National Bank	Loan

DEVELOPMENT TYPE
Multi-phase, new construction, rental flats and for-sale homes.

RESIDENT PROFILE
Mix of market-rate and affordable. Low- and moderate-income households, incomes $15,000–33,740.

DENSITY
22 units/acre

DEVELOPMENT PROFILE

Type	N°/Units	Size (sf)	Rents/Sale Prices
I BR	115	650	$380–450/na
2 BR	265	750–1,100	$530–545/na
3 BR	12	1,300	$780–830/na
TOTAL	392		

Laundry: in each unit
Courtyard/play: pool and I acre of green space
Parking: 588 surface
Retail: adjacent to new retail center of 145,000 sf
Total site area: 18 acres

CONSTRUCTION TYPE
Two- and three-story woodframe, masonry and vinyl siding, comp. shingle roofs.

COSTS
Land Cost: $3.50/sf before demo and env. work; Constr. Cost: $31,200,000; Other Costs: $17,287,000; **Total Development Cost: $48,487,000 (w/out land) ($45 to $54/sf). (Completed 1993)**

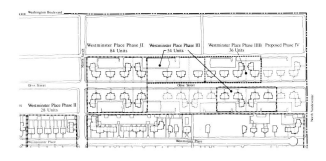

Site plan

0   100 feet

New SF house in context of Westminster Place McCormack Baron

Lake Park Townhomes Issaquah, Washington

OWNER/DEVELOPER
Environmental Works

ARCHITECT
Environmental Works Community Design Center

CONTRACTOR
Pacific Component Homes

FUNDERS
King Co. Planning and Comm. Dev.
Continental Mortgage Corp.
WA State Hsg Finance Comm.

TYPE
Loan (land)
Constr. loan
Mortgage financing

DEVELOPMENT TYPE
New construction for-sale duplex townhouses.

RESIDENT PROFILE
Low-income first-time homebuyers below 80% of AMI.

DENSITY
7.8 units/acre

DEVELOPMENT PROFILE

Type	N°/Units	Size (sf)	Sale Prices
3 BR TH	20	1,290	$81,400
3 BR TH	8	1,400	$83,400
TOTAL	**28**		

Parking: 56 garages
Total site area: 3.59 acres

CONSTRUCTION TYPE
Two-story woodframe, horiz. siding, comp. shingle roofs.

COSTS
Land Cost: $378,571; Constr. Costs: $1,365,800; Other Costs: $537,650; **Total Development Cost: $2,282,000 ($81,500/unit).** (Completed 1987)

Completed in 1987, this was the first master plan development undertaken by King County that incorporated on-site housing for families with low to moderate incomes. Community input and a density bonus agreement with the master developer led to the county awarding Community Development Block Grant funds to the non-profit organization, Environmental Works (EW), to purchase a parcel within the Klahanie new town master plan. EW's community design center designed the 14 duplex buildings with the scale of the nearby, more expensive houses in mind. The 1,450-square-foot, attached townhouses connected to garages are sited around a cul-de-sac entrance street, which is a safe place for children to play. Gabled roofs, horizontal siding, and front porch entries give the homes a comfortable traditional feel.

At 3,000 units the larger development is generally more upscale; it has such amenities as 300 acres of open space with a lake, several parks, tennis and other sports courts, a swimming pool, and fishing pier available to all residents. The county helped to make the homes affordable by assuming a silent second mortgage. Vince Tom, project manager for the county noted two important lessons from the development process, "It is important to structure the mortgage so that any appreciation is shared with the county. In developments with narrow qualifying limits, you may have to educate potential buyers to help market the homes."

Site section   0   64 feet

Streetscape Cynthia Richardson

Holladay Avenue Homes San Francisco, California

Completed over a decade ago, the Holladay Avenue Homes (HAH) blend into the neighborhood so well that the fierce opposition which initially faced this housing is difficult to understand. The non-profit developer, the Bernal Heights Housing Corporation (BHHC), organized to fight a developer who wanted to build a wall of market-rate housing across one block of a substandard street. Faced with gentrification, the community's goal was to preserve its mixed-income, multi-ethnic character for both homeowners and renters. HAH was proposed as a small step in this direction. However, fearful of the character of future residents and of the possibility that their property values would fall, neighboring homeowners opposed the housing.

The attached buildings are staggered up the sloping site and oriented southward for maximum daylight and solar heating. The shingled structures were set back from the south property line to preserve existing trees and allow space for a pathway that connects the houses to the street. As limited equity homes, a deed restriction limits their resale to people with low incomes. Neighborhood property values continued to soar through the 1980s, making this development an asset to the community. Buck Bagot, co-director of BHHC at the time, reflected on this award-winning housing, saying, "Affordable housing development is about two kinds of power, organized money and organized people. We have the low income housing tax credit because of the self-interest of organized money. But to get affordable housing we need to mobilize folks behind their direct self-interest for a home."

OWNER / DEVELOPER
Bernal Heights Housing Corporation

ARCHITECT
Herman Stoller Coliver Architects

CONSULTANTS
Landscape Architect: Tito Patri & Assoc.
Development Consultant: Devine & Gong Inc.

CONTRACTOR
B & T General Contractors

FUNDERS	**TYPE**
HUD, Section 235	Loan
City of S.F Mayor's Office of Hsg	Loan
CDBG	Land

DEVELOPMENT TYPE
New construction for-sale (limited-equity) attached townhouses.

RESIDENT PROFILE
Low-income families below 80% of AMI.

DENSITY
16 units/acre

DEVELOPMENT PROFILE

Type	N°/Units	Size (sf)	Sale Prices
2 BR	2	980	$50,000 (5% down)
3 BR	2	1140	$60,000 (5% down)
TOTAL	4		

Large garden: 7,500 sf
Parking: 8 garage and surface
Total site area: 10,950 sf (.25 acre)

CONSTRUCTION TYPE
Two-story woodframe, conc. retaining walls, shingle siding, comp. shingle roofs.

COSTS
Land Cost: $0; Constr. Costs: $350,000; Other Costs: $42,000; **Total Development Cost: $392,000 ($98,000/unit).** (Completed 1983)

South elevation

Four units in context with neighbors Sandy Marks

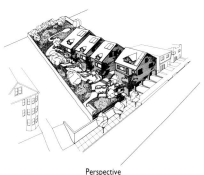

Perspective

Open Doors Los Gatos, California

OWNER/DEVELOPER
Mid-Peninsula Housing Coalition

ARCHITECT
Hooper Olmsted and Hrovat

LANDSCAPE ARCHITECT
Terra Media

CONTRACTOR
Segue Construction

PROPERTY MANAGEMENT
Mid-Peninsula Housing Management Corp.

FUNDERS

	TYPE
State RHCP Funds (Bond Issue)	Perm./constr. loan
Santa Clara County CDBG Funds	Perm. loan
SAMCO Mortgage	
Low Income Hsg. Tax Credits	Perm. loan
purchased by Mission First	Equity
West Valley Open Doors	
(Local non-profit)	Grant
Wells Fargo Bank	Constr. Loan
Local Initiative Support Corporation	Predev. Loan

DEVELOPMENT TYPE
New construction rental flats and townhouses over flats.

RESIDENT PROFILE
Very-low- and low-income families,
incomes $12,000–30,000; 25–60% AMI.

DENSITY
19 units/acre

DEVELOPMENT PROFILE

Type	N°/Units	Size (sf)	Rents
2 BR	32	827–905	$390–650
3 BR	30	1,107–1,138	$430–760
4 BR	2	1,331	$495–725
TOTAL	64		

Parking: 134 spaces, surface
Courtyard/play area: 0.5 acre
Childcare center: 2,000 sf
Total site area: 3.37 acres or 146,797 sf

CONSTRUCTION TYPE
Two- and three-story woodframe, hardboard siding
and comp. shingle roofs.

COSTS
Land Costs: $1,870,000; Constr. Costs $3,875,000 ($61/sf);
Childcare Center: $200,000; Other Costs: $2,785,000;
Total Development Cost: $8,730,000.
(Completed April 1993)

Open Doors is the first housing in Los Gatos designed for families with low incomes. Most of the residents work at the nearby hospital; many have young children. Architect Richard Olmsted designed two- and three-story buildings as stacked flats, and townhouses over flats in a pin-wheel plan that creates a variety of building elevations and setbacks. Different colors highlight separate identities for units in a building cluster. "The housing feels like a village of attached houses rather than a monolithic apartment building," commented Olmsted. Although the apartments have front patios, they do not have private rear yards because they are back-to-back. The clusters are sited around a shared courtyard with a large lawn and a play structure.

The San Juan Bautista Child Development Center of San Jose leases the childcare center for about 36 children from both the wider community and Open Doors. Computer and art classes are also held at the center. The success of Open Doors was difficult to sell to the neighborhood in advance. When the housing was introduced to the neighborhood, strong opposition, including a lawsuit, reduced the unit count from 68 to 64, and added 24 parking spaces. But, supported by the Town of Los Gatos the development went forward after some delay. The residents, many of whom had been living in the area in overcrowded and expensive housing, value the stability to build their lives and the security for their children.

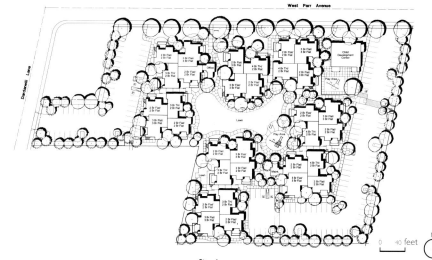

Site plan

Central lawn area Mark Darley/Esto

Lucretia Gardens and Julian Street San Jose, California

Located on two sites, one urban infill, the other a suburban site bordering recreational park land, this was the first public housing for families in Santa Clara County. The 25 units were divided into nine apartments on Julian Street and 16 on Lucretia Avenue. The Housing Authority of the County of Santa Clara's (HACSC) decision to build on two sites stemmed from the opposition of the council person from the Lucretia Gardens site to an overconcentration of families with low incomes. The neighbors at Julian Street were supportive because the site was a vacant lot used as a dump. Although a newly elected council person opposed the housing after it was approved, strong support from the mayor and the rest of the council enabled the housing to be built.

According to the architect, funding from the US Department of Housing and Urban Development (HUD) required that the same design be used for both sites. However, requirements by local planning officials enabled the SCCHA to convince HUD that design standards should be improved. The designers enriched the facades by capping them with curved parapets and by using projecting second-story bays with alternating straight and gabled cornices to shelter the entrances. Each unit has a semi-private front porch, a private back patio, and shares a common open space. Architect Bob Herman noted, "A simple site plan, combined with carefully articulated building elevations can create a dignified yet economical place to live."

OWNER/DEVELOPER
Housing Authority of the County of Santa Clara

ARCHITECT
Herman Stoller Coliver Architects, Inc.

LANDSCAPE ARCHITECT
John Northmore Roberts

CONTRACTOR
Nibbi Brothers

PROPERTY MANAGEMENT
Housing Authority of the County of Santa Clara

FUNDERS	TYPE
HUD Section 8	Capital grant
City of San Jose Housing Department	Grant

DEVELOPMENT TYPE
New construction, rental attached townhouses and flats, Public Housing.

RESIDENT PROFILE
Very-low- and low-income families, incomes $0–36,000.

DENSITY
20 units/acre

DEVELOPMENT PROFILE

Type	N°/Units	Size (sf)	Rents
3 BR flat	1	925	$73–484/mo
3 BR (accessible)	1	925	(30% of HH income)
3 BR TH	23	1,000	
TOTAL	**25**		

Laundry: in each unit.
Open space: shared: 13,500 sf: front yards: 5,100 sf
Parking: 48 surface
Total site area: 53,100 sf (1.22 acres—two sites)

CONSTRUCTION TYPE
Two-story woodframe, hardboard siding, flat roofs.

COSTS
Land Cost: $530,000; Constr. Costs $2,157,000; Other Costs: $230,000; **Total Development Cost: $2,387,000 ($95,480/unit).** (Completed May 1994)

Site plan

0   20 feet

Unit front with tall window Robert Herman

Three-bedroom townhouses looking north Robert Herman

OWNER/DEVELOPER
Mid-Peninsula Housing Coalition

ARCHITECT
Kodama Associates

LANDSCAPE ARCHITECT
Merrill & Assoc.

CONTRACTOR
Dow Builders

PROPERTY MANAGEMENT
Mid-Peninsula Hsg Mgmt. Corp.

FUNDERS   **TYPE**
HUD Section 811   Capital grant and
                              operating subsidy
Belmont Redevelopment Agency   Loan
PG&E   Grant

DEVELOPMENT TYPE
New construction rental flats.

RESIDENT PROFILE
Low-income developmentally disabled adults
and families, incomes averaging $10,975.

DENSITY
30 units/acre

DEVELOPMENT PROFILE

Type	N°/Units	Size (sf)	Rents
Studio	10	430	$270 (ave.)
1 BR	8	540	$270 (ave.)
2 BR	6	800	$270 (ave.)
TOTAL	24		

Community/laundry: 1,500 sf
Parking: 10 surface
Total site area: 35,284 sf (.81 acres)

CONSTRUCTION TYPE
Two-story woodframe, hardboard and board-and-batten
siding, comp. shingle roof.

COSTS
Land Cost: $475,000; Constr. Costs: $1,498,048 ($82/sf);
Other Costs: $297,734; **Total Development Cost:**
$2,270,782. (Completed August 1993)

Horizons is a 24-unit complex designed to provide affordable independent living for families with an adult member who is developmentally disabled. The housing is centrally located near transit and services. Former City Council member Gary Orton supported the development saying, "It is important to build this type of housing in accessible locations, to reduce the long distances people sometimes have to travel." Architect Steven Kodama designed the five residential buildings with heights of one and two stories to vary the massing and to create an intimate scale in the courtyard. The buildings' barn-like forms, open corridors, and board-and-batten siding have a familiar, vernacular character. A community room gives people a place to have tenant association meetings and larger gatherings for holidays and birthdays.

The site's proximity to a commuter rail line and a busy street made noise-abatement an imperative. Project manager for the Mid-Peninsula Housing Coalition (MPHC) Susan Russell said, "The US Department of Housing and Urban Development (HUD) approved the site, and then withdrew its approval after the design was underway due to the estimated noise levels from the train tracks." The architects responded to this problem by upgrading the exterior wall assemblies to reflect the sound, and minimizing the openings facing the tracks. MPHC worked with the neighbors to inform them of progress and issues during the development. Russell also noted, "It is important to alleviate people's concerns ahead of time about the kind of person who would be living there." Fortunately, the neighbors were supportive of the development, and many of those who did not know its purpose assumed it was conventional market-rate housing.

0   14 feet

Street elevation

Community building from covered walkway Russell Abraham

Community building viewed across interior courtyard Russell Abraham

Paula Avenue Apartments San Jose, California

Stretched along a narrow street in a stable neighborhood with good schools, the Paula Avenue Apartments house families with low and very low incomes in buildings that are designed to evoke the image of neighboring market-rate condominium complexes. The alternating two and three stories of stacked flats look like townhouses; shared stairways are hidden between buildings, and no parking is visible from the street. The third-floor units have vaulted ceilings, and all the units have sunny, south-facing balconies. Four of the ground-floor units are arranged for transitional families to share living accommodation for a short period of time. The city considered the site to be undevelopable because of its odd shape. But the solution proposed by architects, Marquis Associates, which

placed the housing close to the street edge and the parking in back, persuaded the city that the site would work for housing. Terry Wenzl of First San Jose Housing said, "Our task was to design fairly high-density housing without conveying a dense feeling, and I think we achieved this."

The City of San Jose is generally supportive of well-conceived affordable housing developments. Alex Sanchez, housing manager, noted, "Many of the residents are families with very low incomes who were displaced when the convention center was built in the downtown. They now enjoy high-quality design and good property management, and the development has contributed to the stability of the neighborhood."

OWNER/DEVELOPER
First San Jose Housing

ARCHITECT
Marquis Associates

LANDSCAPE ARCHITECT
Richard Vignolo

CONTRACTOR
Yamaoka Builders, Inc.

PROPERTY MANAGEMENT
The John Stewart Company

FUNDERS	TYPE
City of San Jose	Perm. loan
Silicon Valley Bank	Constr. loan
Low Income Housing Tax Credits purchased by SAMCO	Equity

DEVELOPMENT TYPE
New construction rental stacked flats.

RESIDENT PROFILE
Very-low- and low-income families, incomes $12,000–28,000.

DENSITY
31 units/acre

DEVELOPMENT PROFILE

Type	N°/Units	Size (sf)	Rents
2 BR	21	864	$414–725
TOTAL	**21**		

Community/laundry: 2,270 sf
Courtyard/play: 800 sf
Parking: 40 surface/tuck-under
Total site area: 29,621 sf (.68 acres)

CONSTRUCTION TYPE
Two- and three-story woodframe, hardboard siding, comp. shingle roofs.

COSTS
Land Cost: $425,000; Constr. Costs: $1,200,000 ($54/sf); Other Costs: $637,000; **Total Development Cost: $2,136,539.** (Completed 1991)

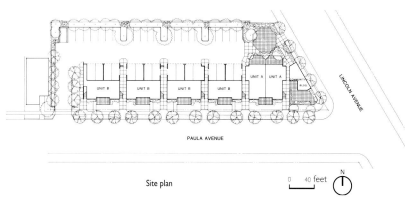

Site plan

0   40 feet   N

View from the street Alan Geller

View from the main road Alan Geller

Blacklands Transitional Housing Austin, Texas

OWNER/DEVELOPER
Owner: Blackland Community Development Corp.
Developer: Texas Low Income Housing Info. Service

ARCHITECT
Tom Hatch Architects
Construction Admin: Haynes-Eaglin Waters

LANDSCAPE ARCHITECT
City of Austin Xeriscape Program

CONTRACTOR
Morales Construction

PROPERTY MANAGEMENT
Frederick Johnson

FUNDERS   **TYPE**
CDBG, City of Austin   Grant
University of Texas   Land

DEVELOPMENT TYPE
Renovation of existing houses into rental duplexes.

RESIDENT PROFILE
Homeless families, transitional program.

DENSITY
8 units/acre

DEVELOPMENT PROFILE

Type	Nº/Units	Size (sf)	Rents
2 BR	8	672	$50–200
TOTAL	8		

Parking: 8 surface
Total site area: 41,340 sf (.95 acres)

CONSTRUCTION TYPE
One-story woodframe, horiz. siding, comp. shingle roofs.

COSTS
Land Cost: $1/yr for 30 years; Constr. Costs: $181,000;
Other Costs: $3,200; **Total Development Cost: $184,200**
($23,025/unit). (Completed April 1993)

The University of Texas in Austin (U.T.) bought the houses in this development as part of a plan to acquire one-half of Blackland, a vital and well-maintained African-American neighborhood, for investment purposes. The community opposed the plan and started its own acquisition program for housing development. A homeless advocacy group proposed to use several university-owned buildings to house homeless people, a plan which community residents were initially hesitant about but eventually adopted. The university donated the houses and moving costs and leased a new site to the community for 30 years at a dollar per year. However, rehabilitation of the houses was delayed for four years due to opposition from City of Austin planning and development staff.

Architect, Tom Hatch, provided design, construction documents, and technical assistance on a pro bono basis. The houses were located to face the street and were given standard setbacks to reflect the character of the Blackland neighborhood. The design was kept simple, and basic materials were used. Front porches with wood trim and railings were added to the existing board-and-batten houses. Storage rooms were attached between two units to form a duplex in order to satisfy city zoning requirements.

Karen Paup, development manager, said that even with neighborhood sponsorship, an architect with good design skills, and the perseverance of the sponsor and their development manager, Blackland Housing took 8 years to accomplish. The housing that now stands proudly in the neighborhood, converted a vacant lot to a home for previously homeless people.

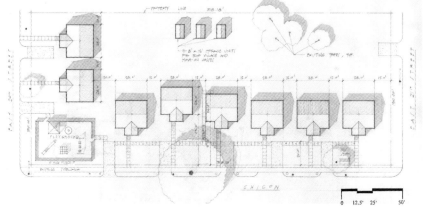

Site plan

Detail of decoration at gable Paul Bardagjy

Streetscape along Chicon Street Paul Bardagjy

La'ilani at Kealakehe · Kona, Hawaii

Many resort developers realize that it is in their interest to provide decent affordable housing for their workers. The State of Hawaii and the County of Hawaii Island has a program that requires resort developers to build affordable housing for every market-rate or hotel unit developed. La'ilani, which is managed by the State of Hawaii Housing Authority, is part of a master plan for the area which includes a range of housing types, a school, and other community facilities.

Nestled into a sloped site with panoramic views, the buildings are grouped around automobile courts paved and landscaped to reduce the visual presence of parked cars. The housing is designed as eightplex buildings—all corner-unit stacked flats —and each apartment has a private on-grade fenced area and a front porch or balcony. The buildings are designed as modified "plantation manor houses", and have roof-mounted solar hot-water panels. Lush planting and lava rock paving at entry drives help the housing blend into the Hawaiian landscape. Community facilities include a childcare center, laundry pavilions with adjoining play areas, a basketball court, and community gardens. Architect Owen Chock remarked, "La'ilani has set a new standard for public affordable housing in the state. This is the result of Mauna Lani Resort executive vice president Tom Yamamoto's insistence on building high quality housing in contrast to the usual public rental housing."

OWNER/DEVELOPER
Mauna Lani Resort, Inc. (MLR)

ARCHITECT
Design Partners Incorporated

LANDSCAPE ARCHITECT
David Tamura

CONTRACTOR
CAS Ltd.

PROPERTY MANAGEMENT
Hawaii Housing Authority

FUNDERS — **TYPE**
State of Hawaii Hsg Fin.
& Dev. Corp. — Tax-exempt bonds
Mauna Lani Resort — Equity

DEVELOPMENT TYPE
New construction rental housing, eightplexes.

RESIDENT PROFILE
Low-income families, resort workers.

DENSITY
13 units/acre

DEVELOPMENT PROFILE

Type	N°/Units	Size (sf)	Rents
1 BR	32	592	$275–450
2 BR	144	765	$475–650
3 BR	24	1,023	$600–775
TOTAL	**200**		

Community/laundry: 1,080 sf
Parking: 250 surface
Total site area: 15.5 acres

CONSTRUCTION TYPE
Two-story woodframe, slab on-grade, horiz. siding, comp. shingle roof.

COSTS
Land Cost: $0 (donated by State of Hawaii);
Constr. Costs: $11.9m; Other Costs: $.8m;
Total Development Cost: $12.7m ($63,500/unit).
(Completed November 1989)

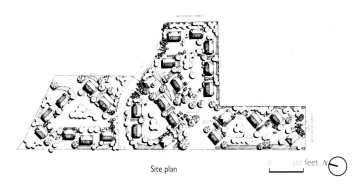

Site plan

0   200 feet N

View of building entries David Franzen

Eight-plex buildings at walkway David Franzen

La Ramona Morales Apartments Benson, Arizona

OWNER/DEVELOPER
Project P.P.E.P.

ARCHITECT
Tucson Community Development/Design Center
Centro de Arquitectura y Urbanismo para la Comunidad

CONTRACTOR
Carnes Construction

PROPERTY MANAGEMENT
Project P.P.E.P.

FUNDERS	**TYPE**
HUD 202	Loan
HUD Section 8	Rent subsidy

DEVELOPMENT TYPE
New construction rental flats.

RESIDENT PROFILE
Low-income seniors and persons with disabilities.

DENSITY
23 units/acre

DEVELOPMENT PROFILE

Type	N°/Units	Size (sf)	Rents	
Studio	4	402	$130	(HUD pays diff. FMR
1 BR	27	402	$130	and 30% income)
TOTAL	**31**			

Community/laundry: 818 sf (includes office)
Courtyard: 8,650 sf
Parking: 20 surface
Total site area: 58,300 sf or 1.34 acre

CONSTRUCTION TYPE
One-story tilt-up concrete, slab on-grade, woodframe
roof/int. walls.

COSTS
Land Cost: $76,000; Constr. Costs: $842,000; Other
Costs: $98,640; **Total Development Cost: $1,016,640
($32,795/unit).** (Completed 1987)

Located in a small rural town in south-eastern Arizona, these apartments have 30 units for the elderly and people with disabilities who typically pay 25 per cent of their monthly incomes for rent. At 402 square feet, the units are quite small, but they are set around a common outdoor area. Architect Jody Gibbs of the Tucson Community Development/ Design Center stated that because of the desert climate with high temperatures and scant rainfall, he had designed other Arizona housing with individual courtyards. However, the Reagan administration in 1986 had decreed that low-income housing not have courtyards. The tree-lined common area is, therefore, technically a "circulation" area. However, it is defined by the three entry gates and acts as a shaded interior street typical of desert regions. Because the grade changes by 10 feet from the west to the east of the site, each group of four units shares a tree-shaded level area which acts as a courtyard. Each such area is connected to the next level by a ramp. The construction technology is tilt-up concrete with 4.5-inch thick walls cast with patterns in various colors drawn from regional textiles, pottery and woodcarving. This use of standard technology to enrich simple forms demonstrates that housing for people with low incomes need not be aesthetically impoverished, but can incorporate the dignity and richness of local cultures.

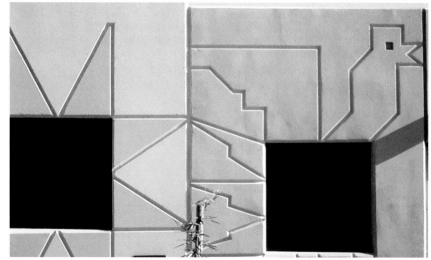

Window design in stair motif Jody Gibbs

West facade showing bird motifs on tilt-up panels Jody Gibbs

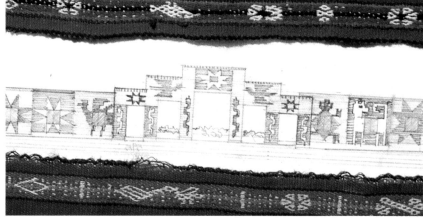

Elevation study based on Latin-American textiles Jody Gibbs

Viviendas Asistenciales   Tucson, Arizona

The Viviendas Asistenciales housing for the elderly and people with disabilities has 31 completely accessible units with individual courtyards grouped around a common courtyard. In its use of courtyards the design reflects desert architecture the world over. Desert trees and an operable dacron canopy shield the main courtyard from the hot sun to improve the comfort of the residents. The housing is located next to a county facility offering health and social services, across the street from a large private full-service shopping center, and one block from the city's main hospital. This location is a boon to residents who cannot afford or do not drive automobiles.

The Tucson Community Development/ Design Center, which developed and owns Viviendas Asistenciales, paid $37,600 for the property—instead of the $400,000 at which the land was valued—because Pima County offered the land via a public process to any developer who would agree to provide 30 units of fully subsidized elderly and handicapped housing for 40 years, and who offered to return title of the property to Pima County at the end of that period. Although it is not strictly family housing, Viviendas illustrates two important points: 1) that economical and attractive design can be climatically appropriate, and 2) that elderly and disabled people can enjoy the opportunity to create a larger "family" within their housing complex.

OWNER/DEVELOPER
Tucson Community Development/Design Center

ARCHITECT
Tucson Community Development/Design Center
Centro de Arquitectura y Urbanismo para la Comunidad

CONTRACTOR
George Codd and Co.

PROPERTY MANAGEMENT
Biltmore Properties

FUNDERS   **TYPE**
HUD 202   Loan
HUD Section 8   Rent subsidy

DEVELOPMENT TYPE
New construction rental flats.

RESIDENT PROFILE
Low-income seniors and persons with disabilities.

DENSITY
25 units/acre

DEVELOPMENT PROFILE

Type	N°/Units	Size (sf)	Rents
1 BR	31	602	$149 (HUD pays diff.
TOTAL	**31**		FMR and 30% income)

Community/laundry: 552 (includes office & kitchen)
Courtyard: 6800 sf
Parking: 20 surface
Total site area: 53,784 sf (1.24 acres)

CONSTRUCTION TYPE
Glue-laminated main beams on steel posts on drilled concrete piers; woodframe rafters and non-bearing walls, stucco exterior finish.

COSTS
Land Cost: $37,600; Constr. Costs: $962,539; Other Costs: $116,749; **Total Development Cost: $1,116,976 ($36,031/unit).** (Completed 1983)

Resident seated in courtyard   Jody Gibbs

Common courtyard looking west   Jody Gibbs

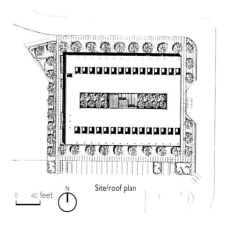
0   40 feet   N   Site/roof plan

West Hopkins Townhouses Aspen, Colorado

OWNER/DEVELOPER
Aspen/Pitkin County Housing Authority

ARCHITECT
Cottle Grabeal Yaw Architects, Ltd.

LANDSCAPE ARCHITECT
Mark Bedell

CONTRACTOR
Vannice

FUNDERS	**TYPE**
City of Aspen Hsg Dept.	Grant/grant for land

DEVELOPMENT TYPE
New construction for-sale attached townhouses.

RESIDENT PROFILE
Families with incomes 25–75% of AMI.

DENSITY
40 units/acre

DEVELOPMENT PROFILE

Type	N°/Units	Size (sf)	Sale Prices
Studio	3	610	$55,000–60,000
2 BR	6	960	$79,000–100,500
3 BR	2	1,100	$89,000–116,000
TOTAL	**11**		

Laundry: in each unit
Courtyard: 1,800 sf
Parking: 11 surface and carport
Total site area: 12,000 sf (.275 acres)

CONSTRUCTION TYPE
Two-story woodframe, plywood and batten siding, metal roofs.

COSTS
Land Cost: $0; Constr. Costs: $1,000,000; Other Costs: $225,000; **Total Development Cost: $1,225,000 ($118/sf).** (Completed 1993)

The West Hopkins townhouses are designed for working families who are permanent residents in the resort community of Aspen where high costs of living place housing beyond the range of many families of working people. This situation has compelled many such families to live far from their place of employment. The West Hopkins housing was a test infill development of only 11 units built on a vacant parcel of land. The scale and architectural character of the three groups of buildings are compatible with the existing context; the buildings are oriented to the street with the living spaces on the ground level to promote neighborhood interaction; they have an internal, semi-private open space. The required one space of parking per unit is on-site and accessed from an alley.

Developed by the Aspen-Pitkin County Housing Authority, architect Larry Yaw designed the units with steep metal roofs and board and batten siding to recall Colorado's turn-of-the-century miners cottages. Higher density was achieved by placing smaller one-bedroom "carriage houses" over garages off the rear drive. The West Hopkins homes have proven to be successful and their design quality was recognized by a Colorado AIA Honor Award in 1994.

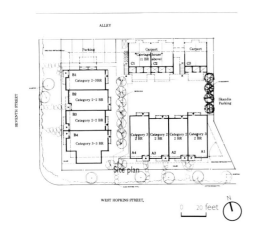

Site plan

Hopkins Street facade Larry Yaw, FAIA

Fineview Crest Pittsburgh, Pennsylvania

Fineview Crest was initiated by local community groups in the heart of Pittsburgh's working-class Fineview neighborhood. To increase home ownership in the neighborhood and to add diversity to the typical narrow townhouses, the Fineview Citizen's Council (FCC) chose to build detached homes on fee-simple lots. Despite general community support, a few neighbors waged a year-long legal battle against the housing, based on the claim that the proposed density and setbacks were not permitted by zoning. Affordable housing advocates worked with city staff and the Pittsburgh City Council to create an ordinance that allowed density and setbacks based on the averages in the area, a solution that has affected developments citywide.

The 12 homes were built in three phases of four homes each, which enabled the developers to borrow less money and use the sales proceeds from one phase to help fund the remaining phases. As they were being constructed, people of various ages and races bought the homes with assistance from the city in the form of 99-year deferred, second mortgages. The homes feature front porches, gabled roofs, and horizontal siding; the rhythm and textures of the homes help them to fit comfortably into the existing neighborhood. Through modest design and the use of cost-saving, energy-efficient materials, the architects were able to make construction and maintenance more affordable. Fineview Crest serves as a model for affordable infill home development in Pittsburgh.

DEVELOPER
Northside Civic Development Council, Inc.

ARCHITECT
Tai + Lee Architects, PC

CONTRACTOR
Kee Construction

FUNDERS

	TYPE
Urban Redevelopment Authority	Deferred loans
Pittsburgh Partnership for	
N'hood Devel.	Loan/grant
Pittsburgh National Bank	Loan/mortgage

DEVELOPMENT TYPE
New construction for-sale single-family homes.

RESIDENT PROFILE
Low- and moderate-income families.

DENSITY
16 units/acre

DEVELOPMENT PROFILE

Type	N°/Units	Size (sf)	Rents/Sale Prices
3 BR	12	2,040–2,067	$78,000+deferred
TOTAL	**12**		2nd mortgage

Laundry: W/D in each house
Courtyard/play: private yards
Parking: 24 garages
Total site area: 32,760

CONSTRUCTION TYPE
Two-story plus basement, woodframe with horiz. siding, comp. shingle roofs

COSTS
Land Cost: $71,600; Constr. Costs: $1,054,635; Other Costs: $295,765; **Total Development Cost: $1,350,391 ($96,110/unit).**
(Completed September 1992)

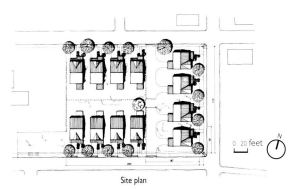

Site plan

Front facade and porch of wide body unit Dutch MacDonald

Kitchen and dining room interior Lockwood Hoehl

Capen Green Dorchester, Massachusetts

DEVELOPER
New Boston Housing Enterprises

ARCHITECT
Bergmeyer Associates, Inc.

CONSULTANTS
Landscape Architect: Kevin Keorner
Development Consultant: Sharon Lowenthal

CONTRACTOR
Accubuild Homes, Inc.

FUNDERS	TYPE
Mass. Hsg Finance Authority, HOP	Grant
City of Boston, 747 Program	Donated land
Neighborhood Development Fund	Grant

DEVELOPMENT TYPE
New construction fee-simple duplex townhouses.

RESIDENT PROFILE
First-time homebuyers with incomes $23,000–44,000

DENSITY
17 units/acre

DEVELOPMENT PROFILE

Type	N°/Units	Size (sf)	Sale Prices
3 BR(A)	10	1,200	$96,500
3 BR(B)	10	1,225	$96,500
TOTAL	20		

Courtyard/play: private back yards
Parking: 40 surface
Total site area: 50,094 (1.15 acres)

CONSTRUCTION TYPE
2.5 stories prefabricated woodframe, unfinished basements, vinyl siding, comp. shingle roofs, site built porches

COSTS
Land Cost: $50,000 for 7,500 sf; Constr. Costs: $1.8 m.; Other Costs: $700,000; **Total Development Cost: $2.5m ($125,000/unit).** (Completed June 1994)

Site plan and elevation

The goal for Capen Green was to build fee-simple homes—residents own both the house and the land on which it stands—for families with incomes of 50–80 per cent of the area's median income. The 10 attached-townhouses have 20 units with partially unfinished third floors and basement spaces to enable owners to create in-law apartments.

The buildings were designed to fit with the neighborhood's traditional triple-deckers and single houses. To vary the appearance of the housing from the street, the buildings were placed on their sites with either the end or the side elevation facing it. Architect Lewis Muhfelder said that the two units types were developed using modular construction, which reduced on-site costs of labor, theft of materials, and vandalism, while speeding up the construction process. Porches and entrances were built on the site to individualize the units.

Community support for the goal of restoring single-family home ownership to the neighborhood was crucial to moving the development through the city approval process. The participation of community members in the planning process changed the program by eliminating a central playground and re-distributing the land to increase the private yard space of the townhouses. Developer David Goldman commented that as soon as construction started, the community began to revitalize as neighbors started to repair and improve their own homes.

Type B duplex townhouses Lucy Chen

Detail of front porch Lucy Chen

Capen Street with Type B duplex townhouses and Type A duplex behind Lucy Chen

Columbia/Hampshire St Housing Cambridge, Massachusetts

Early in 1994, the City of Cambridge announced a competition for the development of affordable housing on a small surplus city property. Uniquely, the competition guidelines solicited proposals only for affordable homeownership, limited participants to Cambridge based non-profit entities, and outlined a constructive partnership between the City and the future development entity. Critical to the ultimate implementation strategy was the City's willingness to achieve neighborhood consensus on the proposed design program before selecting a development team. City representatives worked with community representatives in workshops to resolve potential areas of conflict.

The consensus guidelines issued by the City limited the number of units to a range of 12–20, targeted a specific family unit mix, and suggested certain site planning strategies. The project team developed the design to reinforce the context by directly fronting adjacent streets with a minimal landscaped setback and a corner "hinge-block". Parking and a common courtyard are located on the interior of the site with controlled access from the public perimeter. The 16 units are a mixture of flats and townhouses in a variety of two- and three-level configurations with five unit types. Full basements, private yards, double-occupancy bedrooms, and individual heating systems reflect the long-term occupancy implications of home ownership. This housing is an elegant addition to the neighborhood, and a successful example of small-lot infill in the inner city.

DEVELOPERS
Homeowner's Rehab, Inc. and Just-A-Start Corporation

ARCHITECT
Tise, Hurwitz & Diamond, Inc.

CONSULTANTS
Landscape Architect: Schreiber Associates

CONTRACTOR
Travi Construction Corporation

MANAGEMENT
L.E. Smith Management Company, Inc.

FUNDERS	TYPE
Cambridge Community Development Dept.	HUD Home Fund loan
Mass. Exec. Office of Comm. & Dev.	HUD Home Fund loan
Cambridge Banks Housing Association	Construction loan
Local Initiatives Support Corporation	Below-market construction loan
Cambridge Affordable Housing Trust	Loan/land grant
Charlesbank Homes	Grant
Mass. Housing Finance Agency	Below-market permanent loan
Neighborhood Reinvestment Corp.	Grant

DEVELOPMENT TYPE
New construction condominium townhouses and flats.

RESIDENT PROFILE
Half at or below 65% median income.
Half at or below 80% median income.

DENSITY
19 units/acre

DEVELOPMENT PROFILE

Type	N°/Units	Size (sf)	Sale Prices (Subsidized)
2 BR Flat	3	955–1065	$61,000
2 BR TH	3	1,370 (inc. basement)	$75,000
3 BR TH	8	1,675 (inc. basement)	$68–85,000
4 BR TH	2	1,855 (inc. basement)	$77–96,000
TOTAL	16		

Laundry: hook-ups provided in units
Courtyard/Play: 3,400 sf shared, 240 sf/unit (backyards)
Parking: 17 surface
Total site area: 36,610 sf (.84 acres)

CONSTRUCTION TYPE
Woodframe w/poured foundation full-basements.

COSTS
Land: $1 (Donated by City of Cambridge); Const. Costs: $1.625m; Other Costs: $440,000; **Total Development Cost: $2.065 m.** (Completed October 1995)

Site plan

Streetscape along Columbia Street Jim Raycroft

University City Family Housing   Philadelphia, Pennsylvania

OWNER/DEVELOPER
The Altman Companies

ARCHITECT
FRIDAY Architects/Planners and Richard Kline

CONTRACTOR
The Altman Companies

PROPERTY MANAGEMENT
The Altman Companies

FUNDERS   **TYPE**
HUD Section 8   Grant/rent subsidy

DEVELOPMENT TYPE
New construction rental attached townhouses.

RESIDENT PROFILE
Very-low- and low-income families.

DENSITY
25 units/acre

DEVELOPMENT PROFILE

Type	N°/Units	Size (sf)	Rents
2 BR	20	840	(HUD pays diff. bet.
3 BR	40	1,015	FMR & 30% HH income)
4BR	10	1,250	
TOTAL	**70**		

Community/laundry: 750
Courtyard/play: 3 semi-public courtyards, semi-public
           back yards, and play street
Parking: 50 surface
Total site area: 2.8 acres

CONSTRUCTION TYPE
Woodframe, brick masonry fronts and sides,
stucco bay windows

COSTS
Land Cost: $70,000; Constr. Costs: $2,788,100;
Other Costs: $942,160; **Total Development Cost:
$3,730,260 ($53,289/unit).** (Completed in 1983)

The result of a city-sponsored design/developer competition, this affordable housing stands on a 2.8-acre site cleared for redevelopment. The architect/developer team placed 70 townhouses around small courtyards sheltered from the edge of busy Market Street. Building facades with front stoops, typical of housing in the surrounding neighborhood, face each other across the courts to foster resident interaction and child supervision. Two parking courts connect an interior street, which, along with recreation areas and back patios with gardens, create a neighborhood.

Since the housing is on public land, the city required that one per cent of construction costs be spent on public art. The architects were able to apply part of this money to the houses; they worked with artist Michael Webb, who designed decorative motifs for the window surrounds and porch gables. The motifs were executed in a technique called sgraffito in which the design is carved through one layer of stucco into a ground layer of contrasting color. Since similar patterns were a common feature in much of 19th century Philadelphia architecture, the artwork adds a layer of local identity to the housing and is a symbol of pride for its residents. University City is a success—the development received an award for urban design excellence in 1991, and about 70 per cent of the original residents remain, attesting to the stability of affordable housing in the community.

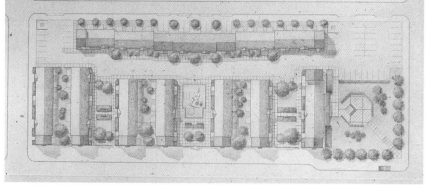
Site plan

Residents at dedication Don Matzkin

View to central courtyard from Market Street Don Matzkin

Dorado Village Philadelphia, Pennsylvania

Dorado Village was developed in the mid-1980s on one-and-a-half city blocks comprising about 2.7 acres in Philadelphia. The buildings' design reflects the understanding developed during the architect's early meetings with the Spanish Merchants Association, which sponsored the development. The goal of the association was to provide large units for families and stabilize the neighborhood that lies between the territory of two divergent ethnic groups.

Despite a density of about 30 units per acre with off-street parking spaces provided for each dwelling unit, the placement of the buildings still permitted a series of sheltered courtyards for the tenants' outdoor

enjoyment. The central courtyard has a tot-lot next to a small building with a community room and laundry. Architect Stephen Mark Goldner used flats, townhouses, and townhouses over flats to provide a variety of unit types and to vary the design of the facades and roofs. Appropriate architectural elements such as arches were incorporated in spite of the budget restraints. Instead of common hallways that reduce unit space, each unit has a private grade-level entrance with private stairs for upper units. Dorado Village, which is maintained by professional management, has proven to be an oasis of pride despite its location in one of the toughest sections of north Philadelphia.

DEVELOPER
Pennrose Properties, Inc.

ARCHITECT
Stephen Mark Goldner Associates

CONTRACTOR
Altman Construction

PROPERTY MANAGEMENT
Pennrose Management Co.

FUNDERS	TYPE
HUD Section 8	Rent subsidy
Penn. Housing Finance Agency	Loan
Pennrose Properties, Inc.	Equity

DEVELOPMENT TYPE
New construction rental flats and townhouses.

RESIDENT PROFILE
Very-low-income large families below 50% of AMI.

DENSITY
29 units/acre

DEVELOPMENT PROFILE

Type	N°/Units	Size (sf)	Rents
1 BR	8	660	HUD pays diff. between
2 BR	24	760	FMR and 30% HH income.
3 BR	40	975	
4 BR	8	115	
TOTAL	80		

Community/laundry: community center, laundry
Courtyard/play: tot-lot
Parking: 80 spaces
Total site area: 117,176 (2.69 acres)

CONSTRUCTION TYPE
Three-story woodframe with stucco and brick masonry facade, comp. shingle roofs

COSTS
Land Cost: $70,648; Constr. Costs: $4,043,844; Other Costs: $621,176; **Total Development Cost: $4,735,668 ($66/sf or $59,196/unit).** (Completed July 1983)

Typical building cluster Stephen Goldner

Site plan/floor plan

LEHIGH AVENUE

OAKDALE STREET

SEVENTH STREET

MARSHALL STREET

WENDLE STREET

HAROLD STREET

HUNTINGTON STREET

0   70 feet   N

View of tot-lot and community room Stephen Goldner

Sojourner Truth Homes Brooklyn, New York

SPONSOR
New York City Housing Partnership

BUILDER/DEVELOPER
Stuyvesant Avenue Housing Corp.
The Hudson Companies, Inc.

ARCHITECT
Harden Van Arnam Architects

CONTRACTOR
Monadnock Construction Inc.

MANAGEMENT
Homeowners Association

FUNDERS	**TYPE**
Chase Community Devel. Corp.	Loan
N.Y. State Affordable Hsg Corp.	Soft loan/grant
N.Y. City Dept. of HPD	Soft loan/grant

DEVELOPMENT TYPE
New construction, for-sale attached townhouses +
basement, with rental unit on 2nd floor of townhouse.

RESIDENT PROFILE
First-time homebuyers, incomes $32,000–53,000.

DENSITY
59 units/acre

DEVELOPMENT PROFILE

Type	N°/Units	Size (sf)	Sale Prices/Rents
2–4 BR TH	68	1,840	$154,683 after subsidy
1–2 BR Flat	68	920	Rental
TOTAL	136		

Laundry: in for-sale unit
Courtyard/play: 980 sf front and rear yards
Parking: 68 surface
Total site area: 150,603 (3.45 acres)

CONSTRUCTION TYPE
Two-story woodframe over concrete basement; brick
veneer in front, aluminum siding in rear over gypsum
sheathing

COSTS
Land Cost: $646,000; Constr. Costs: $10,763,000;
Other Costs: $2,099,000; **Total Development Cost:**
$14,429,000 ($212,191/house and $106,095/unit).
(Completed December 1992)

The Sojourner Truth Homes in the Bedford Stuyvesant area of Brooklyn consists of 68 attached, two-family townhouses in which owners occupy the first level and basement, and tenants rent the second floor unit. If the owner wishes, an extended family may occupy the building. As is typical throughout the neighborhood, these homes have stoops which lead to separate front entrances for each unit; the owner's townhouse has a rear stair leading to the backyard. Architect Cindy Harden commented that concepts such as jogging the building line and adding bay windows were rejected by the developer to make these homes affordable to potential buyers. However, the team was able to provide adequate square footage for families and a brick facade to blend in with the traditional housing in the neighborhood.

Off-street parking was considered to be an important feature for attracting buyers to these new homes. However, in contrast to most similar developments that provide for parking pads in front of the homes, the architect and developer, Alan Bell of The Hudson Companies Inc., agreed to place most of the parking in secure lots at the rear of the homes in order to preserve the traditional townhouse character of the neighborhood. Sojourner Truth Homes was considered highly desirable by local residents and has helped to successfully transform the area by filling vacant, debris-filled lots with new owner-occupied homes.

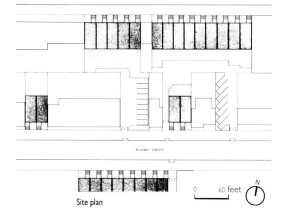

Site plan

0   60 feet   N

Stuyvesant Gardens Brian Rose

Regent Terrace Apartments   Philadelphia, Pennsylvania

103 units/acre

The restoration of these buildings in south-west Philadelphia and their conversion from 36 apartments to 80 units of affordable housing for families and seniors seems an impossible feat in view of their previous deteriorated condition. Citizen groups such as the Tenant Action Group and the Association of Community Organizations for Reform Now (ACORN) worked with elected officials for five years to get this housing built. The City of Philadelphia Redevelopment Authority acquired the land and worked with other city agencies to identify a qualified development team. Tax credits for historic restoration, which fortunately were still available in the 1980s, made the development feasible.

The imposing three-story buildings now look as luxurious as they did in 1910 thanks to present-day restoration techniques that used cast stone column replacements and fiberglass cornices, among other methods. Common rear courtyards and a laundry are shared by the families, while intercom-controlled entries off the front porches serve six units each. The broad porches and graceful stoops create dignified homes for working families and send a signal of positive change through the neighborhood.

DEVELOPER
Co-developer: Pennrose Properties
Co-developer: Pennsylvania Housing Finance Agency

ARCHITECT
Exterior Restoration Architect: Kelly, Maiello Inc.,
   Arch. & Planners
Interior Rehabilitation Architect: Goldner Goldfarb Kline

DEVELOPMENT CONSULTANT
Development Consultant: The Clio Group (Historic)

CONTRACTOR
Allied General Construction Service Corp.

PROPERTY MANAGEMENT
Pennrose Management Co.

FUNDERS	TYPE
Penn. Historical Commission; Historic Tax Credits	Equity
Penn. Housing Finance Authority	Loan
City of Philadelphia, Office of Hsg & Community Dev.	Loan
HUD Section 8 Certs. and Mod. Rehab.	Grant/rent subsidy

DEVELOPMENT TYPE
Gut rehabilitation, reconfiguration, & exterior restoration of 36 three-story apartments to stacked flats.

RESIDENT PROFILE
Very-low-income families, incomes at or below 50% AMI.

DENSITY
103 units/acre

DEVELOPMENT PROFILE

Type	N°/Units	Size (sf)	Rents
1 BR	42	479	(HUD pays diff. bet. FMR
2 BR	38	576	and 30% of HH income.)
TOTAL	**80**		

Community/laundry: yes
Courtyard/play: shared rear yards and front porches
Parking: on-street
Total site area: 32,880 sf

CONSTRUCTION TYPE
Three-story masonry wall-bearing structure with wood frame floor and roof

COSTS
Land Cost: $100,000; Constr. Costs: $4,220,000; Other Costs: $1,980,000; **Total Development Cost: $6,300,000 ($77,500/unit).** (Completed January 1989)

Regent Street before restoration   Howard Brunner

Typical front facade with neighboring buildings   Eric Mitchell

Oak Terrace Boston, Massachusetts

SPONSOR
Asian Community Dev. Corp.

ARCHITECT
Lawrence K. Cheng Assoc. Inc.

CONSULTANTS
Landscape Architect: Williams Associates
Development Consultant: The Community Builders

CONTRACTOR
Beacon Construction Co.

PROPERTY MANAGEMENT
The Community Builders

FUNDERS / **TYPE**

FUNDERS	TYPE
HUD (Section 8)	Rent subsidy
Low Income Hsg Tax Credit via Mass. Hsg Investment Corp.	Equity
Mass Hsg Finance Agency	Loan
Neighborhood Hsg Trust	Grants/subsidies
Federal Home Loan Program	Grant
AFL-CIO Housing Investment Trust	Loan
Boston Redevelopment Authority (BRDA)	Loan/land

DEVELOPMENT TYPE
New construction rental flats and townhouses.

RESIDENT PROFILE
one-third low-, one-third moderate-income, one-third market-rate, families and seniors.

DENSITY
105 units/acre

DEVELOPMENT PROFILE

Type	N°/Units	Size (sf)	Rents
1 BD	14	600	$481–756
2 BD	32	820	$577–975
3 BR	33	1,150	$667–1,175
4 BD	9	1,350	$744–1,375
TOTAL	88		

Community/laundry: both
Courtyard: 6,000
Parking: 44 surface
Retail/commercial: 2,775 sf
Total site area: 36,339 (.83 acres)

CONSTRUCTION TYPE
Steel frame on concrete caissons and grade beams, with exterior finishes of brick veneer and EIFS panel

COSTS
Land Cost: $1,500,000; Constr. Costs: $9,672,620; Other Costs: $3,687,823; **Total Development Cost: $13,360,443 ($151,823/unit).** (Completed January 1995)

In 1987, the Asian Community Development Corporation (ACDC) was awarded the development rights to half of a site with an abandoned building and parking lot. This was the result of a request for proposals from the City of Boston to build 300 units of affordable housing and community facilities, the first new affordable housing in Chinatown in over 20 years. Due to financing constraints, the unit count was reduced to 88 from 120, and the parking was located on an adjacent surface lot instead of underground. The new building makes a transition between a tall hospital on one side and three-story brick townhouses on the other.

The community needed large apartments because 80–90 per cent of the units in Chinatown have only one bedroom. Three- and four-bedroom townhouses surround a secure courtyard, which gives children a supervised play area and acknowledges the traditional Chinese courtyard house. One- and two-bedroom flats occupy the ten-story tower; two retail spaces are offices for dentists and physicians serving Chinatown. The exterior has panels of Exterior Insulated Finish System, and brick to match the older buildings. According to architect Lawrence K. Cheng, "The design and detailing responded to the complex finance and budgetary restraints without sacrificing the quality of the dwellings." Carol Lee, former executive director of ACDC remarked, "Oak Terrace brought out the best of creativity with very limited resources. Many in the community as well as the funders have been impressed by the quality of the design."

View from corner of Washington Street and Oak Street Elton Pope-Lance

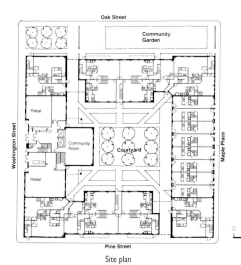

Site plan

Spring Creek Gardens Brooklyn, New York

Spring Creek Gardens is located on 7 acres near Kennedy Airport, and was financed in part by a city program that sells tax abatements for luxury housing in Manhattan to build affordable housing. Since the site is isolated, it was important to create small neighborhoods by grouping buildings around secure courtyards. Five-story buildings are on interior streets; those facing the courtyards, which are built over on-grade parking, residential units, commercial, and community spaces, have four stories. Residents value the secure entries and the safety of the courtyards, which are used by the children for recreation and are overlooked by about 200 families each. The attached buildings house only eight families each, which helps people to get to know their neighbors. The two units on each floor share a covered outdoor stair, a cost-saving and a security measure that eliminates the need for interior corridors, elevators, and fire stairs.

The architects reduced costs by saving time: "SCG was designed for panelized construction (exterior wall and floor panels of lightweight steel with exterior cladding and windows in place.) Wall sections were assembled off-site and trucked to the site; plumbing and mechanical systems were installed on-site. The superstructure was erected in three months." The architects noted, "High density does not have to be dehumanizing. Spring Creek is perceived as lower density than its 6–12-story neighbors. Yet due to the distribution and intended use of open space it is almost twice as dense."

OWNER/DEVELOPER
General Atlantic Realty Corp c/o Millennium Corp

ARCHITECT
The Liebman Melting Partnership

LANDSCAPE ARCHITECT
The Schnadelbach Partnership

CONTRACTOR
Tishman Construction

PROPERTY MANAGEMENT
Phipps Houses Management

FUNDERS	**TYPE**
New York City 421A Program	Tax transfer
Low Income Housing Tax Credits	Equity

DEVELOPMENT TYPE
New construction rental flats and townhouses.

RESIDENT PROFILE
Low-income families.

DENSITY
110 units/acre

DEVELOPMENT PROFILE

Type	N°/Units	Size (sf)	Rents
Studio	184	425	$na
1 BR	107	600	$na
2 BR	420	725	$na
3 BR	54	875	$na
TOTAL	765		

Comm'ty/laundry: 3 laundries, community m'ting room
Courtyard/play: 3 courts, 14,000 sf
Parking: 905 on-grade garage
Retail: small convenience stores
Total site area: 7.8 acres

CONSTRUCTION TYPE
Lightweight panelized steel construction over one-story poured concrete deck

COSTS
na. (First 565 units occupied 1988)

Section

View of town square and main entrance to Spring Creek Gardens Tom Reiss

Courtyard space R.T. Schnadelbach

Lee Goodwin Residence Bronx, New York

OWNER/DEVELOPER
Phipps Houses

ARCHITECT
Levenson, Meltzer, Neuringer

CONTRACTOR
The Jobco Organization

PROPERTY MANAGEMENT
Phipps Houses Management

FUNDERS	TYPE
N.Y. City Capital Budget	
Homeless Hsg Prog.	Loan
N.Y. City	Land

DEVELOPMENT TYPE
Gut rehabilitation of two vacant buildings, permanent and transitional housing.

RESIDENT PROFILE
Homeless female parents with young children

DENSITY
157 units/acre

DEVELOPMENT PROFILE

Type	N°/Units	Size (sf)	Rents
Studio	4	480	Welfare shelter
1 BR	16	670	allowance and
2 BR	16	810	per diem rate.
3 BR	5	950	
TOTAL	**41**		

Community/laundry: 3,750 sf
Courtyard/play: 1,484 sf
Parking: 0
Total site area: 11,500 (.26 acres)

CONSTRUCTION TYPE
Masonry and steel structure

COSTS
Land Cost: $2.00; Constr. Costs: $3,600,000;
Other Costs: $1,300,000; **Total Development Cost:**
$4,900,000. (Completed in 1990)

View of dining area/living room Stephen Fischer

Lee Goodwin Residence houses formerly homeless women and children in two formerly vacant, city-owned, five-story buildings on Prospect Avenue. The goal of the owner/sponsor, Phipps Houses, is to raise both new hope and new housing in the Bronx. Architect Conrad Levenson noted that the re-use of the buildings preserved the neighborhood scale and the density, which would not be allowed in new construction. A social service program providing parenting workshops and other needed assistance, is run by Women in Need.

The combination in one facility of 28 transitional units and 13 permanent units with support services departed from the usual approach to housing homeless families. Four of the transitional units were designed with the living/dining and kitchen areas to be shared by two single-parent families. An unusual feature was two "swing" bedrooms that can be included in adjoining apartments to accommodate larger families. These last two features have had mixed success. Compatibility of families sharing units is unpredictable, and the flexibility of the swing bedrooms only works when adjacent apartments are vacant at the same time. A palette of bright colors was used on the interior for decorative glazed tiles, painted walls, and doors; each floor has its own color scheme. In addition to a variety of spaces that serve residents' needs, neighborhood businesses, such as a dentist office, a pharmacy, and retail shops, contribute to the economic stability of the building and the neighborhood.

Exterior entry Stephen Fischer

One of the largest housing rehabilitation projects in New York City, Crotona Park West, completed in 1994, involved the complete design and reconstruction of an entire community to provide 563 apartments in 20 buildings for 2,200 people in homeless families, and families with low and moderate incomes. The sponsor, Phipps Houses, selected the architectural firm of Levenson Meltzer Neuringer to design Crotona Park West. The development was subdivided into clusters of buildings on three sites, each with its own laundry rooms, community center, management and maintenance centers, commercial space, and adjacent open areas for recreation. Special service facilities such as daycare, a training center, and a large tenant meeting room are located in one cluster but are shared by all residents and available to the larger community.

Facades of the long vacant buildings were restored, preserving their traditional ornament and detail. Custom ironwork designed to be gates and other features, unifies the various architectural styles. The rear elevations are textured and colored to create a cheerful graphic composition that incorporates the fencing, lighting, windows, fire escapes, parapets, and other elements. Architect Conrad Levenson described the project goals as, "To promote community by design in all dimensions: within apartment units, among units on floors, among floors within buildings, between buildings, within each cluster, and between the three clusters." The rebirth of the Crotona Park community sparked revitalization of the larger neighborhood, and serves as a model and inspiration for development throughout the Bronx.

OWNER/DEVELOPER
Phipps Houses

ARCHITECT
Levenson, Meltzer, Neuringer

LANDSCAPE ARCHITECT
James Hadley

CONTRACTOR
Melcara Corp.

PROPERTY MANAGEMENT
Phipps House Services, Inc.

FUNDERS	TYPE
N.Y. City—Vacant Cluster Program	Loan/land

DEVELOPMENT TYPE
Gut rehabilitation of 20 vacant buildings into 563 rental flats and retail.

RESIDENT PROFILE
Formerly homeless, low-income, and moderate-income families.

DENSITY
164 units/acre

DEVELOPMENT PROFILE

Type	N°/Units	Size (sf)	Rents
Studio	7	500	$328–388
1 BR	203	650	$351–539
2 BR	304	800	$492–783
3 BR	49	950	$489–798
TOTAL	563		

Community: 27,000 + daycare & clinic
Courtyard/play: 10,790 sf
Parking: on-street
Retail: 5 stores
Total site area: 151,602 (3.48 acres)

CONSTRUCTION TYPE
Masonry with woodframe interiors.

COSTS
Land Cost: $20; Constr. Costs: $35,000,000; Other Costs: $8,000,000; **Total Development Cost: $43,000,000.** (Completed in 1994)

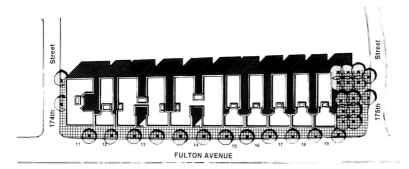

Site plan

Cluster 'C' from Crotona Park (after renovation) Conrad Levenson

Sarah Powell Huntington House   Manhattan, New York

OWNER/DEVELOPER
Women's Prison Assoc. & Hopper Home

ARCHITECT
Roberta Washington Architects, P.C.

CONTRACTOR
Ironstraw Construction
Phoenix Builders

PROPERTY MANAGEMENT
Women's Prison Association

FUNDERS	TYPE
N.Y. State Homeless Hsg	
Assistance. Corp.	Loan/grant
N.Y. City Dept. of Homeless Services	Subsidy
N.Y.C.	Land

DEVELOPMENT TYPE
Gut rehabilitation of six-story apartment building to flats and services.

RESIDENT PROFILE
Transitional housing for mothers who have been in prison to reunite them with their children.

DENSITY
182 units/acre

DEVELOPMENT PROFILE

Type	N°/Units	Size (sf)	Rents
1 BR	1	390	(NYC pays $100/night
2 BR	27	450–515	for social services and
TOTAL	28		operating costs.)

Community/laundry: 649 + office space
Courtyard/play: 1,014 childcare
Parking: none
Total site area: 6,696 (.15 acres)

CONSTRUCTION TYPE
Masonry exterior wall, steel girders, wood joists, metal stud partitions

COSTS
Land Cost : $2; Constr. Costs: $3,000,000;
Other Costs: $333,000; **Total Development Cost: $3,564,000.** (Completed 1993)

Sarah Powell Huntington House addresses a vicious trap that keeps homeless women leaving prison from reuniting with their children: without housing, mothers cannot get the welfare system to grant them custody of their children; unless the children are in hand, the homeless system will not provide housing for the mother. This groundbreaking development required the special support of city and state agencies that serve the homeless. After years of community pressure to provide sites for affordable housing in the neighborhood, the city agreed to allocate 50 per cent of the vacant buildings in the area for low- to middle-income housing. Architect Roberta Washington, in association with architect Steven Campbell, converted two 19th-century buildings facing a large park into one six-story

structure with 28 apartments, social services, two childcare rooms, and a multi-purpose room on the first floor.

Half the residents live as room-mates while they qualify for the return of their children, a process which can take up to nine months. The other half have already been reunited, and mothers and children occupy the apartment as a family. It can take another nine months after reunification to move into permanent housing in the community. During this time, government pays a rate of approximately $100 a day per apartment for all expenses associated with operating the building and providing on-site case management, social services, and childcare. Sarah P. Huntington House is a sensible safe haven for women and children finding their way back into family life together.

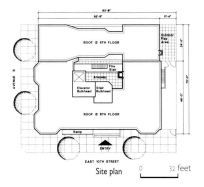

Site plan

View from Avenue B and 10th Street   John J. Gallagher

Close-up of front entry as seen from Manhattan Avenue   John J. Gallagher

Middle Towne Arch   Norfolk, Virginia

A multi-phase development in Norfolk, Virginia, Middle Towne Arch was designed as an extension of the Haynes tract neighborhood. The predominantly African-American community was successful in changing the project to for-sale housing in the affordable range by organizing against the development of the former World War II housing site as an industrial park.

Norfolk's flexibility in the zoning of planned developments within urban redevelopment areas assisted the adoption of a plan that, although it appears unusual, was based on that of the historic Norfolk neighborhoods of Ghent, Colonial Place, and other neighborhoods chosen by the community as a model. In phase I the concentric pattern of curved streets, called the "arch", focuses on a public

space; the focus of phase II is a retention pond around a wooded island. The location of parking on alleys made it possible to create a main street frontage without curb-cuts or garages that conveys the impression of the "good" neighborhood. The lot and block sizes match those of the surrounding area. For this conservative market, UDA Architects has reused the region's colonial architecture with skill and conviction. The close relationship between the private spaces of the dwellings and the community life of the street helps create a secure neighborhood. The success of Middle Towne Arch encouraged the revitalization of the area, which demonstrates that developing affordable middle-income housing can be an effective way to stabilize neighborhoods.

DEVELOPER
Norfolk Redevelopment and Housing Authority (NRHA)

ARCHITECT
UDA Architects

CONTRACTOR
Lasting Development
Various other local firms

FUNDERS	TYPE
Local Banks	Mortgages
NRHA	Grant/loan

DEVELOPMENT TYPE
New construction for-sale single-family homes.

RESIDENT PROFILE
Moderate-income families.

DENSITY
5 units/acre

DEVELOPMENT PROFILE

Type	N°/Units	Size (sf)	Sale Prices
3 BR	188	1,400–2,000	$90,000–140,000
TOTAL	**188** (phase I)		

Laundry: in each unit
Courtyard/play: park and lake, private back yards
Parking: 376 surface and garage
Total site area: 110 acres

CONSTRUCTION TYPE
Two-story woodframe, brick veneer and vinyl siding, comp. shingle roofs

COSTS
Constr. Costs: $9,200,000; Other Costs: $4,339,000;
Total Development Cost: $13,539,000 + land costs.
(Phase I ongoing)

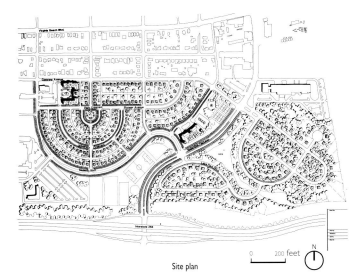

Site plan

0   200 feet   N

Aerial view of Crescent Tom Bernard

Homes on Crescent Tom Bernard

Dermott Villas Dermott, Arkansas

OWNER/DEVELOPER
Marshall Planning and Development (MPD)

ARCHITECT
Wenzel & Associates

CONTRACTOR
Champion Builders, Inc.

PROPERTY MANAGEMENT
Tri-state Management Corp.

FUNDERS	TYPE
Farmers Home Admin. Section 515	95% loan
MPD	5% equity
Rural rental housing loan program	Loan

DEVELOPMENT TYPE
New construction rental flats and townhouses.

RESIDENT PROFILE
Farm and household worker families,
incomes $4,000–12,000.

DENSITY
8 units/acre

DEVELOPMENT PROFILE

Type	N°/Units	Size (sf)	Rents
1 BR	8	520	$0–230
2 BR	15	700	$0–265
2 BR Handicap	2	772	$0–265
2 BR TH	8	878	$0–265
TOTAL	**33**		

Community/laundry: 840 sf
Courtyard/play: playground
Parking: 46 surface
Total site area: 4 acres

CONSTRUCTION TYPE
One- and two-story woodframe with vinyl siding,
comp. shingle roof

COSTS
Land Cost: $15,000; Constr. Costs: $900,000;
Other Costs: $117,800; **Total Development Cost:**
$1,017,000 ($30,818/unit or $41.83/sf).
(Completed 1989)

Although Mer Rouge Villas and Dermott Villas are built in different states, both of these developments are set in groves of mature pecan trees in residential areas that contain some substantial ante-bellum houses. Both are village-like complexes of white buildings with distinctive roofs and columned porches that contain 33 units of housing for families with low incomes subsidized by the Department of Agriculture's Farmers Home Administration. This housing responds to the particularly strong need for decent affordable housing in rural areas of the South.

Designed by William Wenzel, the buildings fit into their contexts— unlike many examples of public housing. In the case of Mer Rouge Villas, the arrangement of the buildings on a diagonal in a 12-foot grid created diamond-shaped clusters among the trees. Not only were all but two of the much-needed shade trees saved by this strategy, but the units benefited from the creation of entrance allees typical of grand estates. The Dermott Villas site plan has the units stepped around cul-de-sacs with parking. In addition to the 16 one-bedroom units, 12 two-bedroom units, and 5 two-bedroom townhouses, both developments have community centers containing the manager's unit, the administrative office, laundry, and maintenance areas.

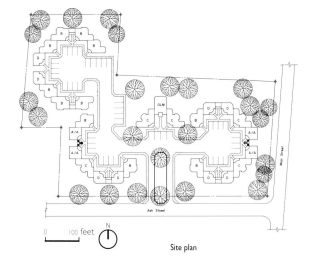

Site plan

Housing clusters and laundry from entry Timothy Hursley

Mer Rouge Villas Mer Rouge, Louisiana

Although the building forms in both developments are closely related—in Mer Rouge Villas they appear to have grown together in a natural way— each has an identity. By using ready made, standardized components supplemented with designed details, the architect achieved economy of design. Since winning his first Farmers Home Administration design competition in 1986, Wenzel has gone on to design affordable housing in several southern states. He declares, "My whole value system changed, and I have gravitated toward the people who have been ignored since FDR and the New Deal." His efforts have not gone unnoticed—in 1992 Mer Rouge Villas received a Presidential Design Award. Developer Thomas B. Marshall commented that since the completion of Dermott Villas, affordable housing developments are accepted more readily by communities. "We have very little political opposition," he said, "since we started building the better designed housing."

OWNER/DEVELOPER
Marshall Planning and Development (MPD)

ARCHITECT
Wenzel & Associates

CONTRACTOR
Champion Builders, Inc.

PROPERTY MANAGEMENT
Tri-state Management Corp.

FUNDERS	TYPE
Farmers Home Administration	95% loan
MPD	5% equity
US Dept. of Agriculture	

DEVELOPMENT TYPE
New construction rental townhouses.

RESIDENT PROFILE
Low- to moderate-income families.

DENSITY
8 units/acre

DEVELOPMENT PROFILE

Type	N°/Units	Size (sf)	Rents
1 BR	16	552	$0–295
2 BR	12	768	$0–330
2 BR TH	5	864	$0–340
TOTAL	33		

Laundry/maintenance: 644 (includes office)
Courtyard/play: tot-lot
Parking: 42 surface
Total site area: 4 acres

CONSTRUCTION TYPE
One-, two- and three-story woodframe, vinyl siding & brick veneer, comp. shingle roofs.

COSTS
Land Cost: $40,000; Constr. Costs: $900,000; Other Costs: $83,083; **Total Development Cost: $983,083 ($28,372 /unit or $32.85/sf).** (Completed November 1987)

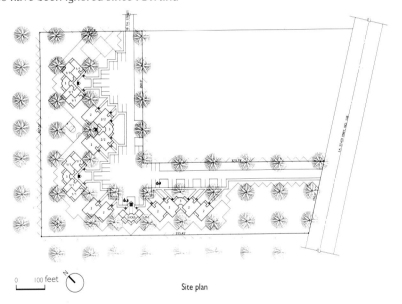

0   100 feet   N

Site plan

Central cluster with basketball hoop Timothy Hursley

RESOURCE GUIDE,
USING THE GUIDES AND INDEXES,
SPECIAL CHARACTERISTICS GUIDE,
COMPARATIVE DESCRIPTION INDEX

Firm name, contact, telephone number, city,
development name, page number for:

- Developers/sponsors/development consultants
- Architects
- Landscape architects
- Contractors
- Property managers
- Photographers
- National housing, design and community
  development organizations
- State affordable housing coalitions

Using the Comparative Description Index and the Special Characteristics Guide

The Comparative Description Index is a reference tool that allows the reader to quickly scan categories, such as density, owner/renter and context, to identify specific developments of the type in which they have an interest. The projects are listed in ascending order of density (units-per-acre) within each regional grouping. The additional category of bed-rooms-per-acre is also included to demonstrate one alternative measure of density that takes into account the impact of family size, not just the number of kitchens in a building.

The Resource Guide

Developers, architects, landscape architects, contractors, property managers, and photographers are listed by profession in alphabetical order in the Resource Guide at the back of the book. The telephone number and city are listed so readers can contact professionals in their area for more information.

SPECIAL CHARACTERISTICS GUIDE

The case studies presented in this book provide examples of developments with the following characteristics.

Affordable housing in affluent communities has become a solution when there is: **a.** strong inclusionary zoning or fair-share policies required by the jurisdiction; **b.** a recognition that the local workforce, which serves the affluent, is part of the community and needs reasonably priced housing.

- Battle Road Farm   See p. 166
- La'ilani at Kealakehe   See p. 229
- West HELP   See p. 172
- West Hopkins Townhouses   See p. 232

Courtyard housing arranges housing around a common court which provides a play area for children and a way to enter dwelling units and facilities.

- Cascade Court Apartments   See p. 116
- Daybreak Grove   See p. 132
- Del Carlo Court   See p. 104
- The Farm   See p. 74
- Frank G. Mar Community Housing   See p. 112
- Hismen Hin-nu Terrace   See p. 100
- Horizons   See p. 226
- Langham Court   See p. 198
- Matsusaka Townhomes   See p. 92
- Melrose Court   See p. 188
- Ninth Square Redevelopment   See p. 196
- Oak Terrace   See p. 240
- Ocean Park Co-op   See p. 146
- La Ramona Morales Apartments   See p. 230
- Roxbury Corners   See p. 192
- Southside Park Co-housing   See p. 84
- Spring Creek Gardens   See p. 241
- Tent City   See p. 202
- Tower Apartments   See p. 90
- Tuscany Villas/Villa Calabria   See p. 78
- Villa Esperanza   See p. 140
- Viviendas Asistenciales   See p. 231
- West HELP   See p. 172
- Willowbrook Green Apartments   See p. 136
- Yorkshire Terrace   See p. 142
- YWCA Family Village   See p. 88
- YWCA Villa Nueva   See p. 106
- 111 Jones/201 Turk   See p. 120

Families, seniors, and/or singles are sometimes combined in developments when the size of the development, the funding, and the demand allows.

- Cascade Court Apartments   See p. 116
- Frank G. Mar Community Housing   See p. 112
- Oak Terrace   See p. 240
- La Ramona Morales Apartments   See p. 230
- Spring Creek Gardens   See p. 241
- Tuscany Villas/Villa Calabria   See p. 78
- Viviendas Asistenciales   See p. 231
- 555 Ellis Street   See p. 108
- 111 Jones/201 Turk   See p. 120
- West Town Cluster Housing   See p. 162

Farmworker housing addresses the needs of a specific category of rural families upon whom the agricultural economy depends. In many locales, state and federal funding programs assist developers in housing these workers.

- Amistad Farm Laborers Housing   See p. 128
- Nuevo Amanecer Apartments   See p. 72
- Rancho Sespe Farmworker Housing   See p. 126

For-profit developers are sometimes relied upon to develop affordable housing when: **a.** there are no local non-profits; **b.** they can bring a market awareness that generates a good development; **c.** the municipality will receive long-term affordability as a condition of providing assistance.

- Battle Road Farm   See p. 166
- Crawford Square   See p. 168
- Dermott Villas   See p. 246
- Harriet Square   See p. 219
- Melrose Court   See p. 188
- Mer Rouge Villas   See p. 247
- Middle Towne Arch   See p. 245
- Ninth Square Redevelopment   See p. 196
- Quincy Homes   See p. 218
- Regent Terrace Apartments   See p. 239
- Westminster Place   See p. 221
- Sojourner Truth Homes   See p. 238
- Southside Park Co-housing   See p. 84

Historic structures rehabilitation restores valuable resources to good use. Although design guidelines and code requirements often increase costs, historic building codes are often flexible, and historic tax credits may improve financing prospects.

- Crotona Park West   See p. 243
- Lee Goodwin Residence   See p. 242
- Regent Terrace Apartments   See p. 239
- Sarah Powell Huntington House   See p. 244

Historic district new construction can significantly affect design and construction costs because of their design guidelines. However, compatibility with surrounding buildings may increase public acceptance and enhance the value of the historic district.

- Catherine Street   See p. 184
- Langham Court   See p. 198
- Ninth Square Redevelopment   See p. 196
- Tent City   See p. 202

Housing for homeless families has become critical in the light of the increasing number of families and children on the streets. These developments are often transitional and include extensive on-site social services to assist families in getting back on their feet.

- Blacklands Transitional Housing   See p. 228
- Lee Goodwin Residence   See p. 242
- Sarah Powell Huntington House   See p. 244
- YWCA Villa Nueva   See p. 106
- West HELP   See p. 172
- YWCA Family Village   See p. 88

Infill housing fills vacant lots and repairs the torn fabric of the streetscape.

- Capen Green   See p. 234
- Cascade Court Apartments   See p. 116
- CEPHAS Housing   See p. 190
- Charleston Infill Housing   See p. 208
- Columbia/Hampshire St Housing   See p. 235
- Dorado Village   See p. 237
- Del Carlo Court   See p. 104
- Field Street   See p. 154
- Fineview Crest   See p. 233
- Frank G. Mar Community Housing   See p. 112
- Harriet Square   See p. 219
- Hismen Hin-nu Terrace   See p. 100
- Holladay Avenue Homes   See p. 223
- Horizons   See p. 226
- Hyde Square Co-op   See p. 176
- International Homes   See p. 220
- Lorin Station   See p. 98
- Langham Court   See p. 198
- Lucretia Gardens/Julian Street   See p. 225
- Matsusaka Townhomes   See p. 92
- Melrose Court   See p. 188
- Oak Terrace   See p. 240
- Paula Avenue Homes   See p. 227
- Parkside Gables   See p. 180
- Parkview Commons   See p. 94
- Quincy Homes   See p. 218
- The Reservoir   See p. 160
- Roxbury Corners   See p. 192
- Sojourner Truth Homes   See p. 238
- Tent City   See p. 202
- Tower Apartments   See p. 90
- University City Family Housing   See p. 236
- Waterside Green   See p. 178
- West Hopkins Townhouses   See p. 232
- West Town Cluster Housing   See p. 162
- West Town II   See p. 156
- 555 Ellis Street   See p. 108
- 201 Turk/111 Jones   See p. 120

Mixed-income housing—typically one-third low-income, one-third moderate-income, one-third market-rate—can be an effective development approach when: **a.** inclusionary zoning requires it; **b.** there are limited public funds, which requires that surplus funds from market-rate units can create an additional subsidy for low-income units; **c.** income diversity is required for community acceptance.

- Crawford Square   See p. 168
- Langham Court   See p. 198
- Ninth Square Redevelopment   See p. 196
- Randolph Neighborhood   See p. 210
- Tent City   See p. 202
- Timberlawn Crescent   See p. 214

Mixed-use developments include retail, commercial, or community spaces at the street level.

- Frank G. Mar Community Housing   See p. 112
- Hismen Hin-nu Terrace   See p. 100
- Lorin Station   See p. 98
- Melrose Court   See p. 188
- Ninth Square Redevelopment   See p. 196
- Roxbury Corners   See p. 192
- Tent City   See p. 202
- YWCA Villa Nueva   See p. 106
- YWCA Family Village   See p. 88
- 555 Ellis Street   See p. 108
- 201 Turk/111 Jones   See p. 120

Mutual housing associations and co-ops provide: **a.** resident equity in their homes; **b.** a larger resident responsibility in management; **c.** access to subsidies not available for homeownership; **d.** greater community acceptance than rental housing.

- Hyde Square Co-op   See p. 176
- Langham Court   See p. 198
- Mutual Housing Association   See p. 186
- Ocean Park Co-op   See p. 146
- Parkside Gables   See p. 180
- Roxbury Corners   See p. 192
- Tent City   See p. 202

New district development utilizes larger scale planning and urban design, and can help revitalize a large area.

- Crawford Square   See p. 168
- Crotona Park West   See p. 243
- Mutual Housing Association   See p. 186
- Ninth Square Redevelopment   See p. 196
- Orchard Village and Oak Hill   See p. 206
- Randolph Neighborhood   See p. 210
- Westminster Place   See p. 221

Partnerships between non-profit and for-profit developers and between grass-roots sponsors and experienced non-profits can be an effective approach when: **a.** the larger developer brings experience and financing capability; **b.** the smaller developer brings access to public funds, community values, and political acceptance; **c.** a combination of market-rate and subsidized housing is desired.

- Dorado Village   See p. 237
- Columbia/Hampshire St Housing   See p. 235
- Frank G. Mar Community Housing   See p. 112
- Hismen Hin-nu Terrace   See p. 100
- Lyton Park Place   See p. 152
- Parkview Commons   See p. 94
- St John's Hospital Housing   See p. 148
- Villa Esperanza   See p. 140
- Waterside Green   See p. 178
- YWCA Villa Nueva   See p. 106
- 201 Turk Street   See p. 120

Public housing authorities (PHAs) have played a key role in developing well-designed affordable housing when: **a.** local non-profits lack capacity; **b.** the PHA has a positive relationship with the community.

- Charleston Infill Housing   See p. 208
- Lucretia Gardens/Julian Street   See p. 225
- Randolph Neighborhood   See p. 210
- West Hopkins Townhouses   See p. 232

Scattered-site developments can be an effective approach to development when: **a.** there are many smaller vacant lots in a neighborhood; **b.** neighborhood acceptance of larger developments is impossible; **c.** local agencies can help acquire and assemble parcels at lower cost.

- Charleston Infill Housing   See p. 208
- Field Street   See p. 154
- International Homes   See p. 220
- Mutual Housing Association   See p. 186
- St John's Hospital Housing   See p. 148
- West Town Cluster Housing   See p. 162

Homeownership developments are built for those families who can qualify for loans and have some resources for downpayments. In most first-time homebuyer programs using government funds, the homeowner receives only limited appreciation in value of the home, and resale is restricted to families with low- to moderate-incomes.

- Battle Road Farm   See p. 166
- Benson Glen   See p. 70
- Capen Green   See p. 234
- Catherine Street   See p. 184
- Columbia/Hampshire St Housing   See p. 235
- Crawford Square   See p. 168
- Fineview Crest   See p. 233
- Harriet Square   See p. 219
- Holladay Avenue Homes   See p. 223
- International Homes   See p. 220
- Lake Park Townhomes   See p. 222
- Lyton Park Place   See p. 152
- Melrose Court   See p. 188
- Middle Towne Arch   See p. 245
- Mutual Housing Association of NY   See p. 186
- Charlestown Navy Yard Rowhouses   See p. 194
- OPAL Commons   See p. 68
- Orchard Village/Oak Hill   See p. 206
- Parkview Commons   See p. 94
- Quincy Homes   See p. 218
- Randolph Neighborhood   See p. 210
- Sojourner Truth Homes   See p. 238
- Southside Park Co-housing   See p. 84
- Waterside Green   See p. 178
- West Hopkins Townhouses   See p. 232

Tax credits are an important source of equity from the federal government for building low-income rental developments. Tax credits are awarded to developments by state allocation boards on a competitive basis, and are then sold to corporations or individuals seeking to shelter their high incomes from taxes.

- Cascade Court Apartments   See p. 116
- Crawford Square   See p. 168
- Daybreak Grove   See p. 132
- Del Carlo Court   See p. 104
- The Farm   See p. 74
- Frank G. Mar Community Housing   See p. 112
- Hismen Hin-nu Terrace   See p. 100
- Lorin Station   See p. 98
- Matsusaka Townhomes   See p. 92
- Nuevo Amanecer   See p. 72
- Oak Terrace   See p. 240
- Open Doors   See p. 224
- Paula Avenue Apartments   See p. 227
- Roxbury Corners   See p. 192
- Spring Creek Gardens   See p. 241
- Stoney Creek Apartments   See p. 82
- Tent City   See p. 202
- Tower Apartments   See p. 90
- Tuscany Villas/Villa Calabria   See p. 78
- Villa Esperanza   See p. 140
- West Town II   See p. 156
- Westminster Place   See p. 221
- Woodlands   See p. 130
- YWCA Family Village   See p. 88
- YWCA Villa Nueva   See p. 106
- 111 Jones Street   See p. 120
- 555 Ellis Street   See p. 108

Page #	Case studies by region — City	# Units	Density: DU/ac	BR/ac	Dwelling type	Rent/own Co-op	Neighborhood context	Childcare etc.
	The Northwest and Northern California							
68	OPAL Commons, Orcas, WA	18	5	11	Single-family	For-sale	Rural Cluster	No
70	Benson Glen, Seattle, WA	43	7	21	Single-family	For-sale	Suburban	No
72	Nuevo Amanecer Apartments, Woodburn, OR	50	10	29	Row/Court	Rental	Suburban	No
74	The Farm, Soquel, CA	39	13	33	Multiplex/Court	Rental	Suburban	Yes
78	Tuscany Villas/Villa Calabria, Davis, CA	36	15	42	Row/Court	Rental	Suburban	No
82	Stoney Creek Apartments, Livermore, CA	70	16	35	Multiplex/Court	Rental	Suburban	No
84	Southside Park Co-housing, Sacramento, CA	25	20	49	Duplex/Court	For-sale	Suburban	No
88	YWCA Family Village, Redmond, WA	20	21	35	Low-rise apts/Mix	Rental	Suburban	Yes
90	Tower Apartments, Rohnert Park, CA	50	25	62	Row/Court	Rental	Suburban	No
92	Matsusaka Townhomes, Tacoma, WA	26	29	84	Row/Court	Rental	Urban Infill	No
94	Parkview Commons, San Francisco, CA	114	44	124	Row/Court	For-sale	Urban Infill	No
98	Lorin Station, Berkeley, CA	14	47	87	Flat/Mix	Rental	Urban Infill	No
100	Hismen Hin-nu Terrace, Oakland, CA	92	55	130	Low/Flat/Mix/Court	Rental	Urban Infill	Yes
104	Del Carlo Court, San Francisco, CA	25	57	139	Walk/Flat/TH/Court	Rental	Urban Infill	No
106	YWCA Villa Nueva, San Jose, CA	63	77	84	Mid/Flat/Mix	Rental	Urban Infill	Yes
108	555 Ellis Street, San Francisco, CA	38	122	277	Low/Mix	Rental	Urban Infill	Yes
112	Frank G. Mar Community Housing, Oakland, CA	119	129	248	Mid/Flat/Mix/Court	Rental	Urban Infill	Yes
116	Cascade Court Apartments, Seattle, WA	100	151	209	Mid/Flat/TH/Court	Rental	Urban Infill	No
120	201 Turk Street, San Francisco, CA	175	200	338	Mid/Flat/Court	Rental	Urban Infill	Yes
120	111 Jones Street, San Francisco, CA	108	251	781	Mid/Flat/Court	Rental	Urban Infill	Yes
	The Southwest and Southern California							
126	Rancho Sespe Farmworker Housing, Piru, CA	100	5	15	Row House	Rental	Rural Cluster	Yes
128	Amistad Farm Laborers Hsg, Hereford, TX	30	8	23	Row House	Rental	Rural Cluster	Yes
130	Woodlands, Boulder, CO	35	12	29	Multiplex/Court	Rental	Suburban	Yes
132	Daybreak Grove, Escondido, CA	13	15	37	Row/Court	Rental	Suburban	No
136	Willowbrook Green Apts, Los Angeles, CA	48	19	35	Row/Court	Rental	Urban Infill	Yes
140	Villa Esperanza, Los Angeles, CA	33	29	96	Row/Flat/Court	Rental	Urban Infill	Yes
142	Yorkshire Terrace, Los Angeles, CA	18	35	70	Flat/Court	Rental	Urban Infill	No
146	Ocean Park Co-op, Santa Monica, CA	43	41	82	Multiplex/Court	Co-op	Urban Infill	No
148	St John's Hospital Hsg, Santa Monica, CA	28	45	121	Flat/Court	Rental	Urban Infill	No
	The Central States							
152	Lyton Park Place, St Paul, MN	21	7	20	Single-family	For-sale	Suburban	No
154	Field Street, Detroit, MI	21	12	30	Multiplex	Rental	Suburban	No
156	West Town II, Chicago, IL	113	17	60	Multiplex	Rental	Urban Infill	No
160	The Reservoir, Madison, WI	28	18	36	Row/Court/Flat	Co-op	Urban Infill	Yes
162	West Town Cluster Housing, Chicago, IL	101	33	65	Multiplex	Rental	Urban Infill	No
	The Northeast							
166	Battle Road Farm, Lincoln, MA	120	10	23	Multiplex	For-sale	Rural Cluster	No
168	Crawford Square, Pittsburgh, PA	301	16	31	Row House	Rent/FS	New District	Yes
172	West HELP, Greenburgh, NY	108	18	18	Row/Court	Rental	Rural Cluster	Yes
176	Hyde Square Co-op, Dorchester, MA	41	22	62	Triplex	Co-op	Urban Infill	No
178	Waterside Green, Stamford, CT	75	27	54	Multiplex	For-sale	Urban Infill	No
180	Parkside Gables, Stamford, CT	69	29	57	Court/Row	Mutual H	Urban Infill	No
184	Catherine Street, Albany, NY	130	37	93	Row House	For-sale	Urban Infill	No
186	Mutual Housing Association, New York, NY	322	54	141	Row House	Mutual H	Urban Rehab	No
188	Melrose Court, Bronx, NY	265	60	123	Walk-up flat	For-sale	Urban Infill	No
190	CEPHAS Housing, Yonkers, NY	15	65	183	Walk-up flat	Rental	Urban Infill	No
192	Roxbury Corners, Roxbury, MA	54	65	176	Court/Mix	Co-op	Urban Infill	Yes
194	Charlestown Navy Yard Rowhouses, Boston, MA	50	67	114	Row House	For-sale	Urban Infill	No
196	Ninth Square Redevelopment, New Haven, CT	335	84	118	Mid-rise/Mix	Rental	New District	No
198	Langham Court, Boston, MA	84	81	129	Walk-up/Row	Co-op	Urban Infill	Yes
202	Tent City, Boston, MA	269	89	181	Mid-rise/Mix	Co-op	Urban Infill	Yes

Page #	Case studies by region	City	# Units	Density: DU/ac	BR/ac	Dwelling type	Rent/own Co-op	Neighborhood context	Childcare etc.
	The South								
206	Orchard Village and Oak Hill, Chatt'ga, TN		49	7	22	Single-family	For-sale	Suburban	No
208	Charleston Infill Housing, Charleston, SC		67	11	25	Multiplex	Rental	Urban Infill	No
210	Randolph Neighborhood, Richmond, VA		622	20	60	Row/Multiplex	Rent/FS	New District	Yes
214	Timberlawn Crescent, Bethesda, MD		107	22	60	Walk/Court	Rental	Suburban	No

COMPARATIVE DESCRIPTION INDEX: 1 Page CASE STUDIES

Page #	Case studies by region	City	# Units	Density: DU/ac	BR/ac	Dwelling type	Rent/own Co-op	Neighborhood context	Childcare etc.
	The Central States								
218	Quincy Homes, Chicago, IL		40	9	27	Single-family	For-sale	Urban Infill	No
219	Harriet Square, Minneapolis, MN		24	10	22	Row	For-sale	Suburban	No
220	International Homes, Chicago, IL		28	14	42	Multiplex	For-sale	Urban Infill	No
221	Westminster Place, St Louis, MO		392	25	43	SF/Low/Flat/Court	Rent/FS	New District	No
	The Northwest and Northern California								
222	Lake Park Townhomes, Klahanie, WA		28	8	23	Duplex	For-sale	Suburban	No
223	Holladay Avenue Homes, San Francisco, CA		4	16	40	Fourplex	For-sale	Urban Infill	No
224	Open Doors, Los Gatos, CA		64	19	48	Eightplex/Walk	Rental	Suburban	Yes
225	Lucretia G'dns/Julian Street, San Jose, CA		25	20	61	Row/Court	Rental	Suburban	No
226	Horizons, Campbell, CA		24	30	37	Multiplex	Rental	Suburban	Yes
227	Paula Avenue Homes, San Jose, CA		21	31	62	Row/Walk	Rental	Suburban	No
	The Southwest and Southern California								
228	Blacklands Transitional Hsg, Austin, TX		8	8	16	Single-family	Rental	Urban Rehab	No
229	La'ilani at Kealakehe, HI		200	13	25	Multiplex/Walk	Rental	Rural Cluster	No
230	La Ramona Morales Apts, Benson, AZ		31	23	23	Flat/Court	Rental	Rural Cluster	No
231	Viviendas Asistenciales, Tucson AZ		31	25	25	Flat/Court	Rental	Urban Infill	No
232	West Hopkins Townhouses, Aspen, CO		11	40	76	Row/Court	For-sale	Urban Infill	No
	The Northeast								
233	Fineview Crest, Pittsburgh, PA		12	16	48	Single-family	For-sale	Urban Infill	No
234	Capen Green, Stamford, CT		20	17	52	Duplex	For-sale	Urban Infill	No
235	Columbia/Hampshire St Hsg, Cambridge, MA		16	19	52	Walk-up/Row	Rental	Urban Infill	No
236	University City Family Hsg, Philadelphia, PA		70	25	57	Walk-up/Courts	Rental	Urban Infill	No
237	Dorado Village, Philadelphia, PA		80	29	77	Walk-up	Rental	Urban Infill	No
238	Sojourner Truth Homes, Brooklyn, NY		136	59	118	Row/TH/Flat	For-sale	Urban Infill	No
239	Regent Terrace Apts, Philadelphia, PA		80	103	157	Walk-up/Row	Rental	Urban Rehab	No
240	Oak Terrace, Boston, MA		88	105	256	Mid/Mix/Court	Rental	Urban Infill	Yes
241	Spring Creek Gardens, Brooklyn, NY		765	110	166	Court/Walk-up	Rental	Urban Infill	Yes
242	Lee Goodwin Residence, Bronx, NY		41	157	258	Mid/Flat	Rental	Urban Rehab	Yes
243	Crotona Park West, Bronx, NY		563	164	277	Mid/Flat	Rental	Urban Rehab	No
244	Sarah Powell Huntington House, NY, NY		28	182	357	Mid/Flat	Rental	Urban Rehab	Yes
	The South/Southeast								
245	Middle Towne Arch, Norfolk, VA		188	5	15	Single-family	For-sale	New District	No
246	Dermott Villas, Dermott, AR		33	8	13	Multiplex	Rental	Rural Cluster	No
247	Mer Rouge Villas, Mer Rouge, LA		33	8	13	Multiplex	Rental	Rural Cluster	No

DEVELOPER/SPONSOR/DEVELOPMENT CONSULTANTS

Developer/Sponsor/Development Consultants	Contact	Telephone	Address	Development Pg
A.F. Evans Company (Joint Venture)	Arthur Evans	510-837-6756	Alamo, California	201 Turk Street 120
The Altman Companies	Steve Altman	215-884-0500	Glenside, Pennsylvania	University City Family Housing 236
Amistad Housing Development Corporation	Kathy Tyler	301-588-810	Hereford, TX	Amistad Farm Laborers Housing 128
Archdiocesan Housing Authority/Hilltop Housing	Paul Purcell, Josephine Tamayo Murray	206-328-5661	Seattle, Washington	Matsusaka Townhomes 92
Asian Neighborhood Design	Tom Jones, Maurice Lim Miller	415-982-2959	San Francisco, California	555 Ellis Street 108
Asian Community Development Corporation	Jacqui Kay	617-482-2380	Boston, Massachusetts	Oak Terrace 240
Aspin/Pitkin County Housing Authority	Dave Tolan	303-920-5050	Aspen, Colorado	West Hopkins Townhouses 232
Bernal Heights Housing Corporation	Helen Helfer (Buck Bagot)	415-648-0330	San Francisco, California	Holladay Avenue Homes 223
Bickerdike Redevelopment	Andy Soto	312-252-1963	Chicago, Illinois	West Town II 156
Blackland Community Development Corporation	Charles Smith	512-472-4821	Austin, Texas	Blacklands Transitional Housing 228
Boulder Woodlands, L.P.	Roger Lewis	303-441-4213	Boulder, Colorado	Woodlands 130
Bricklayers and Labourors Non-Profit Housing Corporation	Tom McIntyre	617-242-2231	Boston, Massachusetts	Charlestown Navy Yard RH/Frank G. Mar Hsg/Parkview Com. 194, 112, 94
BRIDGE (Co-Sponsor)	Don Terner, Jim Buckley, (Ben Golvin)	415-989-111	San Francisco, California	Frank G. Mar Community Housing 112
Brighton Development Corporation	Peggy Lucas	612-332-5664	Minneapolis, Minnesota	Harriet Square 219
Burbank Housing Development Corporation	Nichols Stewart	707-526-9782	Santa Rosa, California	Tower Apartments 90
Cabrillo Economic Development Corporation	Rodney Fernandez	805-659-3791	Saticoy, California	Rancho Sespe Farmworker Housing 126
CASA of Oregon	Charlie Harris	503-537-0319	Newberg, Oregon	Nuevo Amanecer Apartments 72
Catholic Charities of the Archdiosese of San Francisco	Merle Malakoff	415-487-6831	San Francisco, California	111 Jones Street 120
CEPHAS	Gaby Hodgson	914-332-4144	Yonkers, New York	CEPHAS Housing 190
Chattanooga Neighborhood Enterprise	Brian Clements	615-265-4114	Chattanooga, Tennessee	Orchard Village and Oak Hill 206
Chinese Community Housing Corporation (Joint Venture)	Susie Wong	415-984-1450	San Francisco, California	201 Turk Street 120
Church of Messiah Housing Corporation (CMHC)	Richard Cannon	313-567-7966	Detroit, Michigan	Field Street 154
City of Albany, Dept of Economic Development	Charles Newland	518-439-3462	Albany, New York	Catherine Street 184
CityLands Corporation	Susan McCann	312-626-3300	Chicago, Illinois	Quincy Homes 218
The Community Builders	Nancy Phillips	617-695-9595	Boston, Massachusetts	Tent City/Oak Terrace/Roxbury Corners 202, 240, 192
Community Corporation of Santa Monica	Joan Ling	310-394-8487	Santa Monica, California	Ocean Park Co-op/St John's Hospital Housing 146, 148
Community Economics	Janet Falk, Joel Rubenzohl	510-832-8300	Oakland, California	YWCA Villa Nueva/The Farm/Del Carlo Court/Lorin St'n 106, 74, 104, 98
Community Housing Opportunities Corporation	Keith Bloom	916-757-4444	Davis, California	Tuscany Villas/Villa Calabria 78
Drew Economic Development Corporation	Carla Dartis	213-345-5038	Compton, California	Willowbrook Green Apartments 136
The Dorado Venture c/o Pennrose Properties, Inc	John Rosenthal, Mona Williams	215-979-1100	Philadelphia, Pennsylvania	Dorado Village 237
East Bay Asian Local Development Corporation (EBALDC)	Lynette Lee, Joshua Simon	510-287-5353	Oakland, California	Hismen Hin-nu Terrace/Frank G. Mar Community Housing 100, 112
Eden Housing, Inc.	Catherine Merschel	510-582-1460	Hayward, California	Stoney Creek Apartments 82
Environmental Works, Community Design Center	Bob Fish, Gary Oppenheimer	206-329-8300	Seattle, Washington	Lake Park Townhomes 222
Ergos Developments	Jeff Kester	916-447-7606	Sacramento, California	Southside Park Co-housing 84
Esperanza Community Housing Corporation (Co-Gen. Partner)	Melanie Stephans, Sister Diane Donoghue	213-748-7285	Los Angeles, California	Villa Esperanza 140
Fairfield 2000/New Neighborhood	Howard Quinn, John Madeo	203-359-2215	Stamford, Connecticut	Waterside Green 178
Farmworker Housing Development Corporation (FHDC)	Al Nunez	503-981-1618	Woodburn, Oregon	Nuevo Amanecer Apartments 72
First San Jose Housing	Terry Wenzl	408-291-8650	San Jose, California	Paula Avenue Homes 227
Four Corners Development Corporation	Jeanette Bonne	617-565-8519	Boston, Massachusetts	Langham Court 198
General Atlantic Realty Corp. — c/o Millenium Corp.	Phil Aarons	212-595-1600	New York, New York	Spring Creek Gardens 241
The Habitat Co., Receiver for Chicago Hsg Auth. S.Site Prog.	Phillip A. Hickman	312-527-5400	Chicago, Illinois	West Town Cluster Housing 162
H.E.L.P.	Marc Altheim, Claudia Stepki	212-444-1916	New York, New York	West HELP 172
Homeowners Rehab., Inc. + Just-A-Start Corporation	Shelley Dein	617-868-4858	Cambridge, Massachusetts	Columbia/Hampshire Street Housing 235
Housing Action Council	Rose Noonan	914-332-4144	Tarrytown, New York	CEPHAS Housing 190
Housing Authority of the City of Charleston	Donald J. Cameron	803-720-3970	Charleston, South Carolina	Charleston Infill Housing 208
Housing Authority of the County of Santa Clara	Kathy Robinson	408-993-2907	San Jose, California	Lucretia Gardens/Julian Street 225

Developer/Sponsor/Development Consultants	Contact	Telephone	Address	Development Pg
Housing Development Services Inc.	Noel Sweitzer	213-231-1104	Los Angeles, California	Yorkshire Terrace 142
Housing Finance and Dev. Corporation (HFDC) of Hawaii	Director	808-537-0640	Honolulu, Hawaii	La'ilani at Kealakehe 229
Housing Opportunities Commission of Montgomery County	Tom Doerr	301-929-9732	Kensington, Maryland	Timberlawn Crescent 214
Justin Properties Inc.	David Van Landschoot	612-641-0166	St Paul, Minnesota	Lyton Park Place 152
Keen Development Corporation	Bob Kuehn	617-661-9100	Cambridge, Massachusetts	Battle Road Farm 166
L.A. Community Design Center (Co-General Partner)	Bill Huang	213-629-2702	Los Angeles, California	Villa Esperanza 140
The Low-Income Housing Institute	Kim Travenik, Sharon Lee	206-727-0355	Seattle, Washington	Matsusaka Townhomes 92
Madison Mutual Housing Assoc.	Judith Wilcox (Susan Hobart)	608-255-6642	Madison, Wisconsin	The Reservoir 160
Marshall Planning and Development	Tom Marshall	501-355-2687	Eudora, Arkansas	Dermott Villas/Mer Rouge Villas 246, 247
Mauna Lani Resort, Inc. (MRL)	Tom Yamamoto	808-885-6677	Kalahuipuna, Hawaii	La'ilani at Kealakehe 229
McCormack Baron & Assoc. Inc.	Richard Baron, Tom Cella	314-621-3400	St Louis, Missouri	Westminster Place/Crawford Square/Ninth Square 221, 168, 196
Mercy Charities Housing Development Corporation	Jane Graf	415-487-6825	San Francisco, California	111 Jones Street 120
Mid-Peninsula Housing Coalition	Susan Russell	415-299-8000	Redwood City, California	The Farm/Open Doors/Horizons 74, 224, 226
Mission Housing Development Corporation	Daniel Hernandez	415-864-6432	San Francisco, California	Del Carlo Court 104
Mutual Housing Association of New York	Greg Bauso, Nan Wilson	718-693-9100	Brooklyn, New York	Mutual Housing Association 186
Mutual Housing Association of Southwest Connecticut	Peter Wood	203-359-6940	Stamford, Connecticut	Parkside Gables 180
Neighborhood Development Corporation of Jamaica Plain	Lizbeth Heyer	617-522-2424	Boston, Massachusetts	Hyde Square Co-op 176
New Boston Housing Enterprises	David Goldman, Dennis Kanin	617-525-1523	Boston, Massachusetts	Capen Green 234
NY City Housing Partnership	Kathryn Wylde, Steve Brown	212-493-7435	New York, New York	Sojourner Truth Homes 238
Norfolk Redevelopment and Housing Authority	David Rice, Calvin Alpern	804-623-1111	Norfolk, Virginia	Middle Towne Arch 245
North County Housing Foundation	Amy Rowland	619-432-6878	Escondido, California	Daybreak Grove 132
Northside Civic Development Council Inc.	Juan Garret, Emily Buka	412-322-3523	Pittsburgh, Pennsylvania	Fineview Crest 233
OPAL Community Land Trust	Sarah Ogier, Michael Sky	360-376-3191	Eastsound, Washington	OPAL Commons 68
Pacific Union Development Company (Co-Dev.)	Tom Callinan	415-929-8588	San Francisco, California	Parkview Commons 94
Pennsylvania Housing Finance Agency(Co-Dev.)	Karl Smith	717-780-3800	Philadelphia, Pennsylvania	Regent Terrace Apartments 239
Penrose Properties Inc. (Co-Dev.)	John Rosenthal, Mona Williams	215-979-1100	Philadelphia, Pennsylvania	Regent Terrace Apartments/Dorado Village 239, 237
Phipps Houses	Harry Scanlan	212-243-9090	New York, New York	Lee Goodwin Residence/Crotona Park West 242, 243
Pico Union Housing Corporation	Gloria Farias	213-749-8047	Los Angeles, California	Yorkshire Terrace 142
Procida Construction Corporation	Mario Procida	718-299-7000	Bronx, New York	Melrose Court 188
The Related Companies (Joint Venture Partners)	John A. Onder	212-421-5333	New York, New York	Ninth Square Redevelopment 196
Richmond Redevelopment and Housing Authority	Bob Everton, Mike Zitzow	804-780-4342	Richmond, Virginia	Randolph Neighborhood 210
San Antonio Community Development Council	Don Davenport	510-536-1715	Oakland, California 94606	Hismen Hin-nu Terrace 100
Seattle Housing Resources Group (SHRG)	Nancy Smith	206-623-0506	Seattle, Washington	Cascade Court Apartments 116
Seattle-King County YWCA	Rita Ryder, Sue Sherbrooke	206-461-4854	Seattle, Washington	YWCA Family Village 88
San Francisco Network Ministries Hsg Corporation	Glenda Hope	415-252-5627	San Francisco, California	555 Ellis Street 108
The Santa Clara YWCA	Mary Kelley	408-295-4011	San Jose, California	YWCA Villa Nueva 106
The Shaw Company	Frank Martin	312-943-8800	Chicago, Illinois	Quincy Homes 218
South Berkeley Community Development Corporation	Duane DeJoie	510-653-6230	Berkeley, California	Lorin Station 98
Stamford Neighborhood Housing Services	Madison Smith	203-327-1647	Stamford, Connecticut	Parkside Gables 180
Stamford Waterside Development Corporation	John Madeo	203-351-1150	Stamford, Connecticut	Waterside Green 178
Stuyvesant Ave Housing Corporation/The Hudson Companies	Alan Bell, Nick Lembo, William Fowler	718-875-8500	Brooklyn, New York	Sojourner Truth Homes 238
Tent City Corporation	Patricia Miller	617-262-4103	Boston, Massachusetts	Tent City 202
Texas Low Income Housing Information Services	Karen Paup	512-477-8910	Austin, Texas	Blacklands Transitional Housing 228
Threshold Housing	Joe Borden	206-585-8020	Seattle, Washington	Benson Glen 70
Tucson Community Development/Design Center	Jody Gibbs	520-792-9068	Tucson, Arizona	Viviendas Asistenciales/La Ramona Morales Apartments 231, 230
United South End/Lower Roxbury Dev. Corporation (UDC)	Syvalia Hyman III	617-266-5451	Boston, Massachusetts	Roxbury Corners 192
United Tenants of Albany	Roger Markovicz	518-436-8997	Albany, New York	Catherine Street 184
Voice of the People In Uptown, Inc	Lucy Ascoli (Lisa Beacham/Yittayih Zelalem)	312-769-2442	Chicago, Illinois	International Homes 220
Vulcan Affordable Housing Corporation	Mark Simons	518-270-4711	Troy, New York	Catherine Street 184
Women's Prison Association	Ann Jacobs	212-674-1163	New York, New York	Sarah Powell Huntington House 244

ARCHITECTS

Architect	Contact; (Proj. Architect, not w/firm)	Telephone	Address	Development Pg
Appleton and Associates	Marc Appleton, AIA	310-399-9386	Venice California	Ocean Park Co-Op 146
Architects Collective	Larry Kester, AIA	918-492-2987	Tulsa, Oklahoma	Timberlawn Crescent 214
The Architectural Team (phase II & III)	Michael Liu, AIA	617-889-4402	Chelsea, Massachusetts	Battle Road Farm (phase II & III) 166
Asian Neighborhood Design (AND)	Tom Jones; Harry Ja Wong, AIA	415-982-2959	San Francisco, California	555 Ellis Street 108
David Baker+Associates, Architects	David Baker	415-896-6700	San Francisco, California	Parkview Commons 94
Barker, Rinker, Seacat Partners	Phil Lawrence, AIA	303-455-1366	Denver, Colorado	Woodlands 130
Bergmeyer Associates, Inc	Lewis Muhlfelder	617-542-1025	Boston, Massachusetts	Capen Green 234
Bradfield Richards and Associates Architects	Richard H. Bradfield, FAIA	404-256-6565	Atlanta, Georgia	Charleston Infill Housing 208
Brian Clements, Architect	Brian Clements	615-265-414	Chattanooga, Tennessee	Orchard Village and Oak Hill 206
Co-oper Robertson & Partners	Roland Baer, AIA, Cathlyn Acker	212-247-1717	New York, New York	West HELP 172
Cottle Grabeal Yaw	Larry Yaw, FAIA	303-925-2867	Aspen, Colorado	West Hopkins Townhouses 232
Davids Killory Architects (Design Architect)	Christine Killory	619-285-1299	San Diego, California	Daybreak Grove (Design Architect) 132
Davis and Joyce Architects	Sam Davis, FAIA, Lisa Joyce	510-527-9510	Berkeley, California	Tuscany Villas/Villa Calabria 78
Design Coalition	Lou Host-Jablonsky, AIA; (James Glueck, AIA)	608-251-2551	Madison, Wisconsin	The Reservoir 160
Design Partners Inc.	Alan Taramuro, Owen Chock	808-949-0044	Honolulu, Hawaii	La'ilani at Kealakehe 229
Domenech Hicks Krockmalnic	Fernando J. Domenech Jr., AIA	617-267-6408	Boston, Massachusetts	Roxbury Corners/Hyde Square Co-op 192, 176
Dorgan Architecture and Planning	Kathy Dorgan	518-426-815	Albany, New York	Catherine St 184
Duo Dickinson Architects	Duo Dickinson	203-245-0405	Madison, Connecticut	CEPHAS Housing 190
Ena Dubnoff	Ena Dubnoff	310-396-8627	Santa Monica, California	Willowbrook Green Apartments 136
Arvid Elness	Tim Elness; Paul Madson, AIA	612-332-7026	Minneapolis, Minnesota	Harriet Square 219
Environmental Works - Community Design Ctr.	Mary McCrea; (Steve Johnson, Don King, AIA)	206-329-8300	Seattle, Washington	Lake Park Townhomes 222
FRIDAY Architects/Planners & Richard Kline	Don Matzkin, AIA	215-564-0814	Philadelphia, Pennsylvania	University City Family Housing 236
GGLO Architecture and Interior Design	Christopher D. Libby, AIA	206-467-5828	Seattle, Washington	Cascade Court Apartments 116
Golder Goldfarb Kline	Richard Kline	215-735-7475	Philadelphia, Pennsylvania	Regent Terrace Apartments 239
Goody Clancy and Associates	John M. Clancy, FAIA; Virginia Quinn	617-262-2760	Boston, Massachusetts	Langham Court/Tent City 198, 202
Harden Van Arnam Architects	Cindy Harden, RA; Jan Van Arnam, RA	718-855-8006	Brooklyn New York	Sojourner Truth 238
Hardison Komatsu Ivelich and Tucker (HKIT)	George Ivelich, AIA; Robert Tucker, AIA	415-541-0811	San Francisco, California	111 Jones Street/201 Turk Street 120
Tom Hatch Architects	Tom Hatch, AIA; Joel Martinez	512-474-8548	Austin, Texas	Amistad Farm Laborers Hsg/Blacklands Trad. Hsg 128, 228
Herbert S. Newman and Partners, P.C.	Herbert Newman, FAIA, Robert Godshall, AIA	203-772-1990	New Haven, Connecticut	Ninth Square Redevelopment 196
Herman Stoller Coliver Architects	Robert Herman, FAIA; Susie Coliver, David Hall	415-552-9210	San Francisco, California	Holladay Avenue Homes/Lucretia Gardens/Julian St 223, 225
Hooper Olmsted and Hrovat	Richard H. Olmsted, AIA	415-775-5855	San Francisco, California	Open Doors 224
Kadushin Associates Architects Planners	Abraham Kadushin, AIA	313-663-3519	Ann Arbor, Michigan	Field St 154
Kelly, Maiello Inc., Arch. & Plan. (Ext. Restor. Arch.)	Emanuel Kelly, AIA	215-561-1808	Philadelphia, Pennsylvania	Regent Terrace Apartments (Ext. Restor. Arch.) 239
Fred Klein, AIA Architect	Fred Klein, AIA	360-376-5377	Eastsound, Washington	OPAL Commons 68
Kodama Associates	Steven Kodama, FAIA	415-296-1144	San Francisco, California	Horizons/Lorin Station 226, 98
Koning Eizenburg Architecture, Inc	Julie Eizenburg, Hank Koning, FAIA	310-828-6131	Santa Monica, California	St John's Hospital Housing 148
LA Community Design Ctr.	William K. Huang, AIA	213-629-2702	Los Angeles, California	Villa Esperanza 140
Chris Lamen and Associates	Chris Lamen	415-456-2348	San Rafael, California	Stoney Creek Apartments 82
Langer, Dion Assoc. Archts P.C. w/D. Sadowski	Dan Langer, AIA	518-449-9000	Rensselaer, New York	Catherine Street (Arch. of Record) 184
Lawrence K. Cheng Associates, Inc	Lawrence K. Cheng	617-728-313	Boston, Massachusetts	Oak Terrace 240
The Liebman/Melting Partnership	Alan Melting, AIA, AICP	212-239-8080	New York, New York	Spring Creek Gardens 241
Levenson, Meltzer, Neuringer c/o C. Levenson	Conrad Levenson, AIA	718-858-0555	New York, New York	Lee Goodwin Residence/Crotona Park West 242, 243
LHB Architects and Engineers	Rick Carter, AIA	612-831-8971	Edina, Minnesota	Lyton Park Place 152
MacDonald Architects	Donald MacDonald, FAIA	415-626-9100	San Francisco, California	Frank G. Mar Community Housing 112
Marquis Associates	Gita Dev, FAIA	415-788-2644	San Francisco, California	Paula Avenue Homes 227
Marvin H. Meltzer Architects, P.C.	Marvin H. Meltzer	212-734-5600	New York, New York	Melrose Court 188

Architect	Contact; (Proj. Architect, not w/firm)	Telephone	Address	Development Pg
Mithun Partners Inc.	William Kreager, AIA	206-623-3344	Seattle, Washington	Benson Glen 70
Mogavero Notestine Associates	David Mogavero; Craig Stradley	916-443-1033	Sacramento, California	Southside Park Co-Housing 84
John V. Mutlow, FAIA, Architects	John V. Mutlow, FAIA	213-664-4373	Los Angeles, California	Yorkshire Terrace/Rancho Sespe Farmworker Hsg 142, 126
Nagle Hartray and Associates Co.	Jim Nagle, AIA	312-832-6900	Chicago, Illinois	West Town Cluster Housing 162
Perkins Eastman Architects, P.C.	Bradford Perkins, FAIA, AICP	212-889-1720	New York, New York	Parkside Gables 180
Pratt Planning and Architectural Collaborative	Joan Byron, RA; Perry Winston, RA	718-636-3486	Brooklyn, New York	Mutual Housing Association 186
Pyatok Associates	Michael Pyatok, FAIA	510-465-7010	Oakland, California	Hismen Hin-nu Tce/YWCA Family Vill./Tower Apts 100, 106, 90
Ralph Mechur Architects	Ralph Mechur, AIA	310-399-7975	Santa Monica, California	Ocean Park Co-op 146
The Ratcliff Architects(Architect of Record)	James Vann, AIA	510-652-1972	Emeryville, California	Hismen Hin-nu Terrace(Arch. of Record) 100
William Rawn Associates, Architects	William Rawn, FAIA	617-423-3470	Boston, Massachusetts	Charlestown Navy Yard Rowhouses/Battle Road Farm 208, 106
Robertson, Merryman, Barnes	Nancy Merryman, AIA; Candace Robertson, AI	503-222-3753	Portland, Oregon	Nuevo Amanecer Apartments 72
Schroder Murchie Laya Associates Inc	Kenneth Schroeder, FAIA; Richard T. Laya, AIA	312-829-3355	Chicago, Illinois	Quincy Homes 218
Seeyle, Stevenson, Value & Knecht (Public Impr'ts)	Tim Casey	203-375-0521	Stratford, Connecticut	Ninth Square Redevelopment (Public Improvements) 196
Seidel/Holzman	Alexander Seidel, AIA	415-397-5535	San Francisco, California	The Farm 74
Smith Edwards Architects (Historic Rehab.)	Tyler Smith, FAIA	203-296-7800	Hartford, Connecticut	Ninth Square Redevelopment (Historic Rehab.) 196
SOLOMON Architecture and Urban Design	Daniel Solomon, FAIA	415-227-4081	San Francisco, California	Del Carlo Court 104
The Steinberg Group	Robert T. Steinberg, AIA	408-295-5446	San Jose, California	YWCA Villa Nueva 106
Stephan Mark Goldner Associates	Stephan Goldner (@ GGK Assoc.)	215-735-7475	Philadelphia, Pennsylvania	Dorado Village 237
Stickney & Murphy Architects (Architect of Record)	Ron Murphy, AIA; Ron Hopper	206-623-1104	Seattle, Washington	YWCA Family Village (Arch. of Record) 88
Stroud Watson, Architect	Stroud Watson	615-266-5948	Chattanooga, Tennessee	Orchard Village and Oak Hill 206
Studio E Architects	Brad Burke	619-235-9262	San Diego, California	Daybreak Grove 132
Tai and Lee Architects	Yoko Tai	412-681-8832	Pittsburgh, Pennsylvania	Fineview Crest 233
Tise Hurwitz and Diamond, Inc.	Stephen Tise, AIA; Daniel Glenn	617-739-8420	Brookline, Massachusetts	Columbia/Hampshire Street Housing 235
Tonkin/Hoyne Architects and Planners	Les Tonkin; (John Mclaren)	206-624-7880	Seattle, Washington	Matsusaka Townhomes 92
Trivers Associates	Andrew Trivers, AIA; Paul Berry, AIA	314-241-2900	St Louis, Missouri	Westminster Place/Ninth Square Redevelopment 221, 196
Tucson Community Development and Design Center	Jody Gibbs	520-792-9068	Tucson, Arizona	Vivienda Asistenciales/La Ramona Morales Apartments 231, 196
UDA Architects and Planners	Ray Gindroz, AIA	412-765-1133	Pittsburgh, Pennsylvania	Crawford Sq./M' Towne Arch/Randolph N'hood 168, 245, 210
Roberta Washington Architects, P.C.	Roberta Washington, AIA; Carole Richards	212-749-9807	New York, New York	Sarah Powell Huntington House 244
Weese Langley Weese Architects Ltd	Dennis Langley, AIA	312-642-1820	Chicago, Illinois	International Homes/West Town II 220, 156
Wenzel & Associates	Henry Wenzel, Jr., AIA	601-363-1811	Tunica, Mississippi	Dermott Villas/Mer Rouge Villas 246, 247
Zane Yost and Associates	Zane Yost	203-384-2201	Bridgeport, Connecticut	Waterside Green 178
Lev Zetlin Associates, Inc (Garages)	Abe Gutman	212-741-1300	New York, New York	Ninth Square Redevelopment (Garages) 196

LANDSCAPE ARCHITECTS

Landscape Architect	Telephone	City	Development Pg
AEREA- Leslie Ryan	619-692-3784	San Diego, California	Daybreak Grove 132
Anthony Guzzardo and Associates	415-433-4672	San Francisco, California	The Farm 74
City of Austin Xeriscape Program	512-499-3519	Austin, Texas	Blacklands Transitional Housing 228
Barrio Planners	213-726-7734	Los Angeles, California	Yorkshire Terrace 142
Mark Bedell	303-925-4005	Aspen, Colorado	West Hopkins Townhouses 232
Berger Partnership	206-325-6877	Seattle, Washington	Cascade Court Apartments 116
Bradfield Richards and Associates Architects	404-256-6565	Atlanta, Georgia	Charleston Infill Housing 208
Burton and Spitz	310-828-6373	Santa Monica, California	Ocean Park Co-op 146
Cottong Taniguchi	415-342-9083	Burlingame, California	Stoney Creek Apartments 82
David Gates Associates	510-736-8176	Danville, California	YWCA Villa Nueva 106
David Heldt	415-956-2345	San Francisco, California	111 Jones Street/201 Turk Street 120
David Tamura	808-935-3466	Hilo, Hawaii	La'ilani at Kealakehe 229
Doug Strayer	916-454-3570	Sacramento, California	Southside Park Co-housing 84
Edward Watanabe	206-329-4365	Seattle, Washington	Matsusaka Townhomes 92
Environmental Design Associates	203-762-8020	Wilton, Connecticut	Waterside Green 178
Jane Garrison	206-522-2529	Issaquah, Washington	YWCA Family Village 88
Jody Gibbs	520-792-9068	Tucson, Arizona	Viviendas Asistenciales/La Ramona Morales Apartments 231, 230
Gradjanski & Catz	510-549-0955	Berkeley, California	Lorin Station 98
James Hadley	718-624-2167	Brooklyn, New York	Crotona Park West 243
Hodgson & Douglas	615-327-4447	Nashville, Tennessee	Orchard Village and Oak Hill 206
Jordan and Gilbert	805-642-3641	Ventura, California	Rancho Sespe Farmworker Housing 126
Keller, Mitchell, Caronna	415-391-9987	San Francisco, California	Tuscany Villas/Villa Calabria 78
LaQuatra Bonci	412-322-5888	Pittsburgh, Pennsylvania	Crawford Square 168
Lewis, Scully and Gionet	703-821-2045	Vienna, Virginia	Timberlawn Crescent 214
LHB Architects and Engineers	612-831-8971	Edina, Minnesota	Lyton Park Place 152
Lost West	619-434-5790	Carlsbad, California	Villa Esperanza 140
Carol Mayer-Reed	503-223-5953	Portland, Oregon	Nuevo Amanecer Apartments 72
William Morgan	805-654-1022	Ventura, California	Rancho Sespe Farmworker Housing 126
Mark Morris Associates	212-925-7500	New York, New York	West HELP 172
Mark Morrison Associates	212-677-6887	New York, New York	Melrose Court 188
Matrix Gardens	303-443-0284	Boulder, Colorado	Woodlands 130
Merrill & Associates	415-291-8960	San Francisco, California	Horizons 226
MH Consulting	810-569-8558	Detroit, Michigan	Field Street 154
Omi Lang Associates	415-389-8438	Mill Valley, California	Parkview Commons 94
Orsee Design	408-283-2199	San Francisco, California	555 Ellis Street 108
Chris Patillo Associates	510-465-1284	Oakland, California	Hismen Hin-nu Terrace 100
Rios/Pearson	213-852-6717	Los Angeles, California	Willowbrook Green Apartments 136
John Northmore Roberts	510-843-3666	Berkeley, California	Holladay Avenue Homes 223
Rolland/Towers	203-773-1153	New Haven, Connecticut	Lucretia Gardens/Julian Street 225
Schreiber Associates	617-739-8425	Brookline, Massachusetts	Ninth Square Redevelopment 196
Rich Seyfarth	510-444-7386	Oakland, California	Columbia/Hampshire Street Housing 235
Gary Strang	415-227-4081	San Francisco, California	Tower Apartments 90
Terra Media -Chad Crutcher	415-255-2008	San Francisco, California	Del Carlo Court 104
The Halvorson Company	617-536-0380	Boston, Massachusetts	Open Doors 224
Tito Patri & Associates	415-986-8811	San Francisco, California	Langham Court/Tent City/Roxbury Corners/Hyde Square Co-op 198, 202, 192, 176
Michael Van Valkenburgh	617-864-2079	Cambridge, Massachusetts	Charlestown Navy Yard Rowhouses/Battle Road Farm 194, 166
Vandewalle and Associates	608-255-3988	Madison, Wisconsin	The Reservoir 160
Richard Vignolo	415-956-8664	San Francisco, California	Paula Avenue Homes 227
William Fleming Associates	617-721-2401	Winchester, Massachusetts	Battle Road Farm 166
Steve Wing	203-878-2880	Milford, Connecticut	Parkside Gables 180

CONTRACTORS

Contractor	Telephone	City	Development Pg
Alder/Valentine Assoc. Ltd	914-941-1223	Briarcliff, New York	West HELP 172
Allied General Construction Services Corp.	610-834-0990	Plymouth Meeting, MA	Regent Terrace Apartments 239
Alpha Construction	818-779-5488	Van Nuys, California	Ocean Park Co-op 146
The Altman Companies	215-884-0500	Glenshire, Pennsylvania	University City Family Housing 236
Altman Construction	215-884-8590	Philadelphia, Pennsylvania	Dorado Village 237
Babco Construction Co	708-869-3030	Evanston, Illinois	West Town Cluster Housing 162
Beacon Construction	617-742-8800	Boston, Massachusetts	Oak Terrace 240
Bedell Associates	914-668-0200	Mt Vernon, New York	CEPHAS Housing 190
R.D. Boykin	818-352-4888	Sierra Madre, California	Willowbrook Green Apartments 136
Cabrillo Econ. Development (phase II)	805-659-3791	Ventura, California	Rancho Sespe Farmworker Housing 126
Cahill Construction	415-986-0600	San Francisco, California	111 Jones Street 120
Carnes Construction	520-791-3732	Tucson, Arizona	La Ramona Morales Apartments 230
CAS Ltd	808-329-7533	Kona, Hawaii	La'ilani at Kealakehe 229
Casson Building Corp	303-782-9216	Denver, Colorado	Woodlands 130
Champion Builders	501-221-0063	Little Rock, Arkansas	Dermott Villas/Mer Rouge Villas 246, 247
Clermont General Contractors	718-253-4740	Brooklyn, New York	Mutual Housing Association 186
George Codd and Co.	520-792-3430	Tucson, Arizona	Viviendas Asistenciales 231
Conner Development	206-455-9280	Bellevue, Washington	Benson Glen 70
Connery Bldg Corp	608-221-3804	Madison, Wisconsin	The Reservoir 160
Cracovia Gen. Contractors	718-349-1866	Brooklyn, New York	Mutual Housing Association 186
CWC Builders (phase II and III) + A6	617-965-2800	Newton, Massachusetts	Hyde Square Co-op/Battle Road Farm 176, 166
Dimeo Construction Co.	401-781-9800	Providence, Rhode Island	Langham Court 198
Dow Builders	415-358-9000	San Francisco, California	Horizons 226
Edwin G. Brown Co.	818-352-4422	La Cresenta, California	Villa Esperanza 140
Ergos	916-447-7606	Sacramento, California	Southside Park Co-Housing 84
Fairview Construction	810-377-2600	Auburn Hills, Michigan	Field Street 154
The Frank Mercedes Jr. Construction Group Inc.	203-967-4555	Stamford, Connecticut	Parkside Gables/Waterside Green 180, 178
The Fusco Corp	203-777-7451	New Haven, Connecticut	Ninth Square Redevelopment 196
H & V Allen Construction	718-485-6655	Brooklyn, New York	Mutual Housing Association 186
Hallmark Builders	806-355-9223	Amarillo, Texas	Amistad Farm Laborers Housing 128
Hame Commercial	410-621-1106	Elkridge, Maryland	Timberlawn Crescent 214
E.M. Harris Building Co	314-343-1005	St Louis, Missouri	Westminster Place 221
Hidden Valley Construction	619-740-0911	Escondido, California	Daybreak Grove 132
Hunter and Moffet Contractors	415-567-6332	San Francisco, California	Parkview Commons 94
Ironstraw Construction/Phoenix Builders	212-941-0077	New York, New York	Sarah Powell Huntington House 244
J.M. Hershey Construction	415-525-9761	Santa Rosa, California	Tower Apartments 90
The Jobco Organization	516-246-4770	Great Neck, New York	Lee Goodwin Residence 242
Justin Properties	612-641-0166	St Paul, Minnesota	Lyton Park Place 152
Kee Construction	412-373-1242	Monroeville, Pennsylvania	Crawford Square/Fineview Crest 168, 233
LGD Construction	408-292-0128	San Jose, California	YWCA Villa Nueva 106
Linn Mathes, Inc.	312-454-0200	Chicago, Illinois	West Town II 156
The Loranco Corporation	718-940-1414	Brooklyn, New York	Mutual Housing Association 186

Contractor	Location	Phone	Project
Lugo Construction	Fife, Washington	206-838-7655	Matsusaka Townhomes 92
Lyntrak Construction Company Inc.	Soquel, California	408-476-5591	The Farm 74
McGall Contractors (phase I)	Ventura, California	805-642-3256	Rancho Sespe Farmworker Housing 126
Melcara Corp.	New York, New York	212-734-9191	Crotona Park West 243
Mirabassi Associates	Boston, Massachusetts	617-345-9961	Charlestown Navy Yard Rowhouses 194
Mitchell Construction Company	St Simon, Georgia	912-634-0953	Charleston Infill Housing 208
Monadnock Construction Inc	Brooklyn, New York	718-875-8160	Sojourner Truth 238
Morales Construction	Eagle Lake, Texas	409-234-5438	Blacklands Transitional Housing 228
Nibbi-Lowe Construction	San Francisco, California	415-863-1820	Del Carlo Court 104
Nibbi Brothers	San Francisco, California	415-863-1820	Lucretia Gardens/Julian Street 225
Pacific Component Homes	Seattle, Washingon	206-323-2700	Lake Park Townhomes 222
Peabody Construction	Braintree, Massachusetts	617-848-4410	Roxbury Corners 192
Penn Construction	Brooklyn, New York	718-764-0487	Mutual Housing Association 186
The Procida Organization	Bronx, New York	718-299-7000	Melrose Court 188
John Orevicz (Construction Management)	Berkeley, California	510-845-7173	Lorin Station 98
The Rafn Company	Kirkland, Washington	206-828-0800	Cascade Court Apartments 116
J.E. Roberts/Ohbayashi Corp.	Danville, California	510-820-0600	Hismen Hin-nu Terrace/Frank G. Mar Community Housing 100, 112
J.E. Roberts/Ohbayashi Corp.	Danville, California	510-820-0600	201 Turk Street/Lorin Station 120, 98
Ross Construction	Redwood City, California	415-369-9692	Stoney Creek Apartments 82
Segue Construction	Point Richmond, California	510-234-1800	Open Doors 224
The Shaw Co.	Chicago, Illinois	312-943-8800	Quincy Homes 218
Snavely-Waller-Whiting-Turner	Willoughby Hills, Pennsylvania	216-585-9091	Crawford Square 168
Sound Construction	East Sound, Washington	360-376-5000	OPAL Commons 68
Strategic Construction	Brooklyn, New York	718-857-1100	Mutual Housing Association 186
Strathairn Construction	Brooklyn, New York	718-972-2230	Mutual Housing Association 186
Thrush Construction	Chicago, Illinois	312-787-6641	International Homes 220
Tishman Construction	New York, New York	212-399-3600	Spring Creek Gardens 241
Transworld Construction	San Francisco, California	415-626-5500	555 Ellis Street 108
Travi Construction Corp.	Norwell, Massachusetts	508-871-5160	Columbia/Hampshire Street Housing 235
Turner Construction	Boston, Massachusetts	617-720-5780	Tent City 202
Vannice	Snowmass, Colorado	303-923-5087	West Hopkins Townhouses 232
Vulcan Affordable Housing Corp	Troy, New York	518-270-4711	Catherine Street 184
W.E. O'Neil Construction	Chicago, Illinois	312-327-1611	Ninth Square Redevelopment 196
Louis Waller Contractors	Washington, Pennsylvania	412-223-9680	Crawford Square 168
Watson Forsberg	Minneapolis, Minnesota	612-554-7761	Harriet Square 219
Whiting-Turner Contracting Co.	Baltimore, Maryland	410-821-1100	Crawford Square 168
Walsh Construction	Portland, Oregon	503-222-4375	Nuevo Amanecer Apartments 72
Wolf Construction Corp	Norwood, Massachusetts	617-762-9600	Battle Road Farm 166
Yamaoka Builders, Inc.	Sunnyvale, California	408-720-0500	Paula Avenue Homes 227

MANAGEMENT COMPANIES

Management Company	Telephone	City	Development Pg
Alton Management Corporation	415-693-9263	San Francisco, California	Lorin Station 98
Altman Companies	215-884-0500	Glenshire, Pennsylvania	University City Family Housing 236
Archdiocesean Housing Authority	206-448-3360	Seattle, Washington	Matsusaka Townhomes 92
AWFMEX Inc.	213-747-2790	Los Angeles, California	Yorkshire Terrace 142
Bickerdike Redevelopment Corporation	312-252-1963	Chicago, Illinois	West Town II 156
Biltmore Properties	602-997-0013	Phoenix, Arizona	Viviendas Asistenciales 231
Boulder Project Self Sufficiency	303-441-3929	Boulder, Colorado	Woodlands 130
BRIDGE Housing (Housing)	415-989-1111	San Francisco, California	YWCA Villa Nueva 106
Burbank Housing Mgmt. Corporation	707-526-9733	Santa Rosa, California	Tower Apartments 90
Capitol Hill Improvement Corporation	518-462-9696	Albany, New York	Catherine Street 184
Caritas Managment Corporation.	415-647-7191	San Francisco, California	Del Carlo Court/555 Ellis Street 104, 108
Chattanooga N'hood Enterprise-Real Estate Dept	615-265-4114	Chattanooga, Tennessee	Orchard Village and Oak Hill 206
Church of Messiah Housing Corporation	313-567-7966	Detroit, Michigan	Field Street 154
The CBM Group	916-823-2477	Auburn, California	Daybreak Grove 132
The Community Builders	617-695-9595	Boston, Massachusetts	Oak Terrace/Roxbury Corners/Langham Crt/Tent City 240, 192, 198, 202
Community Corporation of Santa Monica	310-394-8487	Santa Monica, California	Ocean Park Co-op/St John's Hospital Housing 146, 148
DiNardis Assoc., Inc	914-948-9299	N. White Plains, New York	West HELP 172
Drew Economic Development Corporation	213-345-5038	Compton, California	Willowbrook Green Apartments 136
Dryfuss Management	301-656-1465	Bethesda, Maryland	Timberlawn Crescent 214
East Bay Asian Local Development Corporation	510-287-5353	Oakland, California	Hismen Hin-nu Terrace/Frank G. Mar Community Housing 100, 112
Eden Housing Management Inc.	510-582-1460	Hayward, California	Stoney Creek Apartments 82
Evans Property Management	510-837-6756	Alamo, California	201 Turk Street 120
First Realty Management	617-423-7000	Boston, Massachusetts	Battle Road Farm 166
Frederick Johnson	512-479-6577	Austin, Texas	Blacklands Transitional Housing 228
Hawaii Housing Authority	808-832-5960	Honolulu, Hawaii	La'ilani at Kealakehe 229
Housing Authority of City of Charleston	803-720-3970	Charleston, South Carolina	Charleston Infill Housing 208
Housing Authority of the County of Santa Clara	408-993-2907	San Jose, California	Lucretia Gardens/Julian Street 225
Hyder & Company	619-481-3717	Solana Beach, California	Rancho Sespe Farmworker Housing 126
The John Stewart Company	415-391-4321	San Francisco	Paula Avenue Homes 227
Linda Nelson	916-757-4444	Davis, California	Tuscany Villas/Villa Calabria 78
Luthern Social Services of Illinois	312-342-1344	Chicago, Illinois	West Town Cluster Housing 162
Maloney Properties, Inc	617-449-7887	Newton, Massachusetts	Hyde Square Co-op 176
McCormack Baron and Associates, Inc.	314-621-3400	St Louis, Missouri	Crawford Square/Westminster Place 168, 221
Mercy Services Corporation	415-750-5933	San Francisco, California	111 Jones Street 120
Meridian Group, Inc	608-836-1152	Middleton, Wisconsin	The Reservoir 160
Mid-Peninsula Hsg. Mgmt. Corporation	415-299-8050	Redwood City, California	The Farm/Open Doors/Horizons 74, 224, 226
Miguel & Angie Alonzo	806-364-5082	Hereford, Texas	Amistad Farm Laborers Housing 128
Mont Enterprises	203-967-8337	Stamford, Connecticut	Parkside Gables 180
Princeton Property Management	503-794-9004	Milwaukie, Oregon	Nuevo Amanecer Apartments 72
Pennrose Management Co.	215-979-1100	Philadelphia, Pennsylvania	Regent Terrace Apartments/Dorado Village 239, 237
Phipps House Services	212-695-4758	New York, New York	Lee Goodwin Res./Crotona Park West/Spring Creek Gdns 242, 243, 241
Plaza Realty and Management Corporation	203-359-4611	Stamford, Connecticut	Waterside Green 178
Project P.P.E.P.	503-794-9004	Tucson, Arizona	La Ramona Morales Apartments 230
Related Management	203-624-9000	New Haven, Connecticut	Ninth Square Redevelopment 196
Seattle Housing Resources Group	206-623-0506	Seattle, Washington	Cascade Court Apartments 116
L.E. Smith Management Co. Inc.	617-357-7188	Boston, Massachusetts	Columbia/Hampshire Street Housing 235
Solari Enterprises Inc.	714-282-2520	Orange, California	Villa Esperanza 140
Tri-State Management Corporation	501-367-6227	Monticello, Arkansas	Dermott Villas/Mer Rouge Villas 246, 247
Urban Pacific Properties	415-474-4474	San Francisco, California	Parkview Commons 94
WestHab	914-345-2800	Elmsford, New York	CEPHAS Housing 190
Womens Prison Association	212-677-0949	New York, New York	Sarah Powell Huntington House 244
YWCA of Santa Clara County (Facilities)	408-295-4011	San Jose, California	YWCA Villa Nueva 106
YWCA of Seattle and King County	206-461-4854	Seattle, Washington	YWCA Family Village 88

PHOTOGRAPHERS

Photographer	Telephone	City	Development Pg
Russell Abraham	415-896-6400	San Francisco, California	Horizons/Lorin Station 226, 98
Paul Bardagjy	512-452-9636	Austin, Texas	Blacklands Transitional Housing 228
Tom Bernard	412-765-1133	(c/o UDA Archs. and Planners)	Randolph Neighborhood/Middletowne Arch 210, 245
Laurie Black	503-655-5939	Portland, Oregon	Nuevo Amanecer Apartments 72
Hedrich Blessing	312-351-1151	Chicago, Illinois	West Town Cluster Housing 162
Bradfield Richards and Assoc.	404-256-6565	Atlanta, Georgia	Charleston Infill Housing 208
Howard Brunner	610-664-1554	Bala Cynwyd, Pennsylvania	Regent Terrace Apartments 239
Tim Buchman	412-765-1133	(c/o UDA Archs. and Planners)	Crawford Square 168
Butts Photography	303-355-1150	Denver, Colorado	Woodlands 130
Wayne Cable	312-951-1799	Chicago, Illinois	International Homes/West Town II 220, 156
Lucy Chen	617-625-1008	Somersville, Massachusetts	Capen Green/Battle Road Farm 234, 166
Stephen Cridland	503-274-0954	Portland, Oregon	Nuevo Amanecer Apartments 72
Annette del Zoppo Productions	310-559-1999	Culver City, California	Willowbrook Green Apartments 136
Mark Darley	415-381-5452	Mill Valley, California	Open Doors 224
Janet Delaney	510-845-3449	Oakland, California	Hismen Hin-nu Terrace/555 Ellis Street 100, 108
Terence Falk	203-933-9552	West Haven, Connecticut	Ninth Square Redevelopment 196
Fern Tiger Associates	510-763-3867	Oakland, California	Resource Guide Cover 248
Stephen Fischer	212-666-0121	New York, New York	Lee Goodwin Residence 242
David Franzen	808-261-9998	Kailua, Hawaii	La'ilani at Kealakehe 229
John J. Gallegher	718-499-9779	Brooklyn, New York	Sarah Powell Huntington House 244
Allan Geller	415-775-2497	San Francisco, California	Paula Avenue Homes 227
Fred George	212-254-9181	New York, New York	Parkside Gables 180
Jody Gibbs	520-792-9068	Tucson, Arizona	Viviendas Asistenciales/La Ramona Morales Apartments 231, 230
Ron Glassett	360-376-2600	Eastsound, Washington	OPAL Commons 68
Stephen Mark Goldner	215-735-7475	Philadelphia, Pennsylvania	Dorado Village 237
Goody Clancy Associates	617-262-2760	Boston, Massachusetts	Langham Court 198
Jay Graham	415-459-3898	San Anselmo, California	Stoney Creek Apartments 82
Mick Hales	914-228-0106	Carmal, New York	CEPHAS Housing 190
Franz Hall	612-870-8936	Minneapolis, Minnesota	Lyton Park Place/Harriet Square 152, 219
Robert Herman	415-552-9210	San Francisco, California	Lucretia Gardens/Julian Street 225
Lockwood Hoehl	412-421-8285	Pittsburgh, Pennsylvania	Fineview Crest 233
Lou Host-Jablonski	608-246-8846	Madison, Wisconsin	The Reservoir 160
Timothy Hursley	501-372-0640	Little Rock, Arkansas	Dermott Villas/Mer Rouge Villas 246, 247
Ralph Hutchins	617-926-8880	Watertown, Massachusetts	Roxbury Corners 192
Christopher Irion	415-896-0752	San Francisco, California	Del Carlo Court 104
Bob Kerr	518-869-1034	Albany, New York	Catherine Street 184
William Kildow Photography	312-248-9159	Chicago, Illinois	Quincy Homes 218
James Kline	916-736-0177	Sacramento, California	Southside Park Co-housing 84
Conrad Levenson	718-858-0555	New York, New York	Lee Goodwin Residence/Crotona Park West 242, 243
Mimi Levine	301-656-1465	Bethesda, Maryland	Timberlawn Crescent 214
Jane Lidz	415-587-3377	San Francisco, California	Tuscany Villas/Villa Calabria 78
Stanley Livingston	313-665-6401	Ann Arbor, Michigan	Field Street 154
Loisos/Ubbelohde	510-653-6579	Berkeley, California	Daybreak Grove 132
Ford Lowcock	818-284-0449	Alhambra, California	Rancho Sespe Farmworker Housing 126
Dutch MacDonald	412-362-7791	Pittsburgh, Pennsylvania	Fineview Crest 233
Sandy Marks	415-826-2742	San Francisco, California	Holladay Avenue Homes 223

Photographer	Development Pg	City	Telephone
John F. Martin	555 Ellis Street 108	San Francisco, California	415-861-7355
Joel Martinez	Amistad Farm Laborers Housing 128	Austin, Texas	512-474-8548
Don Matzkin	University City Family Housing 236	Philadelphia, Pennsylvania	215-564-0814
Eric Mitchell	Regent Terrace Apartments 239	St Peters, Pennsylvania	610-469-4690
Robb Miller	YWCA Villa Nueva 106	Studio City, California	818-506-5678
Michael Moran	Melrose Court 188	New York, New York	212-226-2596
Grant Mudford	St John's Hospital Housing 148	Los Angeles, California	213-663-9888
Yannis Paris	Cascade Court Apartments 116	Seattle, Washington	206-783-2806
Elton Pope-Lance	Oak Terrace 240	Sudbury, Massachusetts	508-443-4393
Jock Pottle	West HELP 172	New York, New York	212-989-3306
Michael Pyatok	Hismen Hin-nu Terrace/Tower Apartments 100, 90	Oakland, California	510-465-7010
Marvin Rand	Villa Esperanza/Yorkshire Terrace 140, 142	Venice, California	310-396-3441
Jim Raycroft	Columbia/Hampshire Street Housing 235	Boston, Massachusetts	617-542-7229
Maguire Reeder	Daybreak Grove 132	Alexandria, Virginia	703-519-9300
Tom Reiss	Spring Creek Gardens 241	New York, New York	212-673-1550
Paul Rocheleau	Middle Towne Arch 245	(c/o UDA Archs. and Planners)	412-765-1133
Michael Romine	YWCA Family Village 88	Seattle, Washington	206-522-2529
Brian Rose	Sojourner Truth Homes 238	New York, New York	212-260-5029
Steve Rosenthal	Langham Court/Charlestown Navy Yard Rowhouses/Tent City 198, 194, 202	Auburndale, Massachusetts	617-244-2989
Jim Simmons	Willowbrook Green Apartments 136	Los Angeles, California	310-559-1999
Dick Springgate	Benson Glen 70	Seattle, Washington	206-634-3232
Magnus Stark	Frank G. Mar Community Housing 112	Pasadena, California	818-798-6599
John Sutton	Parkview Commons/111 Jones Street/201 Turk Street 94, 120	Pt. San Quentin, California	415-258-8100
David Todd	Waterside Green 178	New Haven, Connecticut	203-929-8873
Les Tonkin	Matsusaka Townhomes 92	Seattle, Washington	206-624-7880
Trivers Associates	Westminster Place 221	St Louis, Missouri	314-241-2900
Peter Vanderwalker	Roxbury Corners/Hyde Square Co-op 192, 176	West Newton, Massachusetts	617-964-2728
Alex Verticoff	Ocean Park Co-op 146	Venice, California	310-450-9442
Paul Warchol	Melrose Court 188	New York, New York	212-431-3461
Larry Yaw	West Hopkins Townhouses 232	Aspen, Colorado	303-925-2867

NATIONAL HOUSING, DESIGN, AND COMMUNITY DEVELOPMENT ORGANIZATIONS

Codes

Information—I   Technical assistance—T   Funding—F   Policy—P

Organization	Codes	Telephone	City
American Institute of Architects, Community Design and Development	I/T/P	202-626-7532	Washington, D.C.
American Institute of Certified Planners	I/T	202-872-0611	Washington, D.C.
American Planning Association	I/T/P	202-872-0611	Washington, D.C.
Association of Community Design Centers (West Coast)	I/T/P	503-281-8011	Portland, Oregon
Association of Community Design Centers (East Coast)	I/T/P	718-636-3486	Brooklyn, New York
Center for Budget and Policy Priorities	I	202-408-1080	Washington, D.C.
Center for Community Change	I/T	202-342-0519	Washington, D.C.
Community Information Exchange	I	202-628-2981	Washington, D.C.
Congress for the New Urbanism	I/P	415-291-9619	San Francisco, California
Corporation for Supportive Housing (West Coast)	I/T/F/P	510-251-1910	Oakland, California
Corporation for Supportive Housing (East Coast)	I/T/F/P	212-986-2966	New York, New York
Council of Large Public Housing Authorities	I/T/P	202-638-1300	Washington, D.C.
Development Training Institute	T	301-764-0780	Baltimore, Maryland
Enterprise Foundation	I/T/F/P	800-624-4298	Columbia, Maryland
Housing Assistance Council	I/T/F/P	202-842-8600	Washington, D.C.
Institute for Community Economics	I/T/F/P	413-746-8660	Springfield, Massachusetts
Local Initiatives Support Corporation	I/T/F/P	212-454-5929	New York, New York
Low-Income Housing Information Service	I/T/P	202-662-1530	Washington, D.C.
National Alliance to End Homelessness	I/P	202-638-1526	Washington, D.C.
National Association of Affordable Housing Lenders	I/T/F/P	202-861-5770	Washington, D.C.
National Association of Community Action Agencies	I/T/P	202-265-7546	Washington, D.C.
National Association of Community Development Loan Funds	F/T	215-923-4754	Philadelphia, Pennsylvania
National Association of Counties	I/T/P	202-393-6226	Washington, D.C.
National Association of Development Companies	I/T/P	703-812-9000	Arlington, Virginia
National Association of Development Organizations	I/T/P	202-624-7806	Washington, D.C.
National Association of Home Builders	I/T	202-822-0200	Washington, D.C.
National Association of Housing and Redevelopment Officials	I/T/P	202-429-2960	Washington, D.C.
National Association of Neighborhoods	I/T/P	202-332-7766	Washington, D.C.
National Association of Towns and Townships	I/T/P	202-624-3550	Washington, D.C.
National Coalition for the Homeless	I/P	202-775-1322	Washington, D.C.
National Congress for Community Economic Development	I/T/F/P	202-234-5009	Washington, D.C.
National Council for Urban Economic Development	I/P	202-223-4735	Washington, D.C.
National Council of State Housing Agencies	I/T/P	202-624-7710	Washington, D.C.
National Economic and Development Law Center	I/T	510-251-2600	Oakland, California
National Housing Conference	I/T/P	202-393-5772	Washington, D.C.
National Housing Law Project	I/T/P	510-251-9400	Oakland, California
National Housing Services of America	F	510-832-5542	Oakland, California
National League of Cities	I/T/P	202-626-3000	Washington, D.C.
National Low-Income Housing Coalition	I/T/P	202-662-1530	Washington, D.C.
National Multi-Housing Council	I/T/P	202-559-3381	Washington, D.C.
National Rural Housing Coalition	I/T/P	202-393-5229	Washington, D.C.
Neighborhood Reinvestment Corporation	I/T	202-376-2400	Washington, D.C.
National Training and Information Center	I/T	312-243-3035	Chicago, Illinois
Partners for Livable Communities	I/P	202-887-5990	Washington, D.C.
Urban Institute	I/T/P	202-833-7200	Washington, D.C.
Urban Land Institute	I/T/P	202-624-7000	Washington, D.C.
Women's Institute for Housing and Economic Development	I/T	617-423-2296	Boston, Massachusetts

STATE AFFORDABLE HOUSING COALITIONS CONTACT LIST

Organization	Telephone	City/State
Alaska Homeless Coalition	907-272-1626	Anchorage, Alaska
Alabama Low-Income Housing Coalition	205-652-9676	Epes, Alaska
Arkansas Low-Income Housing Coalition	501-376-8015	Little Rock, Arkansas
PPEP HDC	800-293-2974	Tucson, Arizona
California Housing and Homeless Coalition	916-447-0458	Sacramento, California
Non-Profit Housing Coalition of Northern California	415-989-8160	San Francisco, California
Southern California Association of Non-Profit Housing	213-480-1249	Los Angeles, California
Colorado Affordable Housing Partnership	303-297-2548	Denver, Colorado
Connecticut Housing Coalition	203-563-2943	Wethersfield, Connecticut
Delaware Housing Coalition	302-678-2286	Dover, Delaware
Florida Housing Coalition	904-878-4219	Tallahassee, Florida
Atlanta Mutual Housing Association	404-892-4824	Atlanta, Georgia
Affordable Housing Alliance	808-946-2244	Honolulu, Hawaii
Iowa Coalition on Housing and Homelessness	515-288-5022	Des Moines, Iowa
Idaho Housing Coalition	208-338-7066	Boise, Idaho
Statewide Housing Action Coalition	312-939-6074	Chicago, Illinois
Indiana Coalition on Housing and Homelessness Issues	317-636-8819	Indianapolis, Indiana
Housing and Credit Counseling	913-234-0217	Topeka, Kansas
Housing and Homeless Coalition of Kentucky	502-223-1834	Frankfort, Kentucky
Louisiana for Low-Income Housing Today	504-482-3822	New Orleans, Louisiana
Massachusetts Affordable Housing Alliance	617-728-9100	Boston, Massachusetts
Maryland Low-Income Housing Coalition	410-727-4200	Baltimore, Maryland
Michigan Housing Coalition	517-377-0509	Lansing, Michigan
Minnesota Housing Partnership	612-874-0112	Minneapolis, Minnesota
Adequate Housing for Missourians	314-993-3398	St Louis, Missouri
Mississippi Housing Coalition	601-483-4838	Meridien, Mississippi
Montana Low-Income Coalition	406-449-8801	Helena, Montana
North Carolina Low-Income Housing Coalition	919-881-0707	Raleigh, North Carolina
North Dakota Coalition for Homeless People	701-241-8559	Fargo, North Dakota
Nebraska Coalition for the Homeless	402-559-7115	Omaha, Nebraska
New Hampshire Coalition for the Homeless	603-228-2753	Concord, New Hampshire
Non-Profit Affordable Housing Coalition of New Jersey	609-393-3752	Trenton, New Jersey
New Mexico Housing Alliance	505-242-4406	Albuquerque, New Mexico
Nevada Homeless Coalition	702-329-2727	Reno, Nevada
New York State Rural Housing Coalition	518-434-1314	Albany, New York
New York State Tenant and Neighborhood Information Service	212-695-4204	New York, New York
Coalition on Housing and Homelessness in Ohio	614-291-1984	Columbus, Ohio
Oklahoma Coalition for the Homeless	405-232-7164	Oklahoma City, Oklahoma
Oregon Housing Now	503-288-0317	Portland, Oregon
Pennsylvania Low-Income Housing Coalition	215-576-7044	Glenside, Pennsylvania
Rhode Island Statewide Housing Action Coalition	401-751-5566	Providence, Rhode Island
South Carolina Low-Income Housing Coalition	803-737-5916	Hopkins, South Carolina
Tennessee Coalition for the Homeless	615-757-5551	Chattanooga, Tennessee
Texas Low-Income Housing Information Service	512-477-8910	Austin, Texas
Utah Homeless Coordinating Center	801-359-4929	Salt Lake City, Utah
Virginia Housing Coalition	703-486-0626	Arlington, Virginia
Vermont Affordable housing Network	802-241-2646	Waterbury, Vermont
Washington Low-Income Housing Network	206-442-9455	Seattle, Washington
Wisconsin Partnership for Housing Development	608-258-5560	Madison, Wisconsin
Southwest Community Action Council	304-529-2456	Huntington, West Virginia
Wyoming Coalition for the Homeless	307-634-4548	Cheyenne, Wyoming

The information and illustrations in this publication have been prepared and supplied by the architects, developers, and others involved in each project, and the authors. While all reasonable efforts have been made to ensure accuracy, the publishers do not, under any circumstance, accept responsibility for errors, omissions and representations express or implied.

The authors acknowledge that the Los Angeles Housing Department has printed a booklet named "Good Neighbors: Housing that Supports Stable Communities". LAHD has agreed to share the name "Good Neighbors" with this publication. For copies of their booklet please call 213-847-7483.

"Good Neighbors: Affordable Family Housing" Case Studies Slide Library Order Form

SOLD TO

Name_____

Firm/Organization_____ AIA Membership No._____

Address_____

City/State/Zip_____

Phone_____ Fax_____

SETS SELECTED

Primary Case Studies by Region	Unit Cost $	Total Cost
1. Northwest and Northern California (171 slides)	345/310.50 AIA	$_____
2. Southwest and Southern California (78 slides)	160/144.00 AIA	$_____
3. Central States (43 slides)	90/81.00 AIA	$_____
4. Northeast (129 slides)	260/234.00 AIA	$_____
5. South/Southeast (31 slides)	75/67.50 AIA	$_____
Secondary Case Studies by Region		
6. Northwest and Northern California (40 slides)	80/72.00 AIA	$_____
7. Southwest and Southern California (36 slides)	75/67.50 AIA	$_____
8. Central States (24 slides)	50/45.00 AIA	$_____
9. Northeast (76 slides)	155/139.50 AIA	$_____
10. South/Southeast (10 slides)	20/18.00 AIA	$_____
Case Studies in Groupings of Development		
11. Affordable Housing in Affluent Communities (34 slides)	70/63.00 AIA	$_____
12. Courtyard Housing (240 slides)	480/432.00 AIA	$_____
13. Families, Seniors and/or Singles (84 slides)	170/153.00 AIA	$_____
14. Farmworker Housing (28 slides)	60/54.00 AIA	$_____
15. For-Profit Developers (80)	160/144.00 AIA	$_____
16. Historic Structures Rehabilitation (29 slides)	60/54.00 AIA	$_____
17. Historic District New Construction (29 slides)	60/54.00 AIA	$_____
18. Housing for Homeless Families (45 slides)	90/81.00 AIA	$_____
19. Infill Housing (291 slides)	585/526.50 AIA	$_____
20. Mixed-Income Housing (49 slides)	100/90.00 AIA	$_____
21. Mixed-Use Developments (95 slides)	190/171.00 AIA	$_____
22. Mutual Housing Association (60 slides)	120/108.00 AIA	$_____
23. New District Development (55 slides)	90/81.00 AIA	$_____
24. Partnerships (94 slides)	190/171.00 AIA	$_____
25. Public Housing Authorities (25 slides)	50/45.00 AIA	$_____
26. Scattered-Site Developments (43 slides)	90/81.00 AIA	$_____
Complete Slide Library (all slides, all regions—638 slides)	1180/1060.00 AIA	$_____
	Shipping/Handling	$ 5.00
	Total Payment Due	$_____

PAYMENT

Enclosed is my cheque payable to the AIA ☐

Charge my credit card ☐ Visa ☐ Mastercard

Card Number _____ Expiration Date_____

Name on card _____

Signature_____

RETURN THIS FORM WITH PAYMENT TO:

AIA Library and Archives
The American Institute of Architects
1735 New York Avenue, N.W.
Washington D.C. 20006, USA

FOR PREPAID OR CREDIT CARD PAYMENTS:

Fax this form to (202) 626-7587
Any questions?
Call Michelle Boxley (202) 626-7495

cut along this line

Notes